Momentum

Momentum

The Responsibility Paradigm and Virtuous Cycles of Change in Colleges and Universities

Daniel Seymour

ROWMAN & LITTLEFIELD
Lanham • Boulder • New York • London

Published by Rowman & Littlefield
A wholly owned subsidiary of The Rowman & Littlefield Publishing Group, Inc.
4501 Forbes Boulevard, Suite 200, Lanham, Maryland 20706
www.rowman.com

Unit A, Whitacre Mews, 26-34 Stannary Street, London SE11 4AB

British Library Cataloguing in Publication Data

Library of Congress Cataloging-in-Publication Data Available
ISBN 978-1-4758-2102-4 (cloth : alk. paper)
ISBN 978-1-4758-2103-1 (pbk. : alk. paper)
ISBN 978-1-4758-2104-8 (electronic)

∞ ™ The paper used in this publication meets the minimum requirements of American National Standard for Information Sciences—Permanence of Paper for Printed Library Materials, ANSI/NISO Z39.48-1992.

Printed in the United States of America

The Family—Rhonda, Manci, Kurt, Olive, and Bridgette

Contents

Preface

On a blustery day in early December, 2013, Virginia Tech held a news conference to celebrate a "momentous and happy occasion." The day stood in stark contrast to the events of six years earlier when a gunman killed thirty-two students and faculty members on the Blacksburg campus. The devastating tragedy led to a national debate on gun violence, campus security, and emergency response procedures. Charles Steger, himself a graduate of Virginia Tech, was the president at the time of the horrific event. Over the intervening days, months, and years he did a laudable job of helping the campus community—and the entire Hokie Nation—grieve their loss, heal from their wounds, and attempt to build a better future that would honor those who were wounded or died. But in May, he had announced that he would be stepping down as president.

The "momentous and happy occasion" on this day was to announce the appointment of a new leader for the institution. Mike Quillen, the rector of the Board of Visitors, began by describing the search process and went out of his way to thank the undergraduate and graduate students and faculty members on the search committee who had shown an extreme amount of dedication in reviewing the 238 applicants. And then, after stating that hiring a president was the single most important task of the board, he introduced as the institution's sixteenth president Timothy D. Sands.

Dr. Sands, the provost at Purdue University, spoke about the magnitude of the job ahead of him while recognizing the great work that had been done to get Virginia Tech to that point. He specifically referenced the work President Steger and the Board of Visitors had done in moving the university forward over the last decade and a half, and then went on to say that his main goal was "to maintain that momentum and build on it." Finally, he added: "This is a place that clearly is not happy with the status quo and that's the kind of institution that I want to be associated with."

Dr. Sands is not alone. Everyone wants to be associated with an organization that has a sense of momentum—that is "on a roll."

The concept of momentum has both specific and ambiguous meanings. At one end of the spectrum are the mathematical formulas associated with Newton's laws of motion. They involve the precise calculation of mass and velocity. But then there is the more equivocal meaning that is part of our everyday life—in the arts, politics, and sports:

- "I tend to tell stories that have a lot of momentum; it's not like 'and then months later. . . .' I like things where the momentum of one action rolls into the next one so everything is the sum of that." Joss Whedon, screenwriter
- "It is often when night looks darkest, it is often before the fever breaks that one senses the gathering momentum for change, when one feels that resurrection of hope in the midst of despair and apathy." Hillary Clinton, former senator and secretary of state
- "Sliding headfirst is the safest way to get to the next base, I think, and the fastest. You don't lose your momentum, and there's one more important reason I slide headfirst, it gets my picture in the paper." Pete Rose, former baseball player

But what is the relationship between momentum and higher education?

To begin to answer that question, let me explore an initial observation: There is a large and growing gap in this country between what we think we do in higher education and how others perceive those efforts. Here are several illustrations:

- In a survey of business and higher education leaders conducted by the Lumina Foundation and Gallup called "What America Needs to Know about High Education Redesign," 96 percent of college and university *chief academic officers* said they were "extremely or somewhat confident" in their institution's ability to prepare students for success in the workforce. In contrast, when asked whether today's college graduates had the skills and competencies their businesses needed, a mere 11 percent of *business leaders* responded "strongly agree."[1]
- Another recent Gallup "lifestyle" poll found that 70 percent of Americans believe that having a college education is "very important." That is up from just 36 percent in 1978 and the highest level since Gallup began asking the question.[2] But a Pew Research Center survey found that 75 percent of adults also said that college is too expensive for most Americans to afford. Moreover, 57 percent said that the higher education system in the United

States fails to provide students with good value for the money they and their families spend.[3]

Various points of view have been expressed as to why such gaps have emerged. The basic rhetoric, however, breaks down along the traditional town-and-gown divide. For many who represent our external stakeholders, the theme is that we are vestiges of a bygone era, unwilling or unable to adapt to a new normal. Tenure is usually a part of this narrative as well as various references to our elitist tendencies—"what a bunch of snobs." Our spendthrift ways are also described in exhausting detail from the climbing walls to the Olympic swimming pools. Every round of tuition increases is met with headlines and stories concluding that higher education is out of control.

For those of us who wear regalia in the late spring every year, we often parry these accusations with our own set of raw generalizations. The first of these refrains centers around our uniqueness as institutions of higher learning and that others just don't understand who we are and the importance of what we do. Next, we often invoke the fad defense by labeling any idea that doesn't emerge whole cloth from our own institutions to be a whim that represents the commodification of higher education and deserving of our disdain.

Such scorn was on full display in an article, "A Field Guide to American Higher-Ed Reformers," which identified some of the "important species and subspecies that now occupy the higher education landscape." According to the author, recognizing these various species (eleven) has become particularly important in this period of drastic university climate change and species migration. They include:

- Venture philanthropists and foundations (Species: *Benevolentia disrumpo*)
  - Habitat/range: Found throughout the Unites States with important subspecies clusters located around Seattle (the extremely large and various Gatesian variant) and Indianapolis (the Lumina conversion variant).
  - Description: Sometimes mistaken for its docile cousin *Benevolentia humanitas*, this aggressive, leechlike species often attaches itself to a host, injects its venom, and slowly transforms it into a food source.
- Business-minded boards of regents and trustees (Species: *Negotium rex*)
  - Habitat/range: Various locales through the United States. This species is known to gather every couple of months to hold very loud and blusterous squawking sessions.
  - Description: This crass, peacock-like species is known for its elaborate preening sessions and mating dances but rarely produces a viable egg.[4]

The divide: plodding Luddite or besieged victim?

Still, if perception is reality, then we need to be seriously concerned, not because of the views expressed by a few thousand people in a survey but because of what those perceptions have wrought. Over the years the gap has produced an eager resolve among many to fix us, disrupt us, reinvent us, redesign us, and . . . reform us. Indeed, what has emerged is an entire ecosystem of "solutions" to higher education's "problems." This paternalistic, and some would say opportunistic, transformation of higher education can be divided into four broad categories: (1) funding mechanisms, (2) scorecard initiatives, (3) commercial enterprises, and (4) ideological entities.

The first way that higher education can be "fixed" is through the pocketbook. Around the country, legislators have rushed to adopt systems that allocate funding based partly or mostly on performance measures rather than the traditional method of student FTEs (full-time equivalent). The simple argument for this approach is that institutions shouldn't be rewarded just for "butts in seats" but for their ability to design systems and processes capable of converting input into output. This logic really began to take hold as state budgets were being cut while disconcerting completion data (and the ensuing "Completion Agenda") were gaining national headlines.

The combination gave rise to a "doing more with less" refrain that swept the nation. Groups outside academe like Complete College America and the National Center for Higher Education Management Systems have aggressively advocated for performance funding and the states have obliged with, at recent count, thirty-four states rewarding and/or penalizing colleges based in part on the numbers of students they graduate.[5]

While many acknowledge that at least some shift toward results is useful, the concern from within the academy is about quality, tone, and micromanagement. The understandable fear is that a reductionist shift to a quantity metric and "throughput" leaves other more robust academic quality metrics in the dust. Also, in some states the tone has taken on "starve the beast" rhetoric by using anecdotes about liberal professors, silly course titles, and the feckless nature of the liberal arts to increase control over how colleges and universities use public funds.

And then there is the problem of strings. While total state support for higher education has bounced back off their "disinvestment" lows (up 5.7 percent from 2013 to 2014), increasingly the added dollars are part of "reciprocal" arrangements between colleges and legislatures.[6] An illustration of this thinking is the recent California Student Success Act for community colleges, which divides up a majority of matriculation funds to colleges based on a formula that rewards seven specific activities—for example, initial orientation (10 percent), initial assessment (10 percent), counseling/advising (15 percent), and so on. Every dollar seems to be coming with strings attached.

A second way to get higher education's attention is to empower consumers with scorecards. As government and accrediting entities began demanding increased effectiveness and efficiency, colleges and universities began developing institutional datasets to create a "culture of evidence," which, in turn, has quickly evolved into a prevailing scorecard mentality. This mindset suggests that a good way to fix us is to advance transparency by creating systems that enable the public to compare and contrast institutions of higher education. As an example, the Texas Higher Education Coordinating Board has its Higher Education Accountability System. Under "Interactive Access to Data" on the system's website it touts: "Use this tool to customize data by time periods, to select components of individual accountability measures, and to specify institutional choices. Select an institution type from the drop-down. Then press 'Go.'"

And the result? Voila! You have a bullet-proof system for establishing culpability.

Of course, not wanting to be left out, the federal government has decided to get into the scorecard game. According to President Obama, who introduced it in his 2013 State of the Union Address, the U.S. Department of Education's College Scorecard is supposed to be a source for prospective students to "compare schools based on a simple criterion—where you can get the most bang for your education buck." While the current College Affordability and Transparency Center has the Scorecard as well as a College Navigator and Net Price Calculator, the proposal to "shake up" higher education comes in the form of a rating system that would link student aid to these ratings such that students who enrolled at high-performing colleges would receive larger Pell grants and more favorable rates on student loans.

Next on the transformation hit parade are those commercial enterprises for which the ranking and sorting of college and universities is part of an apparently profitable business model. In 1983, *U.S. News & World Report* published its first "America's Best Colleges" report and the rest, as they say, is history. Other publishers have joined in over the years with their own versions, and most institutions, while publicly decrying the methodologies being used, privately work hard to move up the rankings. Predictably, a few institutions (usually admissions officials) have responded to the perverse incentives by even fudging the numbers.

Other enterprises focus on the business side of the house. Moody's Investor Services, for example, garners headlines on a regular basis based on their assessment of the financial health of the industry. Their December 2014 report suggests a continued negative outlook for U.S. higher education (in 2015) because of slow growth in tuition revenue among the four-year colleges while declining enrollment is driving the negative outlook among community colleges.

Various consulting firms have offered their business expertise, especially after the beginning of the Great Recession in 2008. Bain & Co., as an example, offers all types of support through their higher education team to address strategic issues such as performance improvement, operating efficiency, cost management and reduction, growth strategy, organizational effectiveness, and funding strategy. Their list of assignments includes:

- Bain helped the University of North Carolina at Chapel Hill identify more than $85 million in cost savings options (5 percent of operating budget) across a range of administrative functions.
- Bain launched a program for an Ivy League university targeting more than $90 million in annual administrative cost savings. We also identified significant alternative revenue growth opportunities to help correct a budget deficit.[7]

There is also the seemingly endless supply of books on higher education. While some involve the rigorous analysis of data such as Richard Arum and Josipa Roksa's much-discussed *Academically Adrift* (2011), and others like Christopher Newfield's *Unmaking the Public University* (2008) are grounded in substantive intellectual and policy debates, still others seek to provoke and titillate—*Higher Education? How Colleges Are Wasting Our Money and Failing Our Kids and What We Can Do About It* (2010), and *The Fall of the Faculty: The Rise of the All-Administrative University and Why It Matters* (2011).

A final group of "transformers" falls under the heading of ideological entities. These are the foundations, think tanks, and centers that have a constituency to represent or simply have a set of beliefs that they wish to give voice to. At the top of the heap is the Lumina Foundation, the nation's largest private foundation focused solely on increasing Americans' success in higher education. According to its strategic plan, its Big Goal is "to increase the proportion of Americans with high-quality degrees, certificates and other credentials to 60 percent by the year 2025," and it produces policy papers and grants to affect that goal.

The Bill & Melinda Gates Foundation largely pursues its higher education agenda by funding other intermediaries such as Jobs for the Future and Complete College America. With a start-up grant of $8 million in 2009, Complete College America has been particularly influential with its reports *Time Is the Enemy* (2011), *Bridge to Nowhere* (2012), and its efforts to persuade states to join an alliance whose members pledge to develop and implement aggressive state and campus-level action plans detailed in *The Game Changers* (2013). Completion by Design, a five-year Bill & Melinda Gates Foundation signature initiative, focuses its work on community colleges in order to increase completion and graduation rates for low-income students.

Then we have the Center for America Progress and its Postsecondary Education Group, which issues reports and policy briefs, the American Enterprise Institute with its Center on Higher Education Reform, the New American

Foundation and its Education Policy Program, and the American Institute for Research and its Delta Cost Project. The Center for College Affordability & Productivity is "dedicated to researching the rising costs and stagnant efficiency in higher education, with special emphasis on the United States" and, interestingly, has partnered with *Forbes* magazine to produce their own college rankings. The Aspen Institute has created a prize—the Aspen Prize for Community College Excellence—in order to incentivize institutions to focus on its criteria of completion outcomes, labor market outcomes, learning outcomes, and equitable outcomes and encourage colleges to claim the "We're #1" mantle.

And this incomplete list does not begin to include the many state-level and institutional-level individuals and groups that are equally enthusiastic about the idea of providing solutions to higher education's problems.

In summary, efforts to transform higher education have become a hyperactive cottage industry of reformers and influencers. From seemingly beneficial initiatives to provide students and parents with better information about colleges and universities to mean-spirited diatribes that are simply designed to generate book sales, the breadth of these efforts is quite significant.

But there is a common element. The commonality is embedded in a theme of accountability. First, the definition:

ac • count • abil • i • ty *(noun)*: the quality or state of being accountable *especially*: an obligation or willingness to accept responsibility or to account for one's actions <public officials lacking *accountability*>.

The language usually associated with the transformation initiatives described above is that higher education needs to be "held accountable." This is, in effect, the quality or state of being accountable when it is "an obligation." The ubiquitous use of the verb *to hold* is not circumstantial. The obligation must be imposed—the individual must explain him- or herself, and the organization needs to be answerable for its actions. With the exception of some entities such as the Lumina Foundation and Complete College America that have advanced critiques coupled with balanced solutions, most of our would-be transformers have enacted language that strongly implies change is something needing to be imposed on our colleges and universities.

This book takes a decidedly different approach to mending the breach between what we perceive we do and how others perceive us. That approach emerges from the second meaning associated with accountability, a "willingness to accept responsibility." More precisely:

re • spon • si • bil • i • ty *(noun)*: the state of being the person who caused something to happen; a duty or task that you are required or expected to do; something that you should do because it is morally right, legally required, etc.

We don't need to be held accountable. We don't need to be transformed. We don't need to be "fixed." What we need is to become responsible for creating our own futures. We need to show that we are capable of embracing change on our own as the means to drive performance improvement that exceeds the expectation of our stakeholders.

The nature of the paradigm shift should be obvious. It is a shift from being reactive to becoming proactive, from allowing others to be the arbiters of quality to creating opportunities for improvement for ourselves. The new responsibility paradigm requires conscious design and professional execution. That is because if we don't do it, if we don't reassert our willingness and ability to create our own future, that future will be directed by others.

Kevin Carey has made this point in an article that suggests the new national ranking initiative is a wake-up call. The lesson for the academy, Carey states, is that unless something happens to change the now-dominant narrative of escalating prices married to stagnant and subpar education results, more and more regulatory imperatives will be forthcoming. He concludes:

> This can't be fixed with a savvy PR campaign. Colleges can only escape the yoke of federal control by achieving dramatic and verifiable improvements in the value of the education they provide to students, in terms of both learning and price. Otherwise, expect more disconcerting ideas to come, and soon.[8]

Several supporting illustrations are useful here. It is clear that "doing more with less" has become a mantra associated with an accountability paradigm. This is an unsustainable algorithm. It begins with the assumption that productivity is low and more efficient means can be used to convert input into output. While virtually any enterprise has processes that can be improved, at some point the exercise necessarily degrades into "doing less with less." Community colleges in this country have proven this point. After being hit with disproportionately larger cuts than comprehensive colleges or research universities, two-year institutions cut staff, froze salaries, and delayed their scheduled maintenance.

And in the end, they did the only thing they really could do—cut classes. At a time when society was calling on them to do more, the only thing they could ultimately do was less.

In contrast, a responsibility paradigm would suggest a different axiom— "doing better with enough." This states that we, not others, are responsible for causing quality to happen. In this case, that something is committing to the design of systems and processes capable of driving continuous performance improvement. All six regional higher education accreditors have adopted this type of "institutional effectiveness" language. The Southern Association of Colleges and Schools (SACS) provides an illustration. One of its core requirements (basic, broad-based foundational requirements an institution must meet) states:

> The institution engages in ongoing, defined, integrated, and institution-wide research-based planning and evaluation processes that (1) incorporate a systematic review of institutional mission, goals, and outcomes; (2) resulting in continuing improvement in institutional quality; and (3) demonstrate the institution is effectively accomplishing it mission.[9]

This commitment to institutional effectiveness should then be coupled with a shift in thinking about how the enterprise is funded—from an expense to an investment. Within a responsibility paradigm, adequate investment must be made such that capacity building and improved outcomes are not jeopardized. There needs to be "enough."

Another illustration is the idea of a "culture of evidence," which emerged as a measure of our willingness to be held accountable. In an accountability paradigm, the resulting data are used to compare and contrast, to rank and sort. The narrative is that we need to be generating data to prove to others we are worthy within a competitive context. Again, the language is punitive. How will higher education be held accountable? We will dutifully gather evidence to identify shortcomings that can then be used to direct changes. Instead, we should be practicing a "culture of inquiry" within which we ask penetrating questions about our systems and processes so we can generate the information needed as feedback to evaluate and then to improve performance. This is what responsible institutions do. They engage, they reflect, and then they decide what to do next.

For example, in early February, 2014, the Department of Education conducted a daylong symposium on the technical challenges facing the administration's college-ratings system. In one of the presentations, Tod Massa, who directs policy research and data warehousing for the State Council of Higher Education in Virginia, attempted to highlight the gaps in data the department collects through its Integrated Postsecondary Education Data Systems (IPEDS). In focusing his remarks on the most important measures of college accountability—graduation rates, net prices, postgraduate wages, and community college outcomes—he began by stating: "To the department, I say this: We need better data. Let me rephrase that: You need better data."[10]

And in the context of this book, let me rephrase that again—*we need better information.*

For accountability purposes, the appropriate pronoun is *you* followed obediently by *data*; that is, the use of datasets and spreadsheets in order to generate rankings and invite comparisons. But if we are serious about being responsible for designing systems and processes capable of organizational learning, then *we* need *information* that enables individuals and groups within our institutions to both ask and answer questions for the express purpose of doing better—always, always better.

While these examples are useful for describing a paradigm shift from "being held accountable" to one in which institutions work hard to "demonstrate their responsibility," they do not necessarily offer specific prescriptions—that is, ways to operationalize the change. We need tools. Or as Ellen Chaffee, a former college president and now senior fellow at the Association of Governing Boards of Universities and Colleges, has remarked, "We don't need a bunch of solutions from outsiders. We need a bunch of tools for people to find their own solutions."[11]

The tool being advocated for in this book is the *virtuous cycle*. Most people are familiar with the idea of a *vicious cycle*:

- Downsizing is likely to reduce an organization's ability to generate revenue and not just costs, which in turn decreases profits and increases pressure to downsize even further.
- Extreme acts of violence perpetrated by one side in a war fuel acts of revenge by the other side, which in turn lead to violent retaliations by the first side and an ongoing escalation by both sides.
- In the subprime mortgage crisis, as housing prices declined, more homeowners went "underwater" (when the market value of a home drops below the mortgage on it). This provided an incentive to walk away from the home, increasing defaults and foreclosures which, in turn, lowered housing values further.

A vicious cycle, then, is an example of a reinforcing loop that produces decay. It compounds change in a downward direction. That is because a reinforcing loop amplifies or adds to any disturbance in the system. How? Take the first example from above. While the first round of downsizing may reduce costs, it also impacts the morale of those who are left behind. Some may decide to jump ship while they can (and those tend to be people who have strong resumes) and others may start coming to work late and leaving early, and caring less and less about the quality of their work. Between the loss of valuable skills and experience of those who have left—involuntarily or voluntarily—and the loss of productivity of the remaining work force, the result is usually expensive mistakes and lost sales from disgruntled customers. All of this cuts into revenue, tempting management to consider even more layoffs to reduce expenses. Down and down we go.

A *virtuous* cycle is also a reinforcing loop, but instead of producing loss and decay, it is an engine of learning and growth. A general illustration is the growth of human knowledge. In prehistoric times, knowledge accumulated very slowly. Individuals learned things about their environment by direct experience. But they had no way to measure precisely, no time to study things that didn't directly affect survival, and no way to record what had been learned. Writing greatly speeded up the accumulation of knowledge, as did the development of mathematics and geometry, which allowed more efficient means of production. Learning in a systematic way—a process known as science—helped, as did the invention of the printing press.

The expansion of knowledge created the problem of coping with the explosion of information and trying to organize it in meaningful ways. The modern computer, a product of that knowledge, became the next platform for advancing knowledge dramatically.[12] It becomes apparent that the more knowledge you have, the easier it is to create new knowledge. And the beat of the virtuous cycle goes on.

But what is the relationship between our gap problem and virtuous cycles?

The growing gap between what we do and what others think we do has resulted in strident calls for colleges and universities to be held accountable. Our knee-jerk response has been defiance, followed by indignation, coupled with indifference, and embellished by the kind of snarky articles described earlier, none of which will pacify the barbarians at our gates.

A different response, however, might involve first "causing" something to happen by embracing our need and ability to create a different future. This responsibility paradigm would then need to develop and use a tool or set of tools to operationalize that change. Virtuous cycles, as we have seen with the knowledge explosion, are not just random events or haphazard occurrences. Instead, one success can, and often does, become the platform for future successes. Confidence is gained, information is shared, and positive feedback begins to build on itself. Such virtuous cycles or upward spirals have very specific characteristics and these dynamics can be used to alter the trajectory of systems. The arc of an organization, then, can be "designed in" by being intentional about the use of such a tool.

It follows that a college or university's algorithm for success in a hyperactive, accountability-driven environment is:

Demonstrating Responsibility (paradigm) +
Virtuous Cycles (tool) = *Momentum*

This is a purposeful approach to change. First, take control of the narrative by eschewing victimhood, then embrace the use of tools that are capable of producing momentum. Be intentional. Be a builder. Be a designer. Be a tool user.

Finally, an important part of this needed paradigm shift involves the unit of analysis. It is often noted how ironic it is that the public's approval rating for

Congress has hit all-time lows of less than 10 percent while incumbents are reelected at a rate of well over 90 percent. In the same way, holding higher education accountable is a worldview that is somewhat understandable when, for example, rising tuition rates are coupled with low completion rates. The unit of analysis here is higher education. It is like Congress.

But as part of the shift to a responsibility paradigm, the nature of the conversation needs to be disaggregated. It is the responsibility of *each* college and *each* university to engage in the conscious design of systems and processes that develop talent and have the capability of improving outcomes over time. As part of a new narrative we need to ditch the defensiveness that helped get us into this mess. Let others engage in the hyperbole and trivial generalizations about the end of higher education or the irresponsible headlines suggesting that attending college is a waste of time.

We—each and every institution—have work to do.

NOTES

1. Cited in Mark Keierleber, "Business and Academic Leaders Disagree on Quality of College Grads, Survey Finds," *Chronicle of Higher Education*, February 25, 2014, http://chronicle.com/article/BusinessAcademic-Leaders/144977/?cid=pm&utm_source=pm&utm_medium=en.

2. Valerie J. Calderon and Shane J. Lopez, "Americans Say Postsecondary Degree Vital, but See Barriers," *Gallup*, February 5, 2013, www.gallup.com/poll/160298/americans-say-postsecondary-degree-vital-barriers.aspx.

3. "Is College Worth It?," Pew Research Center, May 15, 2011, www.pewsocial-trends.org/2011/05/15/is-college-worth-it.

4. Steven Ward, "A Field Guide to American Higher-Ed Reformers," *Chronicle of Higher Education,* April 6, 2015, http://chronicle.com/blogs/conversation/2015/04/06/a-field-guide-to-american-higher-ed-reformers/?cid=pm&utm_source=pm&utm_medium=en.

5. Katherine Mangan, "More States Tie Money to Colleges' Performance, but That May Not Work," *Chronicle of Higher Education*, January 14, 2015, http://chronicle.com/article/More-States-Tie-Money-to/151183.

6. For a detailed analysis of state-by-state allocations, see the annual "Almanac of Higher Education," *Chronicle of Higher Education*, e.g., August 22, 2014, http://chronicle.com/section/Almanac-of-Higher-Education/801.

7. See Bain & Company, www.bain.com/industry-expertise/social-and-public-sector/higher-education.aspx#2.

8. Kevin Carey, "Why President Obama's Rankings Are a Good Place to Start," *Chronicle of Higher Education*, March 14, 2014, http://chronicle.com/article/Why-President-Obama-s/145243.

9. "Principles of Accreditation: Foundations for Quality Enhancement," Southern Association of Schools and Colleges: Commission on Colleges, 2012, 18, www.sac-scoc.org/pdf/2012PrinciplesOfAcreditation.pdf.

10. Cited in Jonah Newman, "What Experts on College-Ratings Systems Mean by 'We Need Better Data,'" *Chronicle of Higher Education*, February 14, 2014, http://chronicle.com/blogs/data/2014/02/14/what-experts-on-college-ratings-system-mean-by-we-need-better-data/?cid=at&utm_source=at&utm_medium=en.

11. Cited in Goldie Blumenstyk, "Swings in Credit Ratings Hint of Challenges Ahead for Colleges," *Chronicle of Higher Education*, March 4, 2014, http://chronicle.com/article/Swings-in-Credit-Ratings-Hint/145095.

12. A more detailed explanation of human knowledge as a positive feedback loop is described in Draper L. Kauffman, *Systems 1: An Introduction to Systems Thinking* (Minneapolis: Future Systems, 1980), 21–23.

Acknowledgments

Years ago, I was on a consulting assignment at a large community college outside of Philadelphia. The workshop was focused on process design and continuous improvement with fifty to sixty individuals. The group was quite eclectic—as I had requested—and so there were professors, administrators, and staff members in the audience. One technique I often used to get people to understand the nature of processes was to ask them, "What do you do?"

So, I chose a woman in the back row and asked my question. She shifted in her chair and glanced around. Finally, in a weak and anxious voice she managed to say, "I am a secretary in Dean of Student's office." This was the typical type of response to my question. People ordinarily reply to the "What do you do?" question by stating their job title. That is understandable. It is a shorthand answer and one can infer a lot with just a little information.

But it does not really answer the question.

What someone *does* is a process question and involves taking various types of input, adding value by transforming it in some ways, and then handing the results off to others. In the workshop, then, I took a few minutes to explore with her the nature of the input she received, what she did to add value, and who benefited from those transformations.

Weeks later, I was on another assignment several hundred miles to the north in New Haven, Connecticut. The group was smaller. We were focused on a specific, serious problem rather than being in a general workshop setting, and the work was scheduled to take a week or so. I engaged the process-improvement team in some just-in-time training and began in a similar fashion by choosing an individual and asking her, "What do you do?"

The woman, in this case seated to my immediate right, gave me a somewhat quizzical look. She seemed to straighten in her chair. And then she said in a confident, matter-of-fact way, "I work at Yale University." It wasn't until

xxiii

later that I found out she was a secretary for an administrator in the Beinecke Library.

Their job titles were similar but their attitudes about their work were very different.

I wish to acknowledge the many colleagues and clients I have worked with as a faculty member, administrator, and consultant over my professional lifetime. I kept thinking about them as I did the research and wrote drafts of this manuscript. My thoughts drifted to scenarios like the one above—*the desire to be a part of something special*. It is a constant. Yes, people want a title and a fatter paycheck. But, perhaps most importantly, they want to be proud of their institution and feel as though they are contributing to its successes. Unfortunately, many do not.

The aspirational vision isn't there, the sense of urgency doesn't exist, and the tools that enable people to come together and create a different future aren't readily available to them. I was driven to write this book because I can still remember the sheer joy in work expressed by that secretary at Yale University. I want others to have that same opportunity to feel good about what they do.

Early feedback on this manuscript came from John van Knorring at Stylus Publishing. As someone with a business and economics background, I was grateful for Dave Richard at Rollins College, who provided me with a better understanding of many of the psychological principles that undergird this work. Martha Oburn, a former colleague and enduring friend, is a crack institutional researcher. Who knew that she is also a wonderful editor with a keen eye for dangling modifiers and irregular verbs? She provided the kind of front-to-back feedback that has turned sentences, paragraphs, and chapters into a completed book. I'd also like to thank the folks at Rowman & Littlefield—specifically, Tom Koerner and Christine Fahey—for their encouragement and guidance along the way.

And to Rhonda, my wife and friend, thank you for the second act.

Introduction

This book is about owning change at the institutional level and how colleges and universities can begin to operationalize a responsibility paradigm. After all, while it is relatively easy to bemoan the fact that we have abdicated our responsibility by not owning it, it is something quite different to enumerate and implement a particular set of tools—in our case, a virtuous cycle—that can empower individuals and catalyze institutions.

This, then, is a call to action in which the "transformees" become the "transformers."

The first chapter of the book, "On Perilous Conduct," begins by examining the environment within which colleges and universities currently operate—that is, those political, economic, social, and technological forces that are influencing our institutions. It concludes that the environment is increasingly unstable but suggests that the real challenge is that these factors are now interacting in unique and powerful ways—*a high-velocity environment*. The chapter then describes the organizational structure of colleges and universities that has enabled them to mitigate past external influences. The last part of the chapter lays out the premise of the book: Institutions no longer have the luxury of seeking some sort of equilibrium. Accommodating change is an insufficient strategy because in a high-velocity environment each and every institution will either be gaining traction (virtuous cycles) or losing ground (vicious cycles).

The second chapter, "Bold Imaginings," lays out a framework for change. It is divided into several parts. The first part speaks to the mechanics of inertia in higher education. Next, there is a description of general systems theory—or a discipline that allows for "thinking in wholes"—as the framework for creating advancement opportunities. There are two building blocks to dynamic systems: balancing loops and reinforcing loops. Since equilibrium (or balance) is less of an option for colleges and universities now and in the future, the discussion shifts to reinforcing loops or engines that compound change in one direction or another. The downward direction produces degradation and decay, and describes how institutions lose ground in high-velocity environments. The final part of the chapter describes in detail the other reinforcing loop, a virtuous cycle, which provides the means for demonstrating responsibility.

The eight chapters that follow are a set of prescriptions that use virtuous-cycle or upward-spiral dynamics to produce momentum in our colleges and universities:

Chapter 3: "Man's Search for Meaning: Striving and Struggling for a Worth-while Goal." This first lesson is about purpose and the need to describe a future that cultivates a sense of urgency in an organization. The self-imposed gap between where we are and what we want to create is the antidote to complacency and the context for momentum.

Chapter 4: "The War Canoe: Aligning People and Processes." A virtu-ous cycle that produces momentum must have the means to harness its resources. The combination of force and direction creates the dynamic for an organization that can build capacity and catalyze growth.

Chapter 5: "The Accumulators: Deciding What Assets You Want to Grow." This dynamic focuses on the use of leverage to activate virtuous cycles. While any college or university has many different assets—"a useful or valuable quality, person, or thing; an advantage or resource"—there needs to be conscious decisions about which ones will have the greatest impact.

Chapter 6: "Icebergs: Understanding What Lies Beneath the Surface." We tend to react to problems without really understanding patterns or root causes. The result is often an institution that spends its time oscillating back and forth in a state of constant crisis management. This dynamic involves the process of exploring fundamental change that advances the institution in sustainable ways.

Chapter 7: "Bootstrapping: Managing the Angle of Approach." Too little change and there is no distinction between "what is" and "what could be"; too much change creates fear and invites opposing forces to gain strength. The primary focus here is about creating patterns such that each success becomes the platform for gaining confidence and additional successes.

Chapter 8: "Peripheral Vision: Sharing Knowledge about How a System Works." A system has a goal and interrelated parts. This chapter suggests that the more people who can see how the system works, the better. Indeed, momentum can't be created by a few. Large numbers of people within the organization must understand what success looks like and know how they can help achieve it.

Chapter 9: "The Examined Life: Embracing Feedback to Learn and Grow." Having the capacity to reflect on what is working and what isn't is at the core of learning organizations. For a college or university to gain traction and build momentum, it must "design in" feedback loops and then be earnest about how to use results to make positive adjustments.

Chapter 10: "Gumption Junction—Demonstrating the Courage to Create." This final prescription acknowledges that the status quo has been the default option for colleges and universities. Embracing a responsibility-driven paradigm that is itself the source of change involves courageous acts and the ability to inspire others to challenge their own assumptions.

Momentum, as Virginia Tech's Timothy Sands reminds us in the preface, is built on a sense of unrest: "This is a place that clearly is not happy with the status quo and that's the kind of institution that I want to be associated with." It is the goal of this book to help institutions take responsibility for nurturing that divine sense of discontent by creating virtuous cycles of change.

Chapter 1

On Perilous Conduct

Inquiring minds want to know. The question posed in large block letters on the front page of *Newsweek* magazine's September 17, 2012 issue was "Is College a Lousy Investment?" The article inside continues the questioning, "Why are we spending so much money on college?," and "Why are we so unhappy about it?," followed by the hook: "Maybe it's time to ask a question that seems almost sacrilegious: Is all this investment in college really worth it?" The next few pages of the article are devoted to examples meant to bemuse and berate: the roller-hockey rink in the student recreation center at one university featuring a Jacuzzi that can fit up to fifty-three people, the virtual golf course at another university, as well as the gourmet meals (including sushi and organic tofu) and valet parking at other institutions.

The cover of the August 2014 edition of *Atlantic Monthly* asks, "Is College Doomed?" The article details why and how universities are in trouble and how for-profit insurgents are tearing down higher education so they can rebuild it. The provocative question asked by the *Atlantic Monthly* was summarily answered the next year by Kevin Carey, the director of the Education Policy program at the New America Foundation, who titled his book *The End of College* (2015).

And then there is the book *The Case Against College*. This headline is followed by 250 pages divided into neat quarters: part 1, "The Young as Victims"; part 2, "The Cost"; part 3, "The Payoffs"; and part 4 "The Alternatives." After describing college as "a graceful way to get away from home," the opening gambit of part 2 begins: "Anywhere you go, any way you count it, a college degree costs more money than entering freshmen and their parents think it will. Never mind how much taxpayers and rich alumni kick in. What students are expected to pay comes as a rude shock even to the best-heeled families. For families in more modest circumstances, the costs can be overwhelming."[1]

It is clear from these less-than-nuanced captions that higher education in the United States is currently under considerable attack. There is only one problem with this straightforward conclusion: the first two articles and Carey's book came out in the 2010s, while Caroline Bird's book, *The Case Against College*, was published almost four decades earlier in 1975—same storylines, different generations.

This is not the first time higher education has struggled with doom and gloom. A 1990 article published in an "On the Lighter Side" section heading for the *Journal of College Admissions* was titled "The Continuing Crisis in Higher Education." The admittedly cursory review started with the "virtual extinction" of higher education institutions in *Education Problems in the College and University* (1921): "Two years and a half ago the higher education institutions of the Unites States were threatened with virtual extinction as the result of plans for mobilizing the man power of the country." The intervening decades were just as harrowing:

1938: "We are witnessing today the 'twilight' of the four-year liberal arts program." —*Journal of Higher Education*

1949: "Every one of America's independent colleges and universities is now staggering under its financial load." —*Association of American Colleges Bulletin*

1952: "The failures of higher education in America have become the concern of millions of people who a few decades ago would have been indifferent." —*The Colleges and the Community*

1960: "In higher education a legacy of acute campus problems is becoming coercive." —*Current Issues in Higher Education*

1972: "American colleges and universities have been buffeted and battered in recent years as never before." —*Journal of Higher Education*

1984: "At the present time, American higher education is at a low ebb." —*Change Magazine*[2]

The "virtual extinction" of higher education in the 1920s had given way to the "twilight" years of the following decade. Colleges and universities then "staggered" through the 1940s, followed by the "failures" of the 1950s. The next decade clearly offered little respite with all of higher education's "acute problems," only to then be "buffeted and battered" during the 1970s. Regrettably, the tide did not turn in 1980s with colleges and universities being marooned like so much flotsam at "low ebb."

There is little doubt that the challenges currently facing higher education in this country are daunting. But this time-travel exercise may at least cause us to reflect on our ripped-from-the-headlines culture. Each generation of faculty, staff, and administrators reacts to their own worldview and reaches their own conclusions about the current state of affairs. The seemingly pervasive and intractable campus problems that academe experienced over the past century were very real to each and every generation.

This opening chapter is organized around three questions. First, *Is the nature of change facing today's colleges and universities as challenging as the headlines suggest?* Change itself is not the issue. The question is really about magnitude and complexity and what we should think and do about it. After all, the psychological state described by Alvin Toffler in *Future Shock* (1970)—"too much change in too short a period of time"—more than four decades ago seems like an apt description today. Organizations are like cells with permeable membranes. The constant flow of stimuli between the organization and its environment provokes continuous modulation. Again, if the accelerated rate of technological and social change described by Toffler left individuals feeling disconnected and suffering from "shattering stress and disorientation" in the 1970s, is it unreasonable to assume that institutions of higher education may be suffering from even more strain and discomfort in the twenty-first century?

The second question follows from the first. If the breadth and depth of environmental change for higher education has created a new, more challenging dynamic, then: *To what degree do colleges and universities maintain the capacity to moderate these external influences?* Our institutions have been remarkably adept at persevering up to this point in history. It is an enviable track record. And with such an enviable track record the tendency is to evoke a "What's past is prologue" Shakespearean armament when responding to current challenges—that is, to dismiss the headlines as unwelcome incursions, label them as fads or the babblings of uninitiated nonmembers of the academy, and assume that the status quo will ultimately prevail.

The final question involves the resolution of the issues and conclusions surrounding the first two questions. If we conclude that this time is different and that there is compelling evidence to suggest that a fundamental change imperative is upon us *and* we assume that the enviable record of higher education to moderate change in the past will not be adequate moving forward, then we need to ask ourselves the final question: *How can individual colleges and universities thrive in the twenty-first century?*

HIGHER EDUCATION'S NEIGHBORHOOD

One of the most informing ways to view organizations is as a set of metaphors. Gareth Morgan described eight different "images" in his classic organizational theory book *The Images of Organization* (1986). He devotes a significant portion of his energy to delineating the difference between "organizations as machines" and "organizations as organisms." He describes the changes in organizations that accompanied the industrial revolution from the mid-1700s to the mid-1800s and the increasing trend toward bureaucratization and routinization of life and work. Of course the major change came half a century later in the form of scientific management as pioneered by Frederick Taylor. The cornerstone of this approach was the division of labor and standardization of work activities that resulted in greater control and efficiency.

While the benefits of "organizations as machines" are well documented and continue to be useful in many industries today, the approach also has severe limitations. For purposes of this discussion, a primary limitation is that mechanistic approaches work best when the environment is *stable, predictable*: Enter "organizations as organisms."

Organizational theory began its foray into biology by developing the idea that employees are people with complex needs that should be satisfied if they are to perform effectively in the workplace. Driven by Maslow's seminal work on motivation, a more integrated view of individuals, organizations, and their environment began to emerge. Organizations as open systems focused on a number of key issues: an emphasis on the environment in which organizations exist, an appreciation for interrelated subsystems, and the need to establish alignment between subsystems and their environment in order to eliminate potential disconnects and dysfunctions.

Within the context of "organizations as organisms," modern colleges and universities are necessarily seen as living, breathing entities that both create knowledge and respond to forces in their environment. It follows, then, that the more dynamic the environment, the more responsive institutions would need to be—hence the importance of our first question: *Is the nature of change facing today's colleges and universities as challenging as the headlines suggest?*

The next four sections constitute an environmental scan of the twenty-first-century higher education landscape. Because of the sheer volume of materials, the approach will be to describe only the most significant themes within each area. The final section posits the idea that the forces themselves—political, economic, social, and technological (PEST)—are interacting in new and significant ways.

Political

The leader of California State University, Charles B. Reed, announced in May of 2012 that he would retire after fourteen years as head of the nation's largest public four-year university system. Search committee members noted, "With so much at stake, finding a replacement who can satisfy the disparate desires of students, faculty, state lawmakers and the public is likely to prove impossible."[3] This dispiriting statement speaks directly to the extent to which members of the academy believe they remain the masters of their own house.

The evidence to suggest that the locus of control has shifted to external constituencies begins with the federal government. The 2006 *Spellings Commission on the Future of Higher Education* was motivated by the belief that our higher education system was failing to prepare the American workforce for the rigors and competitiveness of a globalized marketplace and called for the federal government to play a larger role in promoting accountability and transparency in colleges and universities. It called for a greater focus on student outcomes, a restructured student financial aid system that provided incentives for cost containment, and a federal database to track individual students' performance.[4] While the Obama administration has done a great deal to shine a positive light on community colleges in particular, it too has taken a "we need to fix higher education" approach by proposing a comprehensive college-ratings system tied to federal aid as part of an attempt to minimize tuition and student debt increases.

Individual senators have joined the "fix it" brigade, too. In an essay titled, "Higher Ed Needs Better Data to Spur Reform," senators Ron Wyden and Marco Rubio ask the question, "Why hasn't the quality of the data improved?" They conclude:

A major part of the answer: institutional self-interest. Every school in the country has widely disparate performance outcomes depending on the category, and many college presidents are in no hurry to make their less-than-appealing outcome data available for public scrutiny. There's a fear that students and families will vote with pocketbooks and choose different schools that better meet their needs. The abundance of inaccurate and incomplete data provides institutional leaders a line of defense: so long as such data are the norm upon which they are ranked and rated, they can defend themselves on the basis of flawed methodology.[5]

Other efforts to repair higher education are being played out at the state level. More than half the states have passed laws to base at least some portion of their higher education support on performance measures. Under a 2010 law, Tennessee became the first state to appropriate nearly all of its state higher education dollars based on institutional outcomes such as credit completions and graduations rates. The basic argument on the one side—the accountability side—is that results matter and institutions of higher education need to be incentivized to become more effective (better outcomes) and efficient (more throughput).

Moreover, as state budgets have become healthier after the debilitating recession, it has been apparent that any budget increase needs to be tied to a set of performance indicators (or budgets with strings attached). For example, in Florida the governor's 2014–2015 budget includes $40 million in new money for the state's twelve-university system. Ten different criteria worth a maximum of fifty points are used in the funding formula with universities needing to earn at least twenty-six points to get any new money. Those earning twenty-five points or less risk losing 1 percent of their 2014–2015 base funding.[6]

In addition to the accountability mantra, the states have also picked up on the transparency tune. This supposedly consumer-driven effort is meant to help prospective students and their families compare options, thereby getting more out of their higher education dollars. For example, the California Community College Chancellor's Office has mandated that each of its 112 colleges place on their homepage a Student Success Scorecard. According to the Chancellor's Office, the Scorecard fills a void:

> In its commitment to increase transfer and degree and certificate attainment, the California Community Colleges Board of Governors has established a performance measurement system that tracks student success at all 112 community colleges. This scorecard represents an unprecedented level of transparency and accountability on student progress and success metrics in public higher education in the United States. The data available in this scorecard tell how well colleges are doing in remedial instruction, job training programs, retention of students and graduation and completion rates.[7]

It should also be noted that some of the present state-level politics seem to hearken to the past. In 1967, a month into his term as governor of California, Ronald Reagan assured people that he wouldn't do anything to negatively impact the state's system of public higher education. "But," he added, "we do believe that there are certain intellectual luxuries that perhaps we could do without."

In North Carolina, for example, the John Pope Center for Higher Education Policy describes its mission as making public colleges more accountable to the public by holding them to their "chief goals of scholarly inquiry and responsible teaching." The center's website notes that "taxpayers as well as students and their families pay hefty prices to support a system that often appears to provide little educational value." Jenna Robinson, the center's president, calls the organization a "watchdog" for a university system that has become too expensive for many students because of expanding administrative costs.[8]

While in Wisconsin, the governor has advocated an agenda around holding public colleges more accountable for how they spend their money and how they prepare their students for the workplace. That translated into an original budget proposal that replaced the ideals of "knowledge," "truth," and "public service," embedded in state law as part of the university's mission statement (the Wisconsin Idea) with a demand to concentrate narrowly on the state's workforce needs—and with a sizable budget cut.[9]

Both incidences reflect new efforts to "sharpen the focus" of higher education by eliminating or reducing perceived intellectual luxuries (centers, programs, majors) and the liberal arts that are thought by some elected officials to be an unnecessary indulgence.

Another area of interest is the intersection of commerce and ideology. The *U.S. News & World Report*, the granddaddy of college and university rankings, began in 1983 and has had a profound impact on how institutions invest their scarce resources (to impact their rankings) and market themselves. Over the last thirty years a cottage industry of "publishers as pundits" has successfully designated themselves as arbiters of higher education quality.

But the current crop of arbiters also includes *Forbes* magazine's "America's Top Colleges," which ranks 650 colleges based on their belief in "output" rather than "input" through a partnership with the Center for College Affordability and Productivity and the *Washington Monthly's* "National University Rankings" based on "contribution to the public good" in three broad categories: social mobility, research, and service. The newest entrant (2015) in this crowded field is the Brookings Institute's "value-added" rankings, which compares institutions on the basis of how their alumni perform on three economic measures: mid-career earnings, student loan repayment, and occupational earnings power.

And if that weren't enough commerce for you, there is the business of selling books. Inspired by the success of *The Closing of the American Mind: How Higher Has Failed Democracy and Impoverished the Souls of Today's Students* (1987) and *Imposters in the Temple: American Intellectuals Are Destroying Our Universities and Cheating Our Students of Their Future* (1992), the new decade has seen a spate of freshly minted titles. From *The Fall of the Faculty: The Rise of the All-Administrative University* (2011) to *Why It Matters Excellent Sheep: The Miseducation of the American Elite* (2014), each endeavor seems to increasingly cleave to a defined political narrative.

A final entity deserves some focused attention: college or university boards. Virtually all institutions of higher education have some form of board structure to provide governance and act as the legal agent or "owner" of the institution. Traditionally, the board's governing role has been limited to the selection of the president and policy approval with daily operations and the administration of the institution vested in the president. But things have changed. Boards used to be seen as working with the administration to set broad institutional direction while letting administrators and faculty members, in a shared governance environment, decide on how to get there.

The last decade or so, however, has seen a significant shift from "board as benefactor," in which boards often operated as a buffer to neutralize outside pressure, to "board as boss," in which they became the ones applying the pressure. Why? Because as Rick Legon, president of the Association of Governing Boards of Universities and Colleges, has stated, "Boards are recognizing that the stakes of higher education have risen. The challenges are more difficult, the public trust is more uncertain, and as a bridge between the institution and the public, they're now responsible for an increased level of accountability."[10]

Economic

The economic landscape within which higher education operates is in turmoil. Just as "holding institutions accountable" is the banner associated with the political environment, the current economic environment began with the parallel axiom of "doing more with less." The "doing more" portion of the equation gained traction when enrollments began to increase (especially in community colleges) as the economy turned downward in a counter-cyclical fashion, while the importance of postsecondary education has grown in a knowledge-based economy. The Great Recession also resulted in states slashing the finances of public colleges and universities, which educate more than 70 percent of the country's undergraduate students—hence, "with less." The disinvestment has been shocking, with some states (e.g., Arizona, Wisconsin, Louisiana) making cuts that are beginning to result in a scenario of going from "state supported" to "state assisted" to merely "state located."

That, in turn, began a major cost-shifting exercise with students and their families being forced to pick up the slack. The College Board's *Trends in College Pricing* reported the average sticker price for in-state tuition and fees at public universities was $9,139 in 2014–15 with another $9,804 for room and board charges, while almost 150 private institutions had a total cost of more than $50,000. The challenge, of course, is that the average income for families (adjusted for inflation) remains at levels that are lower than 2002.[11]

An important part of the resulting sticker-shock headlines is the ongoing debate about the causes. Numerous thoughtful analyses on this subject have been aptly detailed in books and articles, especially beginning with Ronald Ehrenberg's *Tuition Rising: Why College Costs So Much* (2002). But what has made it into the popular press is a series of narratives. One such theme attempts to justify the disinvestment in public higher education by the states. Stories that follow this narrative usually try to focus on a lack of faculty productivity or will cherrypick a course title—The Cultural History of Hip

Hop—for ridicule. Another swipe at public institutions is the new "$10,000 degree" being trumpeted by politicians in some states to highlight universities' spendthrift ways. The "starve the beast" argument seems to prevail in this thinking: don't give them any money because they'll just spend it.

For the private institutions, the stories are often about the proverbial arms race of amenities—the rock-climbing walls, sushi bars, and Olympic-sized swimming pools—all seen as being "necessary" for them to remain competitive in their efforts to recruit students and hit enrollment targets.

Another newly emerged issue is the rising level of student debt. As the cost shifting occurred—from state to student—it triggered a concomitant increase in student debt and default rates. And the number that grabbed headlines beginning in 2013 was . . . $1 trillion. That is now the collective student loan debt in this country. It is more than American consumers owe on their credit cards; it is more than the American government owes China. Almost 40 million Americans have these student loans outstanding, with the class of 2014 graduating with an average debt of around $30,000. The implications for sending a whole class of people out into their professional lives with a negative net worth has an extended reach, too, because those same individuals are less likely to purchase cars and homes while dealing with their debt burden.

With states disinvesting, costs shifting, and tuition and debt rising, it necessarily follows that the next shoe to drop would be the argument around the net value of the college-going experience: *Is college worth it?*

The general answer, of course, is "yes," but the more nuanced answer might be "it's complicated." Affirming the positive is a 2014 report by the Pew Research Center, "The Rising Cost of Not Going to College": "On virtually every measure of economic well-being and career attainment—from personal earnings to job satisfaction to the share employed full time—young college graduates are outperforming their peers with less education."[12] Evidence suggests the ROI is even greater for society than it is for the individual. Another 2014 report prepared for the American Association of Community Colleges by Economic Modeling Specialists International found that community college graduates received nearly $5 in benefits for every dollar they spend in their education, while the return to taxpayers is almost six to one.[13]

The qualifier, of course, is that does not mean college is for everyone. There is enormous variation depending on factors such as institution attended, field of study, and whether a student actually graduates.[14] Unfortunately, the nuanced version of events seems often to get lost in the more provocative stories such as the previously mentioned 2012 *Time* magazine cover story, "Is College a Lousy Investment?," or Peter Thiel's "20 Under 20 Thiel Fellowships." The former PayPal CEO started a program in 2011 that encourages kids to forego college and instead start companies by giving them $100,000 in seed money and access to technology mentors. Each year, when a new batch of teen entrepreneurs is announced, there are the inflammatory headlines that infer that a college education is a complete waste of time.

It is impossible to leave this section without a somewhat-detailed observation. In a major speech late in 2013 President Obama stated that income inequality is "the defining issue of our time." That observation (which has a broad political consensus around the problem even though the solutions break down along more conservative-liberal lines) is derived from the fact that economic inequality and the concentration of wealth has changed dramatically. By one measure, U.S. income inequality is the highest it has been since 1928 and more unequal than most of its developed-world peers. Moreover, wealth inequality is even greater than income inequality.

A similar narrative is building in higher education and being reported in the media. It takes two forms: the individual and the institution. The academic version of the "haves and the have nots" made it to the pages of a *New York Times* article titled, "Pay for U.S. College Presidents Continues to Grow," in which it revealed that forty-two college presidents were now making more than $1 million in total compensation.[15] Add to that another headline, "At Private Colleges, 33 Coaches and Athletic Directors Top $1 Million." Add to that a 2014 Delta Cost Project report finding that since 1990, the number of faculty and staff positions per administrator has declined, as the number of executives and professional staff members has climbed, and you begin to get a powerful Wall Street-type narrative.[16]

And the "have nots" in this equation? That would be those who deliver the majority of the instruction at our colleges and universities—adjuncts. A report from the House Education and Workforce Committee titled "The Just-in-Time Professor" found the median pay for a standard three-credit course was $2,700 with an annual salary of $22,041 (below the federal poverty line for a family of four). It went on to state, "The contingent faculty trend appears to mirror trends in the general labor market toward a flexible, 'just-in-time' workforce, with lower compensation and unpredictable schedules for what were once considered middle-class jobs."[17]

At the institutional level this bifurcation exercise—the haves and the have nots—also appears to be gaining strength. According to a 2015 report from Moody's Investors Service, the ten richest institutions held nearly one-third of total cash and investments at four-year schools, while the top forty accounted for two-thirds with a median of $6.3 billion in cash and investments.[18] Other institutions of higher education are not so fortunate. The 1,100 community colleges in the United States enroll 56 percent of our Hispanic students and 48 percent of all black students, the majority of whom receive financial aid to cover their far more modest tuition and fees. Combined, these community colleges earn about $30 million a year from their endowments. That's what Harvard University makes every three days.

Social

Social factors are a broad range of cultural aspects, lifestyle considerations, and demographic variables that influence, in this case, our colleges and universities. As with our first two influencers, a dominant theme has emerged with this environmental factor. If "holding institutions accountable" is the phrase most associated with the political realm and "doing more with less" has been the mantra that seems to accompany the economic conversations within which we operate, then the concept of economic inequality has morphed into a dominant social theme as well. While most of the headlines focus on statistics and stories around the "1 percent," researchers in various fields have dug deep into the implications associated with various forms of inequality.

As an example, epidemiologists Richard Wilkinson and Kate Pickett studied a broad range of health and social problems—physical health, drug abuse, obesity, violence, teenage pregnancies, and so on—across many different countries and found that more unequal societies almost always do worse.[19] And the data suggest that these more unequal societies (and in this country even states) are bad for everyone—the rich and middle class as well as the poor. Joseph Stiglitz, the Nobel Prize winner in economics, has recently detailed how today's divided society endangers our future in his volume *The Price of Inequality* (2012). He argues that the interplay between market forces and political machinations goes beyond economics (slower growth, lower GDP) to threaten our ideals of equal opportunities and fair play.

Inequality, as noted, has many different, yet overlapping, forms. At the core is social inequality in which gender roles, racial stereotyping, and so on can limit access to opportunity. Such limitations inevitably lead to income inequality, which, in turn, leads to wealth inequality. And perhaps most troubling for Americans is that when these forces harden it also leads to a lack of social and economic mobility that smacks at the very foundation of the American dream—"Opportunity is who we are," said the president when describing why inequality was the defining challenge of our time.

Indeed, one begins to question whether the dream is more myth than an actual ladder of opportunity when the Horatio Algers rags-to-riches narrative is not supported by the evidence. Studies of mobility in developed countries show the United States to be less mobile than comparable nations. Those with the greatest intergenerational mobility tend to be the Scandinavian countries—Denmark, Norway, Finland, and Sweden—while the United States and the United Kingdom are at the other end of the spectrum. American society is much "stickier" than most of us assume with the children of the less-advantaged tending to stay at the bottom while the children of the privileged have a greater chance of remaining at the top of the heap.

It is this element of the equation—opportunity—that has specific relevance for higher education because there are two recognized ways to create more equal, less-stratified, societies that are known to have positive effects on the quality and length of life. One is through the redistribution of wealth through such mechanisms as tax policies (progressive taxes, inheritance taxes) and numerous forms of monetary policy that allow various transfer payments such as food stamps and welfare programs. The other is through investment in and access to what is generally regarded as the great equalizer—education. But as we have seen, the patterns that we witness in society bleed across the edges, ooze under the door, and spill over the ramparts until they emerge in various forms in our colleges and universities.

A recent study is illustrative. "Separate and Unequal," a report from Georgetown University's Center for Education and the Workforce, analyzed enrollment trends from 4,400 postsecondary institutions by race and institutional selectivity over the past fifteen years.[20] The key finding is that 82 percent of new white enrollments have gone to the 468 most selective colleges, while 72 percent of new Hispanic enrollment and 68 percent of new African American enrollment have gone to two-year, open-access schools. These two separate postsecondary pathways are not a function of qualifications. For example, more than 30 percent of African Americans and Hispanics with a high school grade point average (GPA) higher than 3.5 go to community colleges compared with only 22 percent of whites with the same GPA.

What is so onerous about these inconvenient truths is that they lead to unequal education and economic outcomes. Selective colleges have greater financial resources and spend two to five times more on instruction per student than open-access institutions. Moreover, selective colleges both have significantly higher completion rates and produce graduates with higher future earnings. The report concludes, "The postsecondary system mimics the racial inequality it inherits from the K-12 education system, then magnifies and projects that inequality into the labor market and society at large."

This separate and unequal theme has been echoed in "Bridging the Higher Education Divide," by the Century Foundation.[21] The task force preparing the report concluded that two-year colleges were being asked to educate those students with the greatest needs using the least funds. One of the most compelling sets of facts used to support a new funding model for community colleges looked at the change in per-pupil total operating expenditures for the ten-year period from 1999 to 2009. The range went from a private-sector increase of $13,912 to the public community colleges, which barely eked out any increase at all—a miserly $1. Again, the conclusion is broad-sweeping: "Our higher education system, like the larger society, is growing more and more unequal."

Perhaps the most disturbing part of this discussion is not simply the pernicious effects that extreme inequality (in all its forms) has on our society but the causal role that higher education may be playing. In an essay adapted from her 2014 book, *Degrees of Inequality*, Suzanne Mettler describes the nature of the crisis:

> Over the past 30 years, it [higher education] has gone from facilitating upward mobility to exacerbating social inequality. College-going, once associated with opportunity, now engenders something that increasingly resembles a caste system: It takes Americans who grew up in different social strata and widens the divisions among them. The consequences are vast, including differences among graduate in employment rates and lifetime earnings, in health, and in civic engagement.[22]

Mettler highlights a series of factors that have helped produce these circumstances. First, federal student aid no longer comes close to covering the cost of tuition, leaving students with little choice other than borrowing more. Next, states have begun to see college degrees less as a public good and more as an individual benefit. Public higher education has, in effect, become increasingly privatized. And finally, lawmakers have permitted the for-profit education industry to capture a huge portion of federal student-aid dollars and also leave many minority and low-income students with stifling debt. It is hard to grasp such a stunning reversal: higher education going from "The Great Equalizer" in American society to "The Great Unleveler."

Technological

It began in the fall of 2011 when two Stanford University professors—Sebastian Thrun and Peter Norvig—offered a course in artificial intelligence. The class was free and online. Enrollment peaked at 160,000, and the MOOC (Massive Open Online Course) had arrived. The MOOC was actually an extension of the already-existing open educational resources movement and the term had been coined years before. But somehow the celebrity status of the instructors, the prestige of Stanford University and the subsequent "massive" enrollment combined to create a firestorm of interest. The following year the *New York Times* dubbed 2012 "The Year of the MOOC" and *Time* magazine declared MOOCs the "Ivy League for the Masses" in an article royally titled, "College Is Dead. Long Live College!"

While traditional online courses charge tuition, offer credit, and limit enrollment to ensure interaction with an instructor, a MOOC is all about access, or as Educause defines it, "a model for delivering learning content

online to any person who wants to take a course, with no limit on attendance."
It follows that this perceived disruption to higher learning has generated a lot
of hype. The headlines initially came from the formation of edX, the nonprofit start-up from Harvard and the Massachusetts Institute of Technology,
Coursera and Udacity, a company formed by Thrun and others. The implications associated with the headlines largely centered on two phenomena: (1)
the democratization of higher education and (2) costs and productivity in
higher education.

First, the ability of people around the world to have access to such courses
and knowledge really is exciting. As an example, a course taught by Professor
Hossam Haick titled "Nanotechnology and Nanosensors" has ten classes of
short lecture videos with weekly quizzes, forum activities, and a final project.
Anyone with an internet connection can participate. It is free. Early on, with
little marketing of the course, there were nearly thirty thousand registrants
including students from Egypt, Saudi Arabia, Jordan, Iraq, and other countries. What is remarkable is that Professor Haick teaches at Technion, Israel
Institute of Technology, and the course was offered through the Coursera
MOOC website *in Arabic and English*.[23]

And second, it was natural that a sexy, new technology was initially
seen as the silver bullet needed to get the cost of a college education under
control. Politicians, in particular, jumped on both the opportunity to appear
forward-looking and the possibility of freeing up money out of state budgets.
As we have already seen, MOOCs also presented an additional opportunity:
the chance to infuse more accountability into the conversation by portraying
many in higher education as being resistant to change.

But what the headlines "giveth," the headlines "taketh" away. Early in
2013, with much publicity including the solid support of California governor
Jerry Brown, San Jose State University announced a partnership with Udacity to offer low-cost introductory MOOC classes for credit. Months later,
the program was pronounced a "flop" after less than a quarter of the algebra
students passed the class while students in all the online courses did worse
than those taking the equivalent traditional classes. Some initial efforts such
as Georgia Tech's MOOC-like online master's degree in computer science
seem destined to succeed. But concerns about the quality of the degrees to
be offered have resulted in a moratorium of MOOCs at American University
while Amherst College's faculty voted down a proposal to join edX, and
Duke University backed out of a deal with nine other universities and 2U, a
provider of cloud-based software.

One of the best things about the MOOC initiative is that the process of
delivering the courses also produces the information to assess them. And the
results are pouring in. A 2014 study of seventeen MOOCs offered by Harvard
and MIT in 2012 and 2013 reveals some intriguing (selected) results:

- 841,687 people registered for the MOOCs.
- 5 percent of all registrants earned a certificate of completion.
- 35 percent never viewed any of the course materials.
- 66 percent already held a bachelor's degree or higher.
- 29 percent of all registrants were female.
- 3 percent of all registrants were from underdeveloped countries.[24]

Another 2014 study from the University of Pennsylvania's Graduate School of Education analyzed the movement of a million users through sixteen Coursera courses offered by the university. The project aimed to identify key transition points for users—such as when users enter and leave courses—as well as when and how users participate in the courses. Course completion ranged from 2 percent to 14 percent with an average of 4 percent across all courses.[25]

A 2015 large-scale study was funded by a Bill & Melinda Gates Foundation grant and sought to answer the question, "Where is research on massive open online courses headed?" Grant money funded twenty-eight separate research efforts, which were then analyzed for the report *Preparing for the Digital University*. The meta-analysis is a 230-page review that covers not only MOOCs but also the history and current state of distance, blended, and online learning.[26]

The clear challenge associated with the MOOC tsunami is the disconnection between the hope associated with access and the reality associated with success in light of the focus on the Completion Agenda. Still, it is a valuable platform for testing new teaching methods and, at the same time, is driving a whole new discussion on research into teaching. It is, in effect, a teaching experiment of unprecedented scale.

And if anyone thinks this roller-coaster ride is over, and the hype has given way to business as usual, they weren't paying attention when in April of 2015 Arizona State University (ASU), in partnership with edX, announced the Global Freshman Academy.[27] Anyone will be able to register for the dozen courses and take them for free. For those who pay a fee, they can have their identity verified at the end of each course, and for those who want to pay the university a separate, larger fee, they can earn credit for their work. After completing the courses, students can receive a transcript from ASU and can transfer to a different program or institution as sophomores. As the edX CEO said in an interview, "What this does is it really opens up new pathways for all students, no matter where they are in the world."[28]

While MOOCs were sucking all the oxygen out of the room, the fact remains that a virtual big bang of technology-driven innovation has begun to impact much of higher education. Perhaps at the most basic level, learning management systems (LMS) are a technology being used on almost every campus to communicate with students and administer the class (share the syllabus, track attendance, record grades). Adaptive learning—technology in which students are constantly given exercises and questions based on their level of mastery—is being used more and more often. Mobile devices are advancing the notion of "learn anywhere at any time."

Lecture capture is another technology that has quickly evolved from an after-class activity into an e-learning platform that seeks to take advantage of a classroom full of laptops and tablets. Initially it allowed faculty members to "flip" their classrooms (asking students to watch video lectures or do online readings for homework and reserving class time for interactive projects, discussions, and clearing up misunderstandings). The technology is now being used to also increase student engagement, to identify intervention opportunities, and to improve student outcomes.

Whether it is MOOCs or adaptive, flipped, or mobile learning, whether it is the transformation of libraries into centralized digital learning centers or the further evolution of voice and video tools in online learning, technology is an equal partner, along with political, economic, and social factors that will impact the future of higher education.

A Case for Strong Emergence

The externally driven narratives that have been covered so far are striking. By themselves, one could easily conclude that the forces that push and pull institutions of higher education are both animated and intensifying. But while the exercise to document these forces is useful and helps to illuminate a truly dynamic context, it still does not give full justice to the environment within which twenty-first-century colleges and universities must now operate. That is because the forces are beginning to interact in significant ways.

This phenomenon is often discussed in various disciplines in terms of magnitude—weak and strong emergence. The notion of weak emergence suggests that any new qualities exhibited by interactions can ultimately be reduced back to the system's parts. An ant hill or traffic jams are simple examples. There is clear interaction taking place but nothing new is being created. Strong emergence, in contrast, is literally a case where "the whole is greater than the sum of its parts" because something new is being created. The results are not additive; they are multiplicative.

These (PEST) interactions are creating a powerful new dynamic that higher education has never seen before.

For example, most states have made a consistent choice to defund higher education over the last decade. But those same lawmakers have become enamored with technology, especially online classes and MOOCs. While the argument for pursuing the use of such technologies is usually stated in terms of driving down costs, a series of questions might also be asked about the learning that is taking place in this digital environment. A new long-term study conducted at Columbia University's Community College Research Center suggests that there may be significant social implications to this trend.[29] Their results suggest that students in certain demographic groups—including black students, male students, younger students, and students with lower grade point averages—whose members typically struggle in traditional classrooms are finding their troubles exacerbated in online courses.

The parts—political, economic, social, and technology—here are not acting independently. Indeed, while the political and economic forces may align with the technology to produce what many believe to be large increases in efficiency, the unintended consequences may have a significant long-term impact on social and economic inequality.

Another illustration of this dynamic is embedded in the national debate over adjunct salaries. In early 2014, a key committee of the Colorado legislature approved a bill that would give community college adjunct instructors seniority rights, some level of job security, and the same pay and benefits on a per-hour basis as full-time instructors. The chairwoman of the committee echoed others on the panel in calling the poor working conditions of adjunct instructors "an issue we just can't ignore."[30]

But while various individuals and groups (e.g., New Faculty Majority, a national advocacy group for adjuncts, and the American Association of University Professors) attempted to frame the political debate in terms of working conditions, it was the community college officials who made the economic argument: forcing community colleges to pay significantly higher salary and benefits would ultimately hurt both adjuncts and students by reducing course offerings to cover the costs. Again, politics are driving an emerging ethical issue that is being debated within the context of budgetary constraints, some of which the politicians themselves created.

A more dramatic illustration of strong emergence in higher education that reverberated across the nation was played out in Charlottesville, Virginia. On June 10 of 2012 Helen E. Dragas, the chair of the Board of Visitors at the University of Virginia, announced the resignation of President Teresa Sullivan. While college and university CEOs are relieved of their duties with some frequency, what made this announcement newsworthy beyond the immediate domain of UVA's historic commons was twofold: first, Sullivan had been appointed president only two years earlier after praiseworthy stints as provost at the University of Michigan and vice president and dean of graduate studies at the University of Texas, Austin; and second, the reasons given for her sudden departure were both sparse and sketchy.

As the story began to unfold over the next several weeks through official statements and e-mails obtained through the Freedom of Information Act, the primary issue appeared to be a political power struggle or clash between two fundamentally different approaches to leading a major academic institution. Much of the language used by board members and others that joined the fray reflected issues of accountability and productivity. The narrative suggested that leadership needed to be bold, dynamic, and perhaps less deferential to faculty members.

Many faculty members and administrators seized on the fact that the board was dominated by hedge fund and real estate executives. They saw the move as a corporate takeover and typical of a top-down, micromanagement mind-set that had no place at such a prestigious institution. The Faculty Senate voted no-confidence in the board. The Southern Association of Colleges and Schools commented that the board's action might have put it out of compliance with three of the organization's standards, among them the "faculty role in governance."

Another dominant theme throughout the fast-moving saga was the role of technology at the university. Ms. Dragas made specific references to the need for the university to embrace the technological shifts that were occurring in higher education in her announcement regarding the president's resignation. Somewhat later she enumerated a series of challenges facing the institution, including "the changing role of technology in adding value to the reach and quality of the education experience of our students," and then discussed the issue of faculty workload and the quality of the student experience by "integrating technology into introductory courses."

As one might expect, deteriorating fiscal conditions were also part of the rationale for moving in such a decisive way against the president. Four of the rectors noted challenges with state and federal funding, heightened pressure for prioritization of scarce resources, declining faculty compensation, and the securing of philanthropic gifts and grants.

But perhaps the most noteworthy, if not headline-grabbing, indictment offered against President Sullivan, and to a large extent the institution as a whole, was a social construct around the rate of change. A self-avowed "incrementalist" who was being asked to lead an institution steeped in tradition came head-to-head with a polar opposite mind-set: "Despite the enduring magic of Mr. Jefferson's University," Ms. Dragas wrote, "the bottom line is the days of incremental decision-making in higher education are over, or should be."

These individual forces reflect the dynamic nature within which "organizations as organisms" must now exist. But that does not explain the consuming firestorm—national press, protest rallies, resignations, PR consultants, a governor's ultimatum—within which UVA found itself within a matter of days. This was more than a philosophical difference that was poorly handled. There was a collective phenomenon, a swarming, that found political ideologies being fueled by social media—a student-led Facebook group swelled to more than 16,000. It was an economic situation that resulted in the board's perceived need to embrace "disruptive innovation" and "strategic dynamism," which threatened the traditional academic values of thoughtful reflection and shared understanding.

The question asked earlier was *Is the rate and nature of change facing today's colleges and universities really as challenging as the headlines suggest?* The answer must be that such environmental factors as political, economic, social, and technology are more dynamic than ever before. But the critical factor is not just the increased weights of the individual elements. What is most critical is the dramatic impact associated with the interaction of these enhanced factors. This is strong emergence: on steroids. The parts are more potent but the interaction of those parts creates a compounding effect that has resulted in a "high velocity environment."[31]

THE POST OFFICE AND SIXTY-TWO UNIVERSITIES

Let's turn to our second question: *To what degree do colleges and universities maintain the capacity to moderate these external influences?* It is evident that higher education often engages in hyperbole when describing its current and future prospects. Even in relatively good times when the perceived utility of a college degree was high, graduates were able to obtain entry-level jobs in their chosen fields, and the flow of resources in the form of financial aid, private giving, and state and federal dollars was robust, there seemed to have always been an undercurrent of impending doom.

But as Joseph Heller wrote in *Catch-22*, "Just because you're paranoid doesn't mean they aren't after you." Continued calls for accountability along with faculty productivity studies and endless iterations of performance-based funding are tough enough. But when you throw in the states' disinvestment in higher education and relentless technology disruptions, it does feel like campuses are engulfed by a maelstrom, a swirl, of challenges. Who can blame a college or university for developing a siege mentality?

And yet, history would appear to be on our side. Irving Kristol, an American columnist and journalist, once noted, "The university has been—with the possible exception of the post office—the least inventive (or even adaptive) of our social institutions since the end of World War II."[32]

Not to be outdone in terms of a command of history, Clark Kerr, the venerated president of the University of California, concluded:

> Taking as a starting point 1530, when the Lutheran Church was founded, some 66 institutions that existed then still exist today in the Western world in recognizable forms. [These are] the Catholic Church, the Lutheran Church, the parliaments of Iceland and the Isle of Man, and 62 universities.[33]

In spite of all the jolts over the centuries, higher education has shown remarkable resiliency. And today, with about 4,100 two- and four-year institutions and 21 million students, the needs of a lot of American students are obviously being met. Moreover, seven of the top ten institutions recognized by Times Higher Education World University Rankings 2014–2015 are in the United States, helping to draw more than 820,000 international students here with more than $24 billion of economic impact in the form of tuition and living expenses. Higher education seems to be a robust, if embattled, industry.

How is this possible? The answer is that, until recently at least, the structural nature of institutions of higher education has allowed it to employ a series of accommodative actions that resulted in relatively stable internal environments. The best explanation of these structural mechanisms has been offered by Henry Mintzberg in his classic work, *Structure in Fives: Designing Effective Organizations* (1983).[34]

According to Mintzberg, an organization consists of five basic parts—strategic apex, middle line, technostructure, support staff, and operating core—that are configured in different ways to form, in turn, five organizational structures. One such structure, the "Professional Bureaucracy," is common to hospitals, school systems, accounting firms, social-work agencies and . . . universities. The key part of this organizational structure is the operating core, which encompasses those members who perform the basic work related to the production of products or services; for example, faculty members at a college or university or medical doctors and nurses at a hospital.

The Professional Bureaucracy relies for coordination on the standardization of skills, training, and indoctrination. Because of their specialization and certification, professionals exercise considerable control over their own work by working closely with the clients they serve (students or patients) without a great deal of interaction with other professionals (Mintzberg uses the example of a complex open-heart operation in which hardly any conversation occurs because every professional so completely understands his or her role). The Professional Bureaucracy is, essentially, bureaucratic because its coordination is achieved by design, by standards that predetermine what is to be done—for example, the requirements associated with obtaining a degree in a particular academic program of study has a similar set of coordinating characteristics.

The major challenges for these structures are: (1) they do not work well in complex unstable environments and (2) they do not have much capacity to develop and pursue a single, integrated strategy. The issue with the first challenge is that the focus of the organization is on pigeonholing by first categorizing or diagnosing the clients' (again, students' or patients') needs and then applying the requisite protocol (major/syllabus or therapeutic treatment). When environmental changes are identified in such "loosely coupled" systems, the professional expects others in the strategic apex to handle the disturbances.[35]

Strategy formulation, the second major challenge identified, is problematic in these structures because the professionals largely act as independent entrepreneurs with little or no interest in negotiating any unified direction. Also, the many professional associations (accreditors who certify the work and the outcomes) affiliated with these organizations reduce the degrees of freedom that other organizational types described by Mintzberg enjoy.

But for those in the operating core, the Professional Bureaucracy is unique among the five configurations because of its democracy, disseminating its power directly to its professional workers and providing them with extensive autonomy to the point of even freeing them of the need to coordinate closely with their peers. As Mintzberg summarizes: "Thus, the professional has the best of both worlds: he is attached to an organization, yet free to serve his clients in his own way, constrained only by the established standards of the profession."[36]

There have been noteworthy efforts to explain the general principles and conditions associated with a Professional Bureaucracy in academe. For example, Robert Birnbaum uses a fictitious institution, Huxley College, in *How Colleges Work: The Cybernetics of Academic Organization and Leadership* to explain how colleges and universities embrace the same self-governing mechanisms used to create stability in other mechanical, biological, and social systems.[37] In describing effective leadership at Huxley, he enumerates a series of approaches:

- *Management by Exception*—Cybernetic leaders, in Huxley's case President Wagestaff, mostly pay attention to what is wrong. They are concerned with identifying and eliminating weaknesses and problems, and much of their time is taken up with responding to disturbances in structure.
- *Designing Systems*—Huxley's system can function effectively only if environmental disturbances are sensed and negative feedback is then generated by organizational subunits and communicated to appropriate groups.
- *Directive Cybernetic Leadership*—The focus is on carrying out routine tasks when things are going well and making minor adjustments and subtle changes of emphasis when problems appear. Shocks to the system can necessitate more direct action.
- *Administrative Intervention*—While some problems may require intervention, administrators must not overcorrect, thereby exacerbating rather than moderating problems. In some situations, the administrators at Huxley should understand that the wise response is to do nothing.
- *The Role of Analysis*—Huxley College does not try to implement comprehensive solutions that take all variables into consideration. Instead, it reacts

to local, short-term problems with correspondingly local, short-term solutions. When other new problems emerge as a consequence, they are dealt with sequentially.

Birnbaum states that good cybernetic leaders, such as his fictitious President Wagestaff, are modest. Recognizing that they preside over black boxes whose internal processes are not fully understood, they adopt three laws of medicine: "If it's working, keep doing it. If it's not working, stop doing it. If you don't know what to do, don't do anything."[38]

Simply put, colleges and universities have incredible accommodative capacities. The University of Bologna was founded in 1088, the University of Oxford in 1167, and University of Cambridge in 1209. In the United States, our relative newcomers are Harvard University in 1650, the College of William and Mary in 1693, and Yale University in 1701. The self-governing systems they have employed place them in the pantheon of organizations along with the Catholic Church, the Lutheran Church, the parliaments of Iceland, and the Isle of Man.

But these organizations were never designed to withstand the type of high-velocity environments they are now experiencing.

A NEW ORDER OF THINGS

We began this opening chapter with a question involving the pace of change: *Is the rate and nature of change facing today's colleges and universities really as challenging as the headlines suggest?* While the hype and hyperbole can confuse the issue, the facts appear to speak clearly and loudly. The high-velocity environment in which colleges and universities find themselves is a function of not only the increasing political, economic, social, and technological forces but also the strength of the interaction these forces have on each other—yes, the whole is greater than the sum of the parts.

Next, while institutions of higher education have shown immense and enduring capabilities to engage in accommodating behaviors going back centuries, many of those organizational proficiencies may have reached their useful limits. The idea that colleges and universities can continue to react and then adjust as President Wagestaff and his colleagues at Huxley College did so successfully in the past seems unworkable moving forward. The status quo, the inherent ability of disturbances to be moderated through self-governing mechanisms, seems unsustainable. Simply put, the Professional Bureaucracy does not appear to have the ability to moderate today's environmental influences, as our second question asked: *To what degree do colleges and universities maintain the capacity to moderate these external influences?*

The conclusion must be that institutions of higher education are and will be in a constant state of imbalance. They will either be winning or losing. They will either be gaining ground or losing traction, but they will not be calmly standing in one place anymore.

The practices used to create stasis by colleges and universities in this high-velocity world no longer work. When state legislatures cut budgets, we will quickly lose the argument that they are "killing quality" and need to restore the funds or we will shut down a high-profile program. When accreditors and other stakeholders want to know about learning outcomes for graduates who have spent two, four, six, or eight years in college, we will not be able to invoke our "specialness" and lecture them about academic freedom. When open-access institutions fail to graduate students in a timely manner, we will not be getting a free pass by falling back on the lack of "college-readiness" of their students.

And when a new approach that comes from other industries or nonacademics is proposed to help create a more viable future for our institutions, we can no longer attack the source and then immediately dismiss the idea as another in a long line of extramural fads. These traditional, reactive responses are now failing to have the desired impact: to cause others to ameliorate their demands and allow us get to back to doing what we have always done.

Still, identifying the nature of the problem is one thing: the crisis is real and approaches that worked so predictably in the past are sure to be far less effective in the future. But—and this is of vital importance to our discussion—it is also clear that proposing a new way of doing things is equally fraught with its own set of challenges.

No less an expert than the celebrated philosopher and politician Niccolo Machiavelli described that challenge in the starkest of terms: "There is nothing more difficult to take in hand, more perilous to conduct, or more uncertain of its success, than to take the lead in the introduction of a new order of things."

Returning to the painfully public example of the University of Virginia provides an illustration of what is at stake and the perilous choices institutions will need to face. Within hours of the President Sullivan's forced resignation, the battle lines began being drawn. The *Wall Street Journal*, for example, jumped into the middle of the fracas with an op-ed piece and an incendiary subheading: "U. Va's faculty revolts when the trustees move against the status quo."[39] Chairwoman Dragas was portrayed as a flawed leader who had the right idea in wanting to undertake sweeping reform but wrongly conducted the board's business in secrecy. The beneficiary of the less-than-transparent process was President Sullivan, who was then able to "pose as a surprised victim" and a "martyr to corporate-style, top-down leadership."

The real antagonist role in the morality play went to the faculty, who were accused by the *Journal* of wanting "an academic Green Zone" separating them from economic reality and willing to destroy anyone who attempted to exercise even modest oversight. As for calls to reinstate the president, the conclusion was that if the board capitulated, "it ought to disband, drop the pretense of outside supervision, and turn the whole place over to the faculty that really run it."

In contrast, others saw the refrain of disruptive innovation and strategic dynamism as an excuse to impose politically motivated changes at a distinguished, public institution of higher education. The headline in one *Chronicle of Higher Education* article said a lot about the view from the trenches of academe: "The Worrisome Ascendance of Business in Higher Education." After reviewing the actions of the rector, vice rector, and a third powerful alum, the author stated, "The trio, having made their chops in real estate, construction, and investing, apparently saw an opportunity to transfer their knowledge to higher education."[40]

More often than not, the reporting from higher education sources characterized Ms. Dragas as "Gordon Gekko-in-heels," who, with her supporting cast of corporate types, shot first and asked questions later. The ensuing reinstatement of Dr. Sullivan was generally hailed as a victory against the twin evils of micromanagement and commodification.

Trying to understand the rules of engagement associated with these dueling positions has not been easy. In fact, Rick Anderson, a dean at the University of Utah, posted the following brain buster to the Scholarly Kitchen blog after reading Peter Kiernan's (a "powerful Virginia alumnus") public release of his e-mail calling on the need for "strategic dynamism" at the University:[41]

Chaos Lobe: Kiernan is right. The environment in which academics, researchers, students, and librarians do their work is changing so quickly and unpredictably that responding to it with incremental measures is simply not feasible.

Order Lobe: Come on. How long have you been working in academia? The university simply isn't like other work environments—it's not realistic to think that a leader can just come in and dictate "strategic dynamism" to a bunch of tenured professors whose tradition and whose culture of decentralized authority have developed over a millennium.

Chaos Lobe: You assume that the academy has a choice. It may control the environment inside its ivied walls, but its circumstances are ultimately determined by events outside, over which the faculty have no control (even if they're full professors). Isn't it the university administrator's job to look outside the cloisters of the university and see what's going on in the wider world, and position the institution to deal with what's coming? In short, isn't it their job to lead?

Order Lobe: Lead, yes, but not necessarily through the constant fomenting of chaos. I'm not saying there's no need for deep and even painful change, only that it matters how you carry it out. Sullivan makes a good point about the surface charms and deep costs of "sweeping change."

Chaos Lobe: She does make a good point there. But you could just as easily argue the obverse: incremental change may be easier for faculty and staff to absorb and may create the comforting aura of wise and prudent leadership, but it too has unintended consequences, and those consequences may lead to costs that are too high to bear.

Order Lobe: So is it better to actively impose chaos, or to try to manage change in such a way as to prevent or at least mitigate chaos?

Chaos Lobe: When your environment is changing quickly and radically, you may not get to choose whether or not you experience chaos. You only get to choose how you'll participate in it. Chaos just doesn't lend itself to incremental management. You have to jump in and flail around if you want to have any impact on its parameters. Pretending otherwise may soothe everyone and make you popular with the faculty in the short term, but serves everyone ill (including faculty and students) in the long term.

He ended this spirited, cerebral debate with the following observation: "The Order Lobe of my brain has to admit that it doesn't have a very good response to that argument yet."

So, who and how will our future be shaped? Anderson's Chaos Lobe has a lot going for it. It acknowledges the need for creativity in a high-velocity environment. It challenges our institutions to be responsive to their stakeholders and their needs. It embraces new technologies and perhaps helps our institutions understand the permeable nature of their boundaries. But the Order Lobe honors those who are responsible for advancing the missions and visions of the institutions. It recognizes that long-lasting change is ultimately successful if, and only if, those that are being asked to change are a significant part of the transformation dialogue.

As such, the answer to our final question—*How can individual colleges and universities thrive in the twenty-first century?*—must involve recognizing and accepting the hyperactive environment within which we operate and then choosing to accept responsibility for taking the lead in creating a new order of things.

PERILOUS SUMMARY

The high-velocity environment that has been described in this chapter is disturbing to many of the professionals who have dedicated lives to higher education in the country. In addition to the major influencers enumerated in the PEST framework (and the interactions), there also seems to be a "death by a thousand paper cuts" scenario being played out in newspapers, magazines, television, the internet, and blog posts. This new media-rich environment appears to delight in focusing on topics such as binge drinking, fraternity and marching band hazing, cheating scandals, racial issues, guns on campus, suicides, votes of no-confidence, and sexual assaults. Indeed, a month after Auburn University trustees gave approval to build the largest video scoreboard in college football, for $13.9 million, Saturday Night Live's opening comedy skit mockingly imagined a world where academic issues were more important than athletic ones.

Of course, if "sunlight is the best disinfectant," there is certainly a chance that some good can come from this additional scrutiny. But from the academics' perspective, the full narrative being developed is one that is hard to fathom. Are we the new tobacco industry? Do we need to be saved from ourselves?

No. What we need is a new order of things. We need to shift the locus of control back to the institutions by understanding the root cause of calls for more accountability and then seeking opportunities to demonstrate our responsibility. Defensiveness is debilitating. Being a victim is incapacitating as well. A new order of things enthusiastically accepts the high expectations being set for us by our stakeholders and then seeks to unleash the creativity and energy of our own people to meet or even exceed those high expectations.

We need to not only accept but also embrace how perilous this journey will be. This new order of things must be about thriving, not just surviving the seemingly endless skirmishes and crises. We know that an institution that is focused on maintaining the status quo is actually losing ground. There is no comfort to be had in the past or even the present. The only comfort will come in developing the capacity to create our own futures.

NOTES

1. Caroline Bird, *The Case Against College* (New York: David McKay, 1975), 27.
2. See Daniel Seymour, "The Continuing Crisis in Higher Education," *The Journal of College Admissions* (Summer 1990): 5–6, and Andy Thomason, "College on the Cover: Doom and Gloom through the Decades," *Chronicle of Higher Education*, August 14, 2014, http://chronicle.com/blogs/ticker/college-on-the-cover-doom-and-gloom-through-the-decades/84003.
3. Cited in Carla Rivera, "Search for Top Exec Puts CSU Issues in Focus," *Los Angeles Times*, July 5, 2012, A1.
4. Cited in Doug Lederman, "Public University Accountability System Expands Ways to Report Student Learning," *Inside Higher Ed*, May 6, 2013, www.

insidehighered.com/news/2013/05/06/public-university-accountability-system-expands-ways-report-student-learning.

5. Ron Wyden and Marco Rubio, "Reform Starts with Good Data," *Inside Higher Ed*, February 6, 2014, www.insidehighered.com/views/2014/02/06/higher-ed-needs-better-data-spur-reform-essay.

6. Tia Mitchell, "Projections Show FAU, UWF and New College Would Lose Money Under Performance Funding Model," *Tampa Bay Times*, February 12, 2014.

7. Student Success Scorecard, California Community Colleges, Chancellor's Office, http://scorecard.cccco.edu/scorecard.aspx.

8. See Eric Kelderman, "Conservative Think Tank Puts Pressure on North Carolina's College," *Chronicle of Higher Education*, May 1, 2015, http://chronicle.com/article/Conservative-Think-Tank-Puts/229837/?cid=at.

9. See Julie Bosman, "2016 Ambitions Seen in Walker's Push for University Cuts in Wisconsin," *New York Times*, February 16, 2015, www.nytimes.com/2015/02/17/us/politics/scott-walker-university-wisconsin.html?_r=0.

10. Cited in Kevin Kiley, "What's Up with Boards These Days," *Inside Higher Ed*, July 2, 2012.

11. "Trends in College Pricing," The College Board, 2014, http://trends.collegeboard.org/sites/default/files/college-pricing-2014-full-report.pdf.

12. "The Rising Cost of Not Going to College," Pew Research, February 11, 2014, www.pewsocialtrends.org/2014/02/11/the-rising-cost-of-not-going-to-college.

13. "Where Value Meets Values: The Economic Impact of Community Colleges," American Association of Community Colleges, February 2014, www.aacc.nche.edu/About/Documents/USA_AGG_MainReport_Final_021114.pdf.

14. Stephanie Owen and Isabel V. Sawhill, "Should Everyone Go to College?," Brookings, May 8, 2012, www.brookings.edu/~/media/research/files/papers/2013/05/07-should-everyone-go-to-college-owen-sawhill/08-should-everyone-go-to-college-owen-sawhill.pdf.

15. Tamar Lewin, "Pay for U.S. College Presidents Continues to Grow," *New York Times*, December 15, 2013, www.nytimes.com/2013/12/16/us/pay-for-us-college-presidents-continues-to-grow.html.

16. Scott Carlson, "Administrative Hiring Drove 28-Precent Boom in College Work Force, Report Says," *Chronicle of Higher Education*, February 5, 2014, http://chronicle.com/article/Administrator-Hiring-Drove-28-/144519.

17. Colleen Flaherty, "House Committee Report Highlights Plight of Adjunct Professors," *Inside Higher Ed*, January 24, 2014, www.insidehighered.com/news/2014/01/24/house-committee-report-highlights-plight-adjunct-professors.

18. Melissa Korn, "For U.S. Universities, the Rich Get Richer Faster," *Wall Street Journal*, April 16, 2015, www.wsj.com/articles/for-u-s-universities-the-rich-get-richer-faster-1429156904.

19. Richard Wilkinson and Kate Pickett, *The Spirit Level: Why Greater Equality Makes Societies Stronger* (New York: Bloomsbury Press, 2009).

20. Anthony P. Carnevale and Jeff Strohl, "Separate & Unequal: How Higher Education Reinforces the Intergenerational Reproduction of White Racial Privilege," Georgetown University, Center on Education and the Workforce, 2013, https://cew.georgetown.edu/report/separate-unequal.

21. The Century Foundation, *Bridging the Higher Education Divide: Strengthening Community College and Restoring the American Dream: The Report of The Century Foundation Task Force on Preventing Community Colleges from Becoming Separate and Unequal* (New York: The Century Foundation, 2013).

22. Suzanne Mettler, "Equalizers No More: Politics Thwart Colleges' Role in Upward Mobility," *Chronicle of Higher Education,* March 3, 2014, http://chronicle.com/article/Equalizers-No-More/144999.

23. Thomas L. Friedman, "Breakfast Before the MOOC," *New York Times,* February 19, 2014.

24. Steve Kolowich, "Completion Rates Aren't the Best Way to Judge MOOCs, Research Say," *Chronicle of Higher Education,* January 22, 2014, http://chronicle.com/blogs/wiredcampus/completion-rates-arent-the-best-way-to-judge-moocs-researchers-say/49721.

25. See Randy Best, "Have MOOCs Helped or Hurt?," *Inside Higher Ed,* January 9, 2015, www.insidehighered.com/views/2015/01/09/essay-ways-moocs-helped-and-hurt-debates-about-future-higher-education.

26. See Casey Fabris, "What Is Being Learned from MOOCs? New Report Takes Stock," *Chronicle of Higher Education,* April 30, 2015, http://chronicle.com/blogs/wiredcampus/what-is-being-learned-from-moocs-new-report-takes-stock/56487?cid=at&utm_source=at&utm_medium=en and http://linkresearchlab.org/PreparingDigitalUniversity.pdf.

27. See www.edx.org/gfa.

28. Carl Straumsheim, "Arizona State, edX Team to Offer Freshman Year Online through MOOCs," Inside Higher Ed, April 23, 2015, www.insidehighered.com/news/2015/04/23/arizona-state-edx-team-offer-freshman-year-online-through-moocs.

29. Di Xu and Shanna Smith Jaggars, "Adaptability to Online Learning: Difference Across Types of Students and Academic Subject Areas," Community College Research Center, February 2013, http://ccrc.tc.columbia.edu/publications/adaptability-to-online-learning.html.

30. Peter Schmidt, "Colorado Lawmakers Take Up Sweeping Overhaul of Adjunct Working Conditions," *Chronicle of Higher Education,* February 4, 2014, http://chronicle.com/article/Colorado-Lawmakers-Take-Up/144397/?cid=at&utm_source=at&utm_medium=en.

31. The term *high-velocity environments* is used by K. M. Eisenhardt in "Making Fast Decisions in High Velocity Environments," *Academy of Management Journal* 32 (1989): 543–76.

32. Irving Kristol, "A Different Way to Restructure the University," *New York Times,* December 8, 1968, 50.

33. As referenced in George Keller, *Academic Strategy: The Management Revolution in American Higher Education* (Baltimore: The Johns Hopkins University Press, 1983), 150.

34. See Henry Mintzberg, *Structure in Fives: Designing Effective Organizations* (Englewood Cliffs, NJ: Prentice Hall, 1983). For those interested in the topic of higher education organizational design, this book remains a touchstone. Particular attention should be given to chapter 10, "The Professional Bureaucracy," and

chapter 13, "Beyond Five," which offer a view of a hybrid model—the Missionary configuration—that aligns more with what is required to create momentum.

35. Karl Weick, "Educational Organizations as Loosely Coupled Systems," *Administrative Science Quarterly* (1976): 1–19.

36. Mintzberg, *Structure in Fives*, 205.

37. See Robert Birnbaum, *How Colleges Work: The Cybernetics of Academic Organization and Leadership* (San Francisco: Jossey-Bass, 1988). Cybernetics is described as a transdisciplinary approach for exploring regulatory systems, their structures, constraints, and possibilities. Cybernetics is applicable when the system being analyzed is involved in a closed signal loop—that is, where action by the system causes some change in its environment and that change is fed to the system via information (feedback) that enables the system to change its behavior.

38. Ibid., 200.

39. "The Virginia Fracas," *Wall Street Journal*, June 25, 2012, www.wsj.com/articles/SB10001424052702304765304577481043087404280.

40. See William Keep, "The Worrisome Ascendance of Business in Higher Education," *Chronicle of Higher Education*, June 21, 2012, http://chronicle.com/article/The-Worrisome-Ascendance-of/132501/?cid=pm&utm_source=pm&utm_medium=en. The headline of this article is a bit more provocative than the substance, which offers a measured critique, including the confession, "As an institution, academe has much more experience resisting change than embracing it."

41. See Rick Anderson, "'Strategic Dynamism' at the University of Virginia: Implications for Scholarly Communications?," *The Scholarly Kitchen Blog*, June 21, 2012, http://scholarlykitchen.sspnet.org/2012/06/21/strategic-dynamism-at-the-university-of-virginia-implications-for-scholarly-communication.

Chapter 2

Bold Imaginings

"Now everyone has a solution for higher education." Not only is that the conclusion one could draw from much of the material presented in the first chapter, but it is also the title of an article written at the end of 2013 that appeared in the *Chronicle of Higher Education.* In it the author observes that rarely does a week go by without an announcement or two of another forum, summit, or major report that proposes to shake up higher education. After reviewing some of the initiatives in more detail, she states, "The public's belief that college is indispensable, coupled with skepticism over cost and quality, means higher education won't be trusted to solve its own problems. There's an appetite for new ideas, especially from outsiders."[1]

The observation being offered should not have come as a surprise to anyone. Everything is pretty straightforward. There really are issues with cost, debt, and inequality of outcomes. Because higher education is seen to be important to both opportunity and success, it is also reasonable to believe that many individuals and organizations, including outsiders, would have an opinion on the subject. Again, there is nothing surprising here at all.

Nonetheless, the article generated thirty-nine comments centered on the threat associated with the proffered new solutions. The following is the initial thread of the conversation:

[archman] begins with: "And the true irony that most educators understand is that nearly all of these do little to help student learning, despite the copious edu-babble-speak thrown about.

When an educator examines most of these initiatives, we find at the heart either . . .

1. cleverly disguised scheme to sell products or services to students and colleges
2. cleverly disguised scheme to cut federal and state funding
3. cleverly disguised political posturing that actually does nothing
4. misguided and heavy-handed bureaucratic interference."

[cao3rd] lends quick confirmation: "Nice stated and spot on."

[hair_seldon] then adds: "There is a lot of truth to this. Sadly, it seems to me that the majority of cleverly disguised schemes fall into the first category."

[cristobal] attempts to deepen the conversation: "I think you're correct on the basic economic factors, but I'd add the wave cycle of HEA reauthorization, the short time since the last reauthorization, heightened fear of debt post-financial collapse, and the elevation of income inequality as a defining umbrella issue. Whether higher ed is functioning as a lever of social mobility gets right to the heart of our concern about social stratification and provides a tangible policy approach to that broader trend."

[archman] doubles down with an analogy: "Perhaps these conferences would have value if they were between professional educators. It seems most of these meetings are attended primarily by non-professionals dipping fingers into the pot for monetary or political gain. Imagine a medical conference convened to create new medical policies, procedures, and qualifications. Now imagine that conference attended entirely by Big Pharm and political appointees. That's what's happening in Higher Education in the 21st century. Control out of the hands of the professional educators, and into the hands of the amateur, the political partisan, and the business sector."

[22260556] somewhat innocently observes: "True enough . . . but one reason is that for twenty years, at least, the 'professionals' inside the sector have either ignored or opposed systemic changes that are in the public interest."

[archman] can't let that idea go unchallenged: "That is quite an uninformed and false opinion. It does however resonate with a great deal of internet and pro-business propaganda thrown out to the masses, so I understand how a lay person might feel this way. I recommend becoming more educated in Higher Education. The Chronicle of Higher Education is a valuable resource to assist with this."

[judi9827] rallies to the defense of [22260556]: "I beg to differ, archman. I am far from a lay person—was a professor for 16 years—but I left the professorate exactly for the reason 22260556 suggests: faculty (and administrators who WERE faculty) resist change and I got tired of it. Now I am truly making a difference from 'outside.'"

[archman] won't concede the point, though: "I am sorry that your personal experiences shape your professional outlook on Higher Education. Many universities and faculty operate very differently than the environment you worked in."

[wiseaftertheevent] unexpectedly throws fuel on the fire: "Hardly. Universities have VERY similar social structures the world over, and these have proved enormously resistant to change. When knowledge preservation was the main job of the university, this mode functioned well. However, the role of the university now is to educate people in knowledge management and functional relational construction. And they're failing badly."

[cao3rd] returns to support [archman]: "No, archman is right. Rapid change is occurring inside the academy and just because you and judi9827 do not believe it is happening, or are unaware of it, it is nonetheless occurring. That certainly does not mean it is occurring everywhere. I have worked at 6 different institutions and I know they are all moving forward with major change, some of it I helped to lead, in on-line, new programming and adjusting to the new realities of regulation without support and becoming more efficient while not losing the core focus on education."

[klwi3329] jumps into the fray: "I've only worked for two, but I can tell you that change comes to government much quicker than it does for education—and that's not saying much."

While many of the comments in this colorful exchange contain valid points, the overall tone of the conversation exhibits many of the characteristics of a threat-rigidity thesis that states that a common reaction to a perceived threat is manifested in two types of rigidity: a restriction in information processing and a constriction of control.[2] For example, disparaging references to a "lay person" is characteristic of a narrowing field of attention that, in this case, limits valid observation and pertinent information to those *within* the academy. An illustration of constriction of control is the stated opinion that the only way conferences (and conversations) have value is if they are *between* professional educators.

There are many other ideas or initiatives that have, over the years, resulted in this same type of maladaptive response in higher education. The principles and practices associated with Total Quality Management (TQM) or continuous quality improvement were quickly labeled a fad and an unwarranted intrusion by business into higher education. The assessment movement and focus on student learning outcomes has been seen by many as an infringement on academic freedom while the recent Completion Agenda is raising concerns among some faculty members that it will lead to the lowering of academic standards and a reduced emphasis on access.

By interpreting so many extramural concepts as threats or "cleverly disguised schemes" according to *archman*, even good ideas or small successes are neutralized, resulting in what is known as oscillating structures.[3] Each step forward is followed by a compensating step that results in reversal and organizational inertia as shown in Figure 2.1. The movement is back and forth, back and forth—lots of action but no forward momentum.

Figure 2.1   Oscillating Structure

This chapter is about operationalizing a responsibility paradigm in higher education such that a second pattern—structural advancement—can emerge. Structural advancement is built on the notion that success becomes the platform for future success. Advancement is all about going from somewhere to somewhere else, whereas oscillation results in organizational inertia.

The first section takes a broad view of systems thinking, which has been defined as a discipline for seeing wholes and popularized by Peter Senge in his seminal book *The Fifth Discipline* (1990). Importantly, much of the discussion in this section goes beyond defining terms to the challenges associated with reconciling "seeing wholes" with the inherent tendencies of higher education to, instead, "see parts." The next section describes the two building blocks of dynamic systems: balancing and reinforcing loops. As we will see, the structure of colleges and universities (the Professional Bureaucracies described in the previous chapter) have proven exceptional at moderating influences through oscillating forces or balancing loops whose purpose is to seek equilibrium. Reinforcing loops, in contrast, compound change in a specific direction. A third section describes one of those directions, that is, when the reinforcing loop acts as an engine of decay or what some refer to as a "doom loop."

Most of the chapter will focus on the other reinforcing loop—virtuous cycles or upward spirals—which acts as an engine of growth. This form of structural advancement and the resulting momentum it produces is offered as the anecdote to organizational inertia in the face of a high-velocity environment and corresponding calls to hold higher education more accountable.

The algorithm for success, then, is to take responsibility for creating our own future by studying and applying the dynamics of virtuous cycles as a tool that can produce momentum in our colleges and universities.

WHEN EVERYTHING TOUCHES EVERYTHING ELSE

In the *Age of Unreason* (1990), Charles Handy, the Irish author/philosopher, summarizes his view about change by stating:

Change is not what it used to be. The status quo will no longer be the best way forward. ... We are entering an Age of Unreason, when the future, in so many areas, is there to be shaped, by us and for us; a time when the only prediction that will hold true is that no predictions will hold true; a time, therefore, for bold imaginings in private life as well as public; for thinking the unlikely and doing the unreasonable.[4]

This narrative aligns with a responsibility paradigm by suggesting the future is there to be shaped—by us and for us—in contrast to an account-ability paradigm in which the future has been ceded to others. But what about bold imaginings? What is so bold about the idea that if colleges and universities don't work hard to shape their own futures those futures will be shaped by others for them? The boldness comes from embracing a proactive systems perspective that focuses on advancement rather than accepting a reactive perspective that suggests our institutions will muddle through as we have done in the past.

What is a systems perspective? Throughout most of human history we believed that the best way to understand something was to take it apart. By focusing on the parts, we would be able to gain deep appreciation for how it worked. This approach was successful in the sciences—physics, chemistry, and biology. One result was the further division of the sciences into special-ized disciplines, each with its own set of theories and accompanying lexicon. But at some point this increasingly reductive methodology led to an illogical conclusion that something was nothing more than the sum of its parts: enter General Systems Theory.

General Systems Theory was appropriately developed by a biologist in 1936; Ludwig von Bertalanffy felt the need for a theory to guide research across several different disciplines. By studying patterns rather than parts, a whole new set of characteristics began to emerge that eventually allowed scholars to better communicate their findings with each other and build on each other's work. For the first time, there was a way of linking together scat-tered and seemingly independent fields of knowledge and revealing what they had in common. The impact was almost immediate across many fields with practical tools being developed such as "systems analysis" in computers and automation as well as "systems thinking" in organization behavior.

A system can be defined as any group of interacting, interrelated, or inter-dependent parts that form a unified whole with a specific purpose. There are many daily examples that help distinguish a collection of parts (also known affectionately as a "heap") from a system. One is to think of your kitchen. The kitchen is full of systems. A refrigerator, a dishwasher, a toaster—each has a set of parts that interact in a specific way in order to achieve a purpose. But the kitchen itself is a collection because the various appliances just mentioned are not interdependent. Another way to see the distinction is by starting with the parts. An auto parts store or a junkyard has plenty of carburetors, bumpers, and tires or everything needed to make an automobile. But these places are heaps, not systems. It isn't until you arrange the parts in a meaningful way that you have an automobile or a system with a purpose (getting you from point A to point B).

As noted, the application of a systems approach to organizations took a leap forward with the publication of *The Fifth Discipline* (1990). In it, Senge couples general systems theory with a broad set of practical tools to advance the idea of a learning organization—"an organization that is continually expanding its capacity to create its future." He explains:

> For such an organization, it is not enough merely to survive. "Survival learning" or what is more often termed "adaptive learning" is important—indeed it is necessary. But for a learning organization, "adaptive learning" must be joined by "generative learning," learning that enhances our capacity to create.[5]

The resulting organization would use systems thinking to integrate four other disciplines (personal mastery, mental models, shared vision, and team learning) in order to learn and grow. Additionally, he described a set of axioms that apply systems thinking in specific ways to the organization. As an example, "today's problems come from yesterday's 'solutions,'" derives from the core idea that in a system everything touches everything else. The phenomenon of unintended consequences is a function of individuals not understanding the interrelationship of elements within a system and how they impact each other over time. Another axiom (a learning disability) is the "fixation on events." By simply reacting to a problematic event in order to accomplish a quick fix, there is a strong likelihood that the symptom will disappear, leaving the fundamental root cause in place (to reappear again in the future).

With just these few illustrations it should be obvious that being able to see and understand the whole in terms of how the parts interact is a powerful force for managing organizations.

A college or university is, by the definition provided, a system. Each one has a set of parts that interact for a stated purpose. The parts include admissions offices, counseling departments, athletics, academic departments, research centers, facilities, public relations, and so on. Clearly, there are many, many parts. There are also many ways to think about purpose. For example, every institution has a mission statement that answers the question, "Why do we exist?," and many have institutional-level learning outcomes that describe the skills, attitudes, and behaviors that graduates hopefully possess. It follows that the actual parts and their combination are idiosyncratic based on the mission-driven nature of each and every institution of higher education.

But do colleges and universities exhibit system characteristics different from businesses, government agencies, and other types of organizations? Karl Weick, an organizational theorist, attempts to answer that question in a seminal article published *in Administrative Science Quarterly* in 1976.[6] In computing and systems design, "loose coupling" is where each of the components has, or makes use of, little or no knowledge of the definitions or capabilities of other separate components. Weick introduced the idea into organizational studies, and "Educational Organizations as Loosely Coupled Systems" became required reading in higher education administration courses over the next four decades.

In educational organizations the idea of loose coupling is simply the observation that things are tied together either weakly or infrequently or slowly or with minimal interdependence (as also previously described by Mintzberg in a Professional Bureaucracy). These loose couplings manifest themselves in many different ways including: occasions when any one of several means will produce the same end; a relative lack of coordination; a relative absence of regulations; and infrequent inspection of activities within the system. Another important loose coupling described by Weick is "the absence of linkages that should be present based on some theory—for example, in education organizations the expected feedback linkage from outcome back to inputs is often nonexistent."[7]

There are a number of potential functions and dysfunctions associated with loose coupling according to Weick. Systems that are not particularly interdependent can be more sensitive to specific aspects of their environment, which can allow some portions of the organization to persist through localized adaptation. They can generate a greater number of mutations or novel solutions than would not be the case with a tightly coupled system. Also, if there is a breakdown in any portion of the organization of a loosely coupled system, then the breakdown can be sealed off and would not affect other portions of the organization. Finally, such systems maximize self-determination of many individuals while minimizing the expense (time and money) needed to coordinate individuals' activities.

All of this comes at a cost, as seen in Figure 2.2. Looking through the list of functions, it is easy to see that adaptive or survival learning (see Senge above) dominates. Any type of coordinated response is problematic because many of the individuals are acting as independent entrepreneurs with little sense of cohesion or unifying obligation, leading Weick to conclude that "loose coupling is also a non-rational system of fund allocation and therefore, unspecifiable, unmodifiable, and incapable of being used as means of change."

Tight   **Loose**

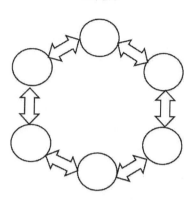

- More interdependency
- More coordination
- More information flow

- Less interdependency
- Less coordination
- Less information flow

Figure 2.2   Tight vs. Loose Coupling

So, while in a system "everything touches everything else," institutions of higher education present a somewhat special case. There is a need to specialize in disciplines and sub-disciplines in order to organize work and advance knowledge. There is also a growing need to more effectively interact with a long list of hyperactive stakeholders. Perhaps we need to be thinking of ways to move away from the extremes of tight and loose. Perhaps we need to pursue the idea of "moderately coupled" systems.

THE BUILDING BLOCKS

We have already seen a wide range of systems from toasters to universities. We have also noted that institutions of higher education can exhibit some very non-system (or heap-like) behaviors because of their loose coupling. But before we even consider the means to create more coordination and better information flow, it is important to begin with a more detailed understanding of the nature of systems. Specifically, all complex systems (biological, social, economic) are built on two principles: balance and reinforcement.

Balancing loops are about constancy. There is a great deal of stability in the world. Indeed, most aspects of life involve the introduction of forces specifically designed to counteract other ones. Such processes are goal-seeking

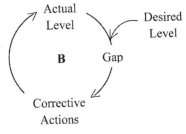

Figure 2.3 Balancing Loop

because there is, at the core, a desired state or level of performance. A thermostat is an obvious illustration. When the thermostat in your home detects that the room temperature is below the desired level, the furnace kicks in and heats the room until it achieves its goal. Then it shuts off. As Figure 2.3 shows, there is always an inherent goal in a balancing process, and what drives a balancing loop (B) is the gap between the desired level and the actual level.

Balancing loops are everywhere. They tend to be somewhat invisible because they quietly function to keep things as they are. You don't notice the temperature of your automobile engine, for example. The manufacturer has decided on an optimal performance depending on the engine type and oil required. The cooling system is designed to take corrective action once the engine begins to heat up too much. For years you are unaware of the balancing loop in place until that fateful day on the 405 freeway when you lose the clamp on the radiator hose and both your engine and you become suddenly unbalanced.

A much more relevant example would be the admissions function at colleges and universities. All institutions have a desired level of freshmen that they wish to admit. Smaller, private, tuition-driven colleges are most vigilant about the goal, while larger, open-access community colleges are the least concerned. Still, all of them have a goal based on a long list of factors including dormitory space, average class size, selectivity, and many others including, most importantly, the budget. So, what happens when Olive College sends out two thousand admittance letters with a goal of one thousand acceptances based on a historical acceptance rate of 50 percent and they get commitments from only nine hundred students?

The built-in corrective mechanism is the wait list. Of course, the reality is much more complicated than this since what needs to be "balanced" involves more than just one goal-seeking number. As an illustration, Massachusetts Institute of Technology (MIT) admitted 1,419 students in fall 2014 out of 18,357 (7.7 percent). Admitted students came from all fifty states and from diverse backgrounds with more than a quarter identified as members of underrepresented minority groups and 17 percent being the first generation in their family to attend college. Even within the 1,419 there are subgoals that would require corrective action if, as an example, the acceptance rate went over 10 percent or the number of states dipped below all fifty.

If balancing loops are about stability through deviation-counteracting feedback, then reinforcing loops (R) are about compounding change through deviation-amplifying feedback (Figure 2.4). Perhaps the most straightforward illustration of this phenomenon is the compounding effect associated with a savings account and earned interest. A causal loop diagram captures the process as savings generate interest, which, in turn, increases the amount of savings, and that new, larger savings then produces even more earned interest. And round and round we go. What is noteworthy is that subsequent growth is not a straight-line function. The behavior over time has exponential growth characteristics.

This change is quite different from what we saw in balancing loops. The difference is in the nature of the feedback. Negative feedback works to cancel out changes. The system "corrects" itself when it gets off target by generating information that can be used for making necessary adjustments. But what happens when the feedback does just the opposite, and each change feeds back through the systems to cause more change? This positive feedback amplifies change in the system. For our savings account this positive feedback loop is a money amplifier. A deposit of $1,000 in a savings account at 5 percent interest each year will double in fifteen years and double again in another fifteen years.

Most people in higher education are familiar with a reinforcing loop because it drives how some institutions implicitly operate—the resources/reputation reinforcing loop—as shown in Figure 2.5.

We can look at some of the criterion in the *U.S. News and World Report's Best Colleges* to see how this works. The first category is "Reputation" and includes the opinions of high school guidance counselors and peer

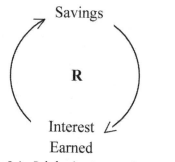
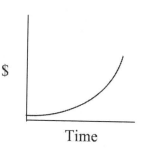

Figure 2.4   **Reinforcing Loop and Exponential Growth**

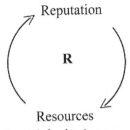

Figure 2.5   Resources-Reputation Reinforcing Loop

assessment, which is a survey of presidents, provosts, and deans of admissions. The category "Student Selectivity" has various subfactors including students' high school standing and acceptance rate, which is defined as, "The ratio of the number of students admitted to the number of applicants for fall 2012 admission. The acceptance rate is equal to the total number of students admitted divided by the total number of applicants." Other categories, however, are related to "Resources." "Faculty Resources" includes the following subfactors: faculty compensation, percent of faculty with terminal degree in their field, percentage of faculty that is full time, student/faculty ratio, and class size. The "Financial Resources" category is the amount of spending per student, and there is an "Alumni Giving" category, or the rate of giving by alums of the institution.

These are not independent (heap-like) factors, though. As an institution gains in reputation, more students apply and student selectivity increases. Demand follows supply and so tuition can be raised and the added revenue can be used to improve faculty compensation, hire more PhDs, and reduce class size. The amount of spending per student naturally increases and that leads to alums who are successful and then . . . give back. This is classic amplification: as reputation improves, resources improve, which then leads to be an improved reputation followed by more resources.

Another, more specific, example draws on the admission illustration used earlier to describe a balancing loop. In the spring of 2014, Stanford University announced that it had hit a new low for acceptances—only 5 percent of those who applied to Stanford were accepted. At first glance it might seem that this is just a matter of Stanford becoming more selective as its reputation increases. But what is really happening? As the word gets out about how difficult it is to get in to prestigious institutions like Stanford, students apply to more institutions. Students applying to seven or more colleges made up just 9 percent of the applicant pool in 1990, but accounted for 29 percent in 2011, according to the National Association for College Admission Counseling, and counselors and admissions officers say they think the figure has gone higher still.[8]

So, Stanford received 42,167 applications for the class of 2018 and sent 2,138 acceptance notices, for a first-year class that, ultimately, numbers about 1,700. The reinforcing loop comes in to play when students, parents, and guidance counselors realize that getting into Stanford, Harvard (6 percent), Princeton (7 percent), University of Chicago (8 percent), and many other elite institutions is a crapshoot and respond by applying to more schools. This in turn drives up the number of students applying for a set number of seats, which decreases the acceptance rate.

Unlike balancing loops, however, reinforcing loops come in two different types: one type compounds change in one direction by being an engine of growth, while the other compounds change in the opposite direction and is an engine of decay.

VICIOUS CYCLES

The critical reason for looking at this type of reinforcing loop or spiral is to understand what is at stake. As you recall from the previous chapter, "On Perilous Conduct," the operating premise is that in a high-velocity environment the traditional capabilities of higher education institutions to moderate influences are severely compromised. The number of institutions that will be in balanced states, able to survive through a series of incremental and individual adjustments, will be fewer and fewer. More likely colleges and universities will be either gaining traction or losing ground. They will either be "on a roll" or they will be suffering extended "losing streaks."

What do these losing streaks look like?

A vicious cycle is a metaphor for decline, a self-reinforcing process that depletes the organization of value. It can best be described as a cycle of disinvestment or deterioration as individuals withdraw resources from a system, an action that reduces its performance and prompts additional withdrawals over time. At its simplest level it can be seen as the opposite of the compounding effect of a savings account. In this case, however, it isn't money that is being withdrawn but rather time, energy, and commitment. It is a pervasive feeling that things are bad and getting worse. So, why would I work late? Why would I care about an organization that doesn't care about me? How can I protect myself? The psychic withdrawal of increasing numbers of individuals will, over time, impact key performance indicators, which, in turn, will reinforce the prevailing narrative of failure and lead to further withdrawal.

There are a number of ways in which these negative and destructive patterns manifest themselves. At the broadest level, there is a sense that trust has been broken. Numerous studies in organization behavior have shown that trust is a significant predictor of performance and organizational commitment or, simply, the ability to focus: the degree to which employees can devote their attention to work, as opposed to "playing politics" or "covering their backside."

Robert Sternberg lasted 135 days as president of the University of Wyoming. Hired in July on 2013, his "brisk tenure" began with an administrative house cleaning that started with ousting the longtime provost. After matter-of-factly observing that he and the provost had serious differences in their interpretations of the university's land-grant mission, most of the associate provosts resigned. One, Nicole Susan Ballenger, stated in an e-mail, "People here, like everywhere, want to be part of their future. When they know they are being left out, disregarded, and at the same time don't understand what the change is meant to be about, they become suspicious about motives, fear takes over, and trust is lost."[9]

Decline is not an event; it is a trajectory. And so, in January of 2014, the University Board of Trustees gave interim president Richard McGinity the job on a permanent basis, seemingly bypassing a university bylaw requiring consulting with a faculty committee. The trustees countered by stating that the need to project a stable image and ensure long-term leadership at UW warranted deviation from the policy.[10] Earlier suspicions effectively are confirmed when deviations from standard protocols are invoked as "necessary." And the destructive narrative builds.

Another very public illustration of a vicious cycle is Houston Community College. One of the largest institutions in the country with more than sixty-five thousand students, the college has had a history of board members using their influence improperly to steer contracts to relatives, friends, and political allies. Its accreditors put the college on probation and a number of trustees had been indicted or forced to resign. Still, as chancellors and key administers came and left, the *Houston Chronicle* was always a strong believer in the mission of the institution and supported the idea that "you can't have a great city without a great community college."

Perhaps with this message in mind, in the fall of 2012 the voters responded positively to a $425 million bond to fund upgrades to facilities across the system. But after four or five years of relative calm, 2013 put the issue of trust back in the headlines. The following op-ed pieces in the *Houston Chronicle* reflect the public's growing concerns:

January 27, 2013, "Houston Community College Concerns: Public Deserves Assurance of Board of Trustees' Commitment to Ethics Reforms": After reiterating a belief in the importance of community colleges and recent ethics reforms, the editors express concerns over the chancellor going on medical leave, the general counsel being appointed as interim, and stated, "We are hearing word of board members with agendas focused on jobs and contracts for favored groups."

April 26, 2013, "Watching HCC's Actions: Community College Board Is Trying to Back Away from a Necessary Commitment": Three months later the college's board is accused of reneging on its assurances to keep an arm's length regarding contracts. The quotes are blunt: "This just smells" and "We'll be watching."

June 6, 2013, "HCC Needs New Leadership: Community College System Board Is Retreating to Bad Old Ways": With five members of the sitting board up for election, the editors issue a call to action: "We encourage HCC supporters throughout the business and education communities to field a reform slate of candidates to challenge those incumbents who have supported the governing board's detour back into its old, discredited ways."

December 27, 2013, "Ethics Cloud at HCC: A Full Investigation Is Needed to Clear Up Questions Raised by Troubling HCC Matter": While, again, restating the pivotal role the college plays in training a skilled workforce and that "our community needs HCC to succeed," the editors are seemingly forced to concede, "Once again, a cloud of suspicion hangs over a trustee of the Houston Community College system."

April 14, 2014, "HCC Mismanagement": The editorial begins, "You can learn a lot about political shenanigans at the Houston Community College System—just not necessarily in the classroom."

April 27, 2015, "HCC Ethics: New, Serious Allegations Fit with History": A whistleblower lawsuit by the former acting chancellor "fit(s) with a long and sordid history of an HCC board that's been more enthusiastic about doling out contracts than educating students."[11]

The arc bends downward and it often begins with a loss of trust.

What follows from a loss of trust is emotional retreat. Individuals within the organization begin to withdraw. Where once people looked for excuses to get together, they now look for opportunities to stay in their respective offices. In a larger group, you simply don't know who to trust or if what you say will be misinterpreted or used against you later. A sense of community that used to give comfort now becomes a source of unease.

This withdrawal from a more collective responsibility and its reduced communication becomes risk aversion as things continue to deteriorate. This level is manifested in reduced information sharing and results in poor decision making. Panic leads to grasping at quick fixes—something, anything to feel better, to feel that action is being taken, or to feel some sense of control. Entropy takes hold as there is less and less willingness to introduce new ideas. Performance begins to suffer as energy is depleted and resources become more constrained.

At some point the decline becomes very personal. It becomes about self-protection. In a deepening downward spiral we see the worst in people.

Random acts of kindness are replaced by random act of selfishness. Everyone is in it for themselves. Empathy is gone because everyone feels vulnerable. The obvious solution for many is to find a way out. Good people, people who have strong resumes and contacts, begin to leave. Most just want better working conditions and will forego a career-advancing position or even more money in order to get to a safe haven. They are exhausted by the drama. New people are hired, but they don't stay—employee churning occurs. As the good people move on, those without options remain and the destructive pattern is reinforced by people who now feel trapped.

The downward trajectory bottoms out in learned helplessness. This is a clinical condition. In experiments on animals, when the animal cannot escape adverse stimuli, it will eventually stop trying to avoid the pain and behave as if it is helpless to change the situation. Even when opportunities to escape are presented, this learned helplessness prevents them from taking action. This same condition is evident when vicious cycles reach rock bottom. There is a palpable sense of resignation with the only coping mechanism being to expend the least amount of energy possible as the pain is inflicted. "Broken trust" followed by "emotional retreat" then "risk aversion" that degrades into "self-protection" and ends with "learned helplessness." The combined impact of these forces makes one feel as if they were circling a drain—caught in the current, pulled ever-downward, with your fate already sealed. Rosabeth Moss Kanter refers to these pathological patterns that are self-perpetuating and mutually reinforcing as "doom loops":

> Losing teams, distressed organizations, declining empires, and even depressed people often run downhill at an accelerating pace. Common reactions to failure prevent success and make losing in the future more likely. Unchecked cycles of decline can easily turn into death spirals. Problems are exacerbated by responses that make them ever harder to solve. Secrecy, blame, isolation, avoidance, lack of respect, and feelings of helplessness create a culture that makes the situation worse and makes changes seem impossible. . . . The system has momentum.[12]

When a reinforcing loop turns downward, the engine of decay can begin to build its own narrative. It is a story that is self-perpetuating. It is a losing streak that will not end because, at some point, the individuals and the organizations seem to forget how to win. Each new negative event is met with a shrug and a feeling of inevitability.

The challenges that Chicago State University currently faces began in 2008 and illustrate the fact that once your reservoir of goodwill is depleted, destructive forces often take hold and will not let go. After a ten-year reign as president, Elnora Daniel announced her retirement in 2008. She had been criticized for controversial spending practices by the auditor general of

Illinois, so it followed that when it was discovered that she authorized spending $18,000 on a coffee-table book honoring herself, it made it to the *Chicago Tribune*. And then:

- When an article on financial-management problems occurred in 2011, it began by stating "the latest" state audit of Chicago State University turned up forty-one problems—up from thirteen the year before.
- When it was found later in the year that nearly 450 students who were academically unqualified were allowed to remain in school and receive student financial aid, it was characterized as a "new scandal."
- When the student newspaper published articles criticizing the university, the advisor was fired followed by a federal judge ordering that he be reinstated.
- When an audit in 2012 found that the university had lost 950 computers worth $3.8 million, a newspaper article managed to connect the loss to both the student financial aid problem from the previous year and the questionable spending practices of the ex-president in 2008.
- When the university implemented (and later rescinded) a policy that forbade faculty and staff members from speaking with the news media, write opinion pieces, or use social media without obtaining permission from public-relations officials, it predictably ended up being featured in the *Chicago Tribune*.
- When it was announced (and later rescinded, too) that president Wayne Watson would step down in 2013, it was a chance to revisit the financial mismanagement problems that plagued his predecessor and remind everyone that enrollment had dropped since he took office and that the faculty had recently voted "no-confidence" in him.
- When the new interim provost, Angela Henderson, was accused of plagiarizing portions of her dissertation, the newspapers connected the dots for the public: Henderson's husband was Watson's personal lawyer and Watson served on her dissertation committee.
- And when in 2014, a jury in Cook County awarded the former legal counsel at the university $2.5 million—$480,000 in back pay plus $2 million in punitive damages plus reinstatement—because he was fired in retaliation for reporting alleged misconduct by top university officials, it followed that the story was reported for all to read in excruciating detail.[13]

There is no benefit of the doubt here. There is only a narrative that has developed over the time and each additional event is examined in that light. Things that feed the narrative stick; things that don't (and there are undoubtedly many positive stories at Chicago State University) are diminished or ignored. Energy and positivity dissipates. The focus is on failure. And a pathology emerges that is vicious and unforgiving. Such is the power of vicious cycles.

VIRTUOUS CYCLES

While the self-defeating dynamics of downward spirals produce incapacitating results as individuals withdraw resources from a system, the same underlying dynamics of reinforcing loops can also be the engines of investment, learning, and growth. As powerful as vicious cycles can be, virtuous cycles are equally as capable of producing change. Fortunately, it would appear that both academics and practitioners have tended to gravitate toward the positive and so the literature, research, and practices around virtuous cycles are both broad and deep.

First, it should be noted that such spirals are all around us. They are seen throughout the world in literature, art, architecture, economics, mathematics, and biology. We have spiral staircases, fiddlehead ferns, and tornadoes. Hawks fly in spirals in their approach to prey. Logarithmic spirals were called *spira mirabilis* (marvelous spirals) by early mathematicians who first studied them. In economics, well-paid workers generate consumer demand that in turn promotes business expansion and hiring. The spiral plays a specific role in symbolism and appears in Galician petroglyphs (rock carvings) from the Stone Age. They are found in structures as small as the double helix structure of DNA and as large as the spiral structure of our galaxy.

Because of the amount of information that is available about spirals and the obvious importance of virtuous cycles to the remainder of this book, the material in this section has been divided into two different groups—individual influences and organizational behavior. Since organizations are made up of individuals, it should be evident that what is really at play here is a nested hierarchy from individuals to groups to organizations. As such, much of the material in the next section also applies to, in our case, colleges and universities as organizations.

Individual Influences

Just as the concept of spirals is relevant when discussing chicken hawks, rock carvings, and weather patterns, it is also relevant in the human sphere, especially at the individual and one-to-one level. The field of psychology has largely focused on what is wrong with people. It has been about dysfunction—mental illness and other psychological problems and how to treat them. But over the last several decades there has been a shift to include the positive along with the negative. Positive psychology is the scientific study of what makes life most worth living. The focus is on building the best things in life as opposed to just identifying and repairing the worst. It complements what has dominated problem-focused psychology for all of its history.

Building on the work of humanistic psychologists including Abraham Maslow, Carl Rogers, and Erich Fromm, positive psychologists have found empirical support for theories of happiness, human good, and flourishing. This "new era of positive psychology" was launched in 1998 when Martin Seligman chose it as the theme for his term as president of the American Psychological Association.[14] He stressed that the disease model (which really focused on making miserable people less miserable) had neglected the majority of people who wanted to move along a continuum from a pleasant life, to an engaged life, to a meaningful life. The field also began advocating a shift in tone from one that solely spoke to victimhood and pathology—the study and diagnosis of disease—to emphasizing responsibility. People have choices and make decisions.

Positive psychology isn't just about feeling good or being happy. It is about doing good and adding value to the world. In her book *Positivity* (2009), Barbara Fredrickson describes this expansive notion:

> People who flourish are highly engaged with their families, work, and communities. They're driven by a sense of purpose; they know why they get up in the morning. Striving to flourish, then, is a noble goal. It's not just about making yourself happy. It's about doing something valuable with your day and with your life. Although flourishing is noble, it need not imply grand or grandiose actions. It simply requires transcending self-interest enough to share and celebrate goodness in others and in the natural world. Flourishing represents your best possible future. Positivity can help you get there.[15]

In their book *Lift* (2009), Ryan and Robert Quinn describe "lift" as a psychological state in which a person is purpose-centered, internally directed, and other-focused. In addition to describing these characteristics in detail, they go on to discuss how our psychological state influences others in at least four ways:

1. Our facial expressions, body language, and tone of voice send new and unexpected cues that people interpret and react to in new and different ways.
2. The emotions that are part of our psychological states are contagious. In other words, people often unconsciously mimic, and then adopt, our feelings.
3. Psychological states sometimes lead us to make different decisions or act in different ways than we would if we had been in a different psychological state, and other people are influenced by these decisions and actions.
4. When we take different actions and perform them in different ways, we generate different results—results that may be more effective, more creative, higher quality, or more beneficial. People pay attention to and try to make sense of unusual or extraordinary results.[16]

Lift, then, is both a psychological state and the effect that this state has on others. We experience it when we focus on purpose rather than problems, or use our values to drive our behavior instead of reacting to circumstances, or when we empathize with others rather than dwelling on our own agendas, or when we seek feedback that enables us to learn and grow instead of insulating ourselves. Moreover, according to Quinn and Quinn, when we experience lift we tend to lift others as well through our thoughts, feelings, actions, and results. We become positive forces in the situations we encounter.

This positive well-being can include a powerful upward-spiral dynamic. First, a positive emotion within an individual can lead to a psychological broadening or an increased receptivity to subsequent positive events, which can in turn lead to further increases in positive emotions (a reinforcing loop). Moreover this same individual positivity can produce "emotional contagion." Well documented in a variety of disciplines—social and developmental psychology, history, cross-cultural psychology, experimental psychology, and psychophysiology—this is the tendency for moods or emotions to spread through small groups and larger populations.[17] All virtuous or vicious cycles in humans have an element of emotional contagion.

For example, in downward spirals, a depressive state emerges in individuals that is spread from one to the other as things appear to progress from bad to worse. We are seemingly more open to bad news and, in turn, we exercise our ability to infect others with negativity as well. Doom loops feed off this negative, infectious energy.

Finally, it should be reiterated that the spirals we are discussing here are not a simple "spread joy" narrative. Flourishing has a much deeper efficacy-based component as both Fredrickson and the Quinns strongly suggest. It is about being purposeful and creating, not just positive feelings, but positive outcomes as well. Research has shown that there is an efficacy-performance spiral. The conviction that one can successfully execute a required behavior has been shown to have a strong, positive effect on performance.[18]

What is key for this book, and the section that we now turn to, is that this same amplifying spiral that can drive individuals to higher levels of performance also exists at the group and organizational level. There exists a "collective efficacy" in which a group or organization's shared belief in its ability to execute a course of action becomes a self-fulfilling prophecy.

Organizational Behavior

As was noted, the advantage of taking a multilevel approach lies in the recognition that individuals, groups, and organizations are not separate entities but parts of a whole (potentially a system) with each affecting and being affected by the other. Such an approach operates as a nested hierarchy much like the Russian nesting dolls (also called matryoshka dolls or Babushka dolls), which are composed of several dolls of decreasing size placed one inside the other. If you think of the individual as the smallest doll, you can easily see a larger doll could be a dyad that includes two individuals and then adding up to a group and finally to an organization. This idea is also consistent with the research and literature noted above about positivity and meaningful lives, flourishing and being other-focused, as well emotional contagion and collective efficacy. All of these concepts involve an extension beyond the individual into larger groups of people.

It is not surprising, therefore, that an entire scholarship has emerged from the linkage of positivity and organizations—Positive Organizational Scholarship (POS). POS is focused primarily on the study of positive outcomes, processes, and attributes of organizations and their members. It encompasses attention to a set of enablers (e.g., processes, structures) as well as motivations (e.g., goodness, unselfishness) and outcomes (e.g., vitality, meaningfulness). As such, POS can be differentiated from more traditional organizational studies by seeking to understand and advance the best of the human condition. A companion approach to organizations, Appreciative Inquiry (AI), follows a similar positive path. Instead of focusing on what is wrong and the narrow, depressing emphasis on solving problems, a more energizing approach is to value the best of what is and envision what might me.

Since POS does not represent a single theory but, instead, looks at a broad set of dynamics, it is difficult to summarize its many theoretical bases and practical applications. However, Kim Cameron, in his work on organizational virtuousness and performance, covers a lot of the POS domain, especially as it relates to positive deviance. The origin of the word *deviant* is from two Latin words: *de* meaning "from" and *via* meaning "road." So, *deviate* means "off the beaten path" and deviant behavior, it follows, is the unexpected or the unconventional.

Within organizational behavior, deviance is seen as intentional behavior. It is not an accident. It is done with a purpose in mind. Deviance is also a significant departure from the norm, which is why it catches peoples' attention. While most discussions about deviance focus on negative behavior, departures from the norm can also be constructive and positive. As such, *positive deviation* can be defined as intentional behaviors that depart from norms in virtuous or honorable ways.

When looking at a basic set of organizational attributes or dimensions such as effectiveness and efficiency, a continuum emerges, as shown in Table 2.1. In the middle is a normal or healthy condition. But the attributes associated with a negative deviation illustrate an almost physiological or psychological illness that results in a reactive, *problem-solving orientation*. In sharp contrast, a positive deviation is about wellness, not illness, and speaks to, among

Table 2.1   Organizational Attributes and Deviation

	Negative Deviation	*Normal*	*Positive Deviation*
Effectiveness	Ineffective	Effective	Excellence
Efficiency	Inefficient	Efficient	Extraordinary
Quality	Error-prone	Reliable	Flawless
Ethics	Unethical	Ethical	Benevolence
Relationships	Harmful	Helpful	Honoring
Adaptation	Threat-rigidity	Coping	Flourishing
Orientation	*Problem solving*		*Virtuousness*

other dynamics, benevolent ethics and honoring relationships that result is a *virtuous orientation*.[19]

Organizational studies are conclusive that virtuousness mitigates negative performance outcomes and is positively associated with higher organizational performance. A major factor in this conclusion is the amplifying effect that virtuousness has on three outcomes: positive emotions, social capital, and prosocial behavior. When organization members observe compassion or witness forgiveness, for example, they increase their pride in the organization and they enjoy work, which creates virtuous cycles of positive feelings. Social capital is the network of social connections that exist between people, and their shared values and norms of behavior, which enable and encourage mutually advantageous social cooperation. Increased social capital is really increased sharing of everything from information to resources. Amplification results because organizational virtuousness increases social capital, which, in turn, improves organizational performance.

Finally, prosocial behavior occurs when individuals behave in ways that benefit other people. Observing and experiencing virtuousness helps to unlock the predisposition toward behaving in ways that benefit others. And, again, this reciprocity tends to create a chain reaction.

A virtuous cycle, then, is a positive-deviation amplification machine.

While many of the ideas developed in POS and AI will be applied in the chapters that follow, it is important to capture two aspects that extend beyond the immediate and direct: resilience and vitality. Resilience involves the maintenance of positive adjustment under challenging conditions. A metaphor that can be used (from materials science) is the image of a kind of super material that can absorb strain or shock and still maintain its shape. What we have already seen is that virtuous processes enhance an organization's overall competence and growth, especially the ability to learn through feedback.

But these processes also enable an organization's ability to restore efficacy by marshaling the necessary knowledge and resources to deal with situations as they arise. And they will arise. Threats—big and small—are always going to occur. The difference is in how the organization responds.

For many organizations, the response follows the standard threat-rigidity pattern. This entails narrow information processing, tightening control, and conservation of resources. Because of this constriction, threats (even moderate ones) can overwhelm the capacity of an organization to deal with them, as we have already seen. But virtuous processes inoculate an organization over time. Virtues such as integrity, courage, and hope are buffers that act as learned optimism (in contrast to learned helplessness) when encountering challenges. These enabling conditions are the processes that support and enhance competence and efficacy and that effectively enable the organization to engage in positive adjustment.[20]

Think of the tragedy at Virginia Tech that provided the backdrop to the story used at the beginning of this book or the national drama that engulfed the University of Virginia as described in the previous chapter. Or how about the sex-abuse scandal at Pennsylvania State University that triggered the dismissal of its legendary football coach, crippling NCAA sanctions, and the indictment of the university president and several other senior administrators? Then there is Cooper Union, founded in 1859 and envisioned as a place where education was "free as air and water." What happens when the institution announces that its most celebrated tradition—free tuition—would end?

Other scandals, layoffs, programs cuts, and votes of "no-confidence" play out every week at colleges and universities across the country. Each threat could begin an unraveling process or add to an existing destructive pattern. But if the capabilities have been developed, the positivity embedded in the culture of the institutions can act as organizational shock absorbers. What could have evolved into a death spiral might, instead, end up being a painful but survivable bump in the road. It is a matter of resilience.

A useful illustration of positive adjustment is the case of the University of Connecticut. As the economic downturn unfolded, the university took a very un-victim-like approach. It aggressively revamped information technologies and centralized purchasing in order to generate savings but also looked for ways to increase revenues. Importantly, the university aligned its long-range planning with the state's $864 million "Bioscience Connecticut" plan designed to bolster its economy by rebuilding the scientific job sector. In 2012, as other institutions continued slashing budgets and announcing plans to freeze hiring, the University of Connecticut announced plans to create nearly three hundred tenure-track positions over the next four years.

Brad Simpson, then an assistant professor of history and international studies at Princeton University, provided personal insight in a *Chronicle of Higher Education* story. He visited UConn and was struck by the vibe—people were optimistic—while interviewing for an associate professor position. "When people are excited about where the institution is going, it's easy to tell," he said; he went on to add, "It's gratifying to join a place with a strategic mission, that's acting proactively instead of reactively."[21]

The second indirect effect that virtuous processes produce is vitality. In contrast to the kind of internally focused coping capabilities just described, an organization that is flourishing and imbued with positive emotions also has developed the potential to move beyond its immediate boundaries—that is, a dynamic in which empowerment is shared. While resilience involves buffering, vitality involves sharing. Simply replace the idea of a "threat" from above with the notion of an "opportunity" and it becomes apparent that power expands when it is shared. The result is what some researchers have labeled "cascading vitality" when vitality extends beyond the boundaries of the organizations and creates vitality in the external environment.[22]

Part of this notion involves how we think about empowerment. Since empowerment involves the generation and use of power, it can also extend to how we share power by connecting with others. It has been found that when individuals are empowered through virtuous processes, they also can access expanded resources. New understandings of the work lead to different goals and the awareness of the potential of other connections. There is an awareness of new sources and types of information that encourages risk-taking and leads to additional opportunities. Success breeds success.

It should be obvious that "cascading vitality" might be an important capability for a college or university operating in a high-velocity environment. Richard Levin became president of Yale in 1993 and has been credited with restoring Yale's financial stability, upgrading its facilities, and dramatically improving its relationship with its community of New Haven, Connecticut. With that background, Yale University was able to undertake the development of the first institution outside of New Haven in its three-hundred-year history. In 2011, Yale and the National University of Singapore collaborated to establish Yale-NUS College. It is the first liberal arts college in Singapore and one of the few in Asia.

But from the beginning, Yale professors questioned whether the university should be operating in a country with a mixed record on civil and political liberties. Singaporeans had their concerns, too: as one of Asia's best institutions, why would they need help from a Western import? What evolved was not a blend of the two institutions but an institution with its own identity. Unlike Yale, Yale-NUS maintains a common curriculum for all its students with no traditional department structure. Hiring is done through interdisciplinary committees. And while decisions about student life and administrative structure are informed by both Yale University and the National University of Singapore, the model that has emerged is uniquely Yale-NUS. Moreover, with many strong connections in the business community, many employers in Singapore stepped forward with internships for the inaugural freshman class in 2013.

It is simply hard to imagine that such an endeavor could emerge from a source of passivity and disconnectedness. Yale-NUS College—"A community of learning, founded by two great universities, in Asia, for the world"—is a product of cascading vitality.

BOLD SUMMARY

It is interesting that Charles Handy, who provided the earlier quote (and the title for this chapter), suggested that "thinking the unlikely" and "doing the unreasonable" was the perfect anecdote for a new age, an age in which change would not be what it used to be. That same idea was used to describe the very nature of deviance earlier. It was labeled as something "unexpected" or "unconventional."

Perhaps this is what bold imaginings, then, is really all about. It is forging an almost divine discontent with the status quo. Accepting our lot in life—whether as individuals or organizations—is really what is expected. We embrace mediocrity. We hone our survival skills every day by showing up and doing the predictable. Life is lived as a bell curve in which most of everything is gathered around the middle.

This suggests the tail ends of the distribution have a much smaller percentage of individuals. On the upper end are the "go-gos." These are the positive-deviation folks. They can't stand average. They don't want to cope or be reliable; they want to be flawless and flourish. They seek out relationships and information. It is all about being a part of something special. Their counterparts are the "no-gos." For them, negativity reigns. Their relationships are cloaked in suspicion and perceived injustices. They tend to be deceitful and lack respect for others. They are the negative-deviation crowd.

And then there are the "go-buts." They are normal and there are lots of them. They want to be good enough because good enough doesn't require anything extra and it also doesn't draw any unwarranted attention. Still, and most importantly, "go-buts" can be swayed. They want to be a part of something special, *but* they aren't sure it will work or if it is worth the effort. Further engagement is conditional. They also don't want to be used. When trust is broken the tug of the "no-gos" becomes real. They do not want to be a part of the dysfunction, *but* they also don't want to be a victim.

This book is about the battle for the hearts and minds of the "go-buts."

If the "no-gos" start to win, then there is a good chance the dynamics of decline will take hold. The downward trajectory will see communication, respect, initiative, and aspirations decreasing while isolation, criticism, and blame increases. Quick fixes and "CYA" thinking will prevail. It will be every man, woman, and child for him- or herself. And the organization runs downhill at an accelerating place until all hope is gone—a doom loop.

But if the "go-gos" can begin to gain traction, their enthusiasm and openness will prove infectious. Hope spreads and a culture of competence emerges. Good enough becomes not nearly good enough. There will be a profound sense of pride in both individual work and collective ambition. And successes will become part of a self-perpetuating, upward trajectory—a virtuous cycle.

This is our future. This is our responsibility.

NOTES

1. Beckie Supiano, "Now Everyone Has a Solution for High Education," *Chronicle of Higher Education*, November 25, 2013, http://chronicle.com/article/Everyone-Has-a-Solution-for/143225.

2. B. M. Staw, I. E. Sandelands, and J. E. Duton, "Threat-Rigidity Effects in Organizational Behavior: A Multi-level Analysis," *Administrative Science Quarterly* 26 (1981): 501–24.

3. See Robert Fritz, *The Path of Least Resistance for Managers* (San Francisco: Berrett-Koehler, 1999).

4. Charles Handy, *The Age of Unreason* (Cambridge: Harvard Business School Press, 1990).

5. Peter M. Senge, *The Fifth Discipline: The Art & Practice of the Learning Organization* (New York: Doubleday, 1990).

6. Karl E. Weick, "Educational Organizations as Loosely Coupled Systems," *Administrative Science Quarterly*, March 21, 1976.

7. Ibid., 12.

8. Richard Perez-Pena, "Best, Brightest and Rejected: Elite Colleges Turn Away up to 95%," *New York Times,* April 9, 2014, www.nytimes.com/2014/04/09/us/led-by-stanfords-5-top-colleges-acceptance-rates-hit-new-lows.html?module=Search&m abReward=relbias%3Ar%2C%7B%222%22%3A%22RI%3A16%22%7D&_r=0.

9. Ry Rivard, "Cleaning House," *Inside Higher Ed*, November 18, 2013, www.insidehighered.com/news/2013/11/18/how-new-president-supposed-clean-house.

10. "University of Wyoming Trustees Tap Dick McGinty for Presidency," *Caspar Star-Tribune*, June 16, 2014, http://trib.com/news/local/education/university-of-wyoming-trustees-tap-dick-mcginity-for-presidency/article_ff9b4c23-6416-5727-9744-24c334c4f27b.html.

11. All materials are taken from *Houston Chronicle* editorials or articles on noted dates with associated titles: www.chron.com.

12. Rosabeth Moss Kanter, *Confidence: How Winning Streaks & Losing Streaks Begin & End* (New York: Crown Business, 2004).

13. All of these references are contained in articles in the *Chronicle of Higher Education*: Sara Jerde, July 4, 2014; Nick DeSantis, March 12, 2014, February 26,

2014, February 26, 2013; Charles Huckabee, November 12, 2013, August 10, 2011; Lawrence Biemeller, April 7, 2012; Joanna Chau, March 15, 2012. Also articles in *Inside Higher Ed*: Ry Rivard, February 27, 2014; Scott Jaschik, February 26, 2014, January 14, 2014, November 28, 2013, November 12, 2013, April 9, 2012, March 23, 2012; J. Andrea Watson, January 13, 2014; Michael Stratford, December 5, 2013; Doug Lederman, August 13, 2011, August 11, 2011, July 26, 2011. Most reference corresponding articles written in the *Chicago Tribune*.

14. See Martin Seligman, "The New Era of Positive Psychology," TED Talk, February 2004, for his discussion of some of these concepts: www.ted.com/talks/martin_seligman_on_the_state_of_psychology.

15. Barbara Fredrickson, *Positivity* (New York: Three Rivers Press, 2009).

16. Ryan W. Quinn and Robert E. Quinn, *Lift: Becoming a Positive Force in Any Situation* (San Francisco: Berrett-Koehler, 2009).

17. Many of the studies in emotion and social interaction are summarized in the book by Elaine Hatfield, John T. Cacioppo, and Richard R. Rapson, *Emotional Contagion* (New York: Cambridge University Press, 1994).

18. Dana H. Lindsey, Daniel J. Brass, and James B. Thomas, "Efficacy-Performance Spirals: A Multilevel Perspective," *Academy of Management Review* 20, no. 3 (1995).

19. Adapted from Kim Cameron, "Organizational Virtuousness and Performance," in Kim S. Cameron, Jane E. Dutton, and Robert E. Quinn (eds.), *Positive Organizational Scholarship* (San Francisco: Berrett-Koehler, 2003).

20. Adapted from Kathleen M. Sutcliffe and Timothy J. Vogus, "Organizing for Resilience," in Kim S. Cameron, Jane E. Dutton, and Robert E. Quinn (eds.), *Positive Organizational Scholarship* (San Francisco: Berrett-Koehler, 2003).

21. Beth Mole, "Bucking the Bad Economy, a Few Universities Plan to Hire Hundreds of Faculty," *Chronicle of Higher Education*, June 25, 2012, http://chronicle.com/article/Now-Hiring-Hundreds-of/132505.

22. Martha S. Feldman and Anne M. Khademian, "Empowerment and Cascading Vitality," in Kim S. Cameron, Jane E. Dutton, and Robert E. Quinn (eds.), *Positive Organizational Scholarship* (San Francisco: Berrett-Koehler, 2003).

Chapter 3

Man's Search for Meaning

Striving and Struggling for a Worthwhile Goal

Viktor Frankl was born in Austria in 1905. He studied medicine at the University of Vienna and completed his residency in neurology and psychiatry at the Steinhof Psychiatric Hospital in Vienna from 1933 to 1937. Then the Nazis invaded. Being Jewish, his professional aspirations were quickly limited and in 1942, he, his wife, and his parents were deported to the Nazi Theresienstadt Ghetto. He was later sent to Auschwitz concentration camp and finally to Dachau, where he worked as a slave laborer. His wife and his parents perished.

After being liberated in 1945, Frankl wrote one of the greatest books of the twentieth century—*Man's Search for Meaning* (1946). The book is less about his particular struggles than it is about his reflections on what it took to survive. He observed, for example, that in many cases prisoners died less from a lack of food or medicine than from a lack of hope or a reason to live. He noted, "Thus it can be seen that mental health is based on a certain degree of tension, the tension between what one has already achieved and what one still ought to accomplish, or the gap between what one is and what one should become."

He considered it a dangerous misconception of mental hygiene to assume that what man needs in the first place is equilibrium or "homeostasis," as it is called in biology. What man actually needs is not a tensionless state but rather the striving and struggling for a worthwhile goal. Moreover, he believed this was a freely chosen task: "There were always choices to make; Every day, every hour, offered an opportunity to make a decision, a decision which determined whether you would or would not submit to those powers which threatened to rob you of your very self, your inner freedom."[1]

This same idea is embedded in much of the research and writing in positivity and Positive Organizational Scholarship that was reviewed in the previous chapter. For example, in *Lift* the authors go into great detail contrasting comfort-centered and purpose-centered people. For them, too often people become comfortable in situations and when problems disrupt—or threaten to disrupt—things, they try to solve those specific problems. The result can be a lifetime of problem solving (oscillation) rather than finding purpose (advancement). Being purpose-centered creates both energy and focus as individuals strive and struggle to attain worthwhile goals. This sense of personal meaning is a critically important psychological facilitator of positive deviance. People feel more vital, are more likely to be proactive (as opposed to being passive), and are also more resilient in the face of "bumps in the road."

There is one more element of *Man's Search for Meaning* that is worth highlighting because it centers on the idea of a responsibility paradigm—"there were always choices to make." Creating a worthwhile goal is a freely chosen task. Again, in *Lift* the parallel discussion embraces the idea that the question "What result do I want to create?" energizes people because it leads them to pursue results that are self-determined and challenges them in a positive way—"Creating implies doing something positive, difficult, and new rather than relying on existing expectations about what can and cannot be done."[2]

Indeed, having a strong sense of purpose or meaning puts individuals into a behavioral orientation in which their own choices result in a desire for making a difference through action.

This first mechanism for creating virtuous cycles of change in colleges and universities moves quickly in our nested hierarchy from the individual to the organization. Initially, a model is presented that frames many of the basic concepts followed by a detailed examination of the practical dimensions associated with the "striving and struggling for a worthwhile goal." Finally, a set of barriers is described that make this momentum-inducing lesson a challenge to achieve in colleges and universities.

THE HEALTH OF AN ORGANIZATION

Of course, Frankl was a psychologist and was narrowly focused on the mental health of the individual. His suffering and observations later formed a strong basis for his logotherapy and existential analysis in which the psychotherapist is generally not concerned with the client's past; instead, the emphasis is on the choices to be made in the present and future. Many individuals have been deeply affected by Frankl's work and his rich legacy has been applied across disciplines.

One such application has been in the area of the creative process as applied to personal effectiveness and has been led by Robert Fritz. A studio musician and composer by training, Fritz began to explore questions about the structural makeup of human motivation. His early books, *The Path of Least Resistance: Principles for Creating What You Want to Create* (1984) and *The Path of Least Resistance: Learning to Become the Creative Force in Your Life* (1989), and consulting practice allowed him to contemplate how his ideas might apply to an organizational setting and the kind of systems discussed in the previous chapter. Working collaboratively with Peter Senge, he began to detail the kind of structural dynamics that could be "designed into" organizations.

At the very core of this design work, this "architectural thinking is structural tension or the difference between what we want and what we have—our desired state as compared to our actual state. Fritz is unequivocal: "I can't say this strongly enough. This principle of structural tension—*knowing what we want to create and knowing where we are in relationship to our goals*—is the most powerful force an organization can have."[3] The nature of this powerful force can be visualized in Fritz's basic model (Figure 3.1).

The difference between an actual state and a desired state creates discrepancy and, in turn, tension. This is nonequilibrium. If Frankl believed that it was a dangerous misconception of mental hygiene to assume that what man needs in the first place is equilibrium or homeostasis, then the idea of purposefully creating discrepancy and tension in a "healthy" organization certainly follows. That is because meaning comes from the struggle to resolve the discrepancy and move along a path leading us to fulfill our aspirations.

This tension-resolution dynamic is at the very heart of designing organizations that thrive. From a structural sense, organizations that create this mechanism are capable of advancement. The discrepancy is purposeful. It is a responsible choice. The mental model is that we are not where we need to be—"We may be good but we could be great." That healthy tension is then the catalyst that inspires action, a set of plans or deeds that can propel the organization forward.

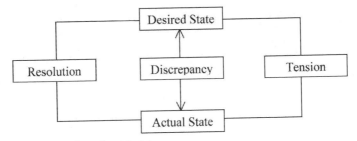

Figure 3.1   **Structural Tension Model**

And a tensionless state? What does that look like? Oscillation. An organizational structure that is not consciously designed to advance is left to rock back and forth. A problem-solving mentality dominates. As soon as one fire is extinguished, another one seems to require our attention. Energy is consumed, as is optimism, because passivity and reactivity is the cultural norm.

It should also be noted that the striving and struggling associated with structural advancement has important implications for virtuous cycles. For example, the language of reinforcing loops can be seen in the language that Fritz uses to describe structural advancement: "There is one major telltale sign that an organization is advancing: its achievements are a platform for further achievements. For an organization that is advancing, everything counts; even those things that don't work are transformed into significant learning that eventually leads to success."[4]

A DESIRED STATE

What does a desired state look like? Most importantly, it is a tangible construct. When setting off on a journey, it is not particularly helpful when, in response to the question "Where do you want to go?," the response is "Anyplace but here" or "North." While it may sound adventurous, that sense of being carefree quickly runs into the reality of making hard choices about gas, food, and money. So, we are not talking here about a cute logo on a website or sweeping proclamations about "quality" or "excellence." Being wispy or vague about our future does not begin to create the discrepancy we need to find meaning and to flourish.

Perhaps the place to start is with the idea of a compelling shared vision, one of the disciplines that Senge discusses as part of a learning organization. At its core, a shared vision is the answer to the question "What do we want to create?" It describes an overarching goal that propels the organization on a path forward and, as such, it challenges the inertia that often dominates the daily activities of many. Without it, the forces associated with the status quo, the comfort-centered norms, are just too overwhelming. But with it, there is a spark, a sense of excitement, about the enterprise. There is joy in work.

Powerful visions also generate pride in those who feel a part of something larger than themselves. Everyone wants to be a part of something special. And then there is courage. There comes a time, in any organization, where individuals are called on to make tough decisions or to sacrifice or take leaps of faith. There is strength inherent in doing whatever is necessary in pursuit of a compelling shared vision.

A useful illustration of the power associated with this type of vision is evident in the numbers associated with one university. How is it possible for an institution to go from nine thousand graduates to more than eighteen thousand in a decade and to have a goal of reaching twenty-five thousand by 2020? How is it possible for that same institution to start at $100 million in funded research and climb to more than $400 million in that same timeframe with a goal of $700 million by the end of this decade as well? How is it possible to do that without adding to the number of faculty members and to actually having 1,800 fewer employees?

At Arizona State University (ASU), the struggle to achieve begins with a vision: "To establish ASU as the model for a New American University, measured not by who we exclude, but rather by who we include and how they succeed; pursuing research and discovery that benefits the public good; assuming major responsibility for the economic, social, and cultural vitality and health and well-being of the community."

What exactly is this New American University?[5] The institution uses a series of eight "design aspirations" to describe their own search for meaning:

Leverage Our Place: ASU embraces its cultural, socioeconomic, and physical setting.

Transform Society: ASU catalyzes social change by being connected to social needs.

Value Entrepreneurship: ASU uses its knowledge and encourages innovation.

Conduct Use-Inspired Research: ASU research has purpose and impact.

Enable Student Success: ASU is committed to the success of each unique student.

Fuse Intellectual Disciplines: ASU creates knowledge by transcending academic disciplines.

Be Socially Embedded: ASU connects with communities through mutually beneficial partnerships.

Engage Globally: ASU engages with people and issues locally, nationally, and internationally.

This is not comfortable stuff. First, stating that you want to be measured "not by who we exclude, but rather by who we include and how they succeed" turns the entire resource-reputation model and its focus on selectivity on its head. But at the core of ASU's striving is the idea of "design aspirations." This language captures the essence of Fritz's basic model. The New American University is a desired state that clearly differentiates itself from the vast majority of universities in this country. As such, it creates dissonance. There is an obvious disconnect between this vision and how other institutions, and even ASU, have traditionally conducted themselves. Aspirations of this kind are exhilarating.

But a vision without a plan is just a dream.

The resolution aspect of the model is embedded in ASU's "design." This speaks to intention. It is a conscious effort to ensure that energy (which is created by the aspiration) is focused on specific means to catalyze change. And, of course, the language of responsibility cannot be overlooked. No one is being held accountable here. Extramural agents are not dictating ASU's future. The institution is not being forced to react or to bolster its defenses against a real or perceived threat. ASU is *choosing* to assume responsibility for its important role in its community and in society.

While the answer to the question "What do we want to create?" is an appropriate starting point to this conversation, it is also worth describing a broader interpretation of meaning that is reflective of our general model. The authors of an important *Harvard Business Review* article, Douglas Ready and Emily Truelove, examined institutions that managed to thrive in spite of the extraordinary challenges associated with the recent Great Recession. After interviewing senior executives and conducting surveys with many mid-level managers, they construct a comprehensive model that reflects the kind of resilience needed to respond to the bumps and bruises inflicted on organizations (as was discussed in the previous chapter).

The model is expressed in what they call "collective ambition"—a summary of how leaders and employees think about why they exist, what they hope to accomplish, how they will collaborate to achieve their ambition, and how their brand promise aligns with their core values. The seven elements of a collective ambition are enumerated as follows:

1. *Purpose:* your company's reason for being; the core mission of the enterprise.
2. *Vision:* the position or status your company aspires to achieve within a reasonable timeframe.
3. *Targets and milestones:* the metrics you use to assess progress toward your vision.
4. *Strategic and operational priorities:* the actions you do or do not take in pursuit of your vision.
5. *Brand promise:* the commitments you make to stakeholders (customers, communities, investors, employees, regulators, and partners) concerning the experience the company will provide.
6. *Core values:* the guiding principles that dictate what you stand for as an organization, in good times and bad.
7. *Leader behaviors:* how leaders act on a daily basis as they seek to implement the company's vision and strategic priorities, strive to fulfill the brand promise, and live up to the values.[6]

This broader construct has been applied to higher education in a 2013 book that focuses on community colleges—*Noble Ambitions: Mission, Vision, and*

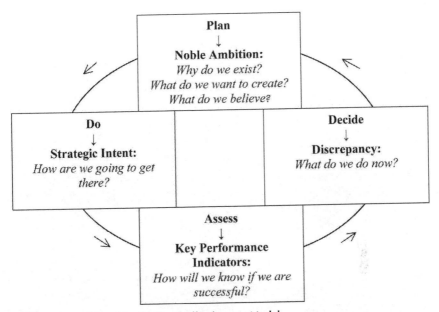

Figure 3.2   A General Institutional Effectiveness Model

Values in American Community Colleges. In addition to the vision question, "What do we want to create?," two additional questions are asked: "Why do we exist?" and "What do we believe?" These mission and values questions, along with the vision question, are then analyzed across more than two hundred community colleges in terms of their ability to create structural tension and then resolution through strategic planning.

While the evidence strongly suggests that individual community colleges are far too comfortable with themselves and fail to express their noble ambitions in a way that drives action and change, a resulting model of institutional effectiveness (Figure 3.2) captures both the comprehensive nature of a collective ambition and the striving associated with continuous improvement.[7]

It should be clear that there is a connection between a generalized notion of improved mental health in individuals and a similar concept in organizations: being able to articulate an aspiration that is meaningful, creates energy, and inspires courage and that, in turn, leads to positive adjustment, upward spirals of change, and momentum.

Within the larger context of purpose, and a search for meaning, another set of dimensions makes the concept of a collective ambition itself more robust and applicable to our efforts to accept responsibility for our own flourishing. These dimensions include: social identity, constancy of purpose, institutional legitimacy, and distinctiveness.

Social Identity

One of the most important dimensions of our search for meaning is embedded in the sharing part of Senge's "compelling shared vision." Social identity is that portion of an individual's self-concept that is derived from membership in a relevant group. A key assumption in social identity theory is that individuals are intrinsically motivated to strive for a positive self-concept. Further, as individuals to varying degrees are defined and informed by their respective social identities, it follows that individuals strive to achieve or maintain positive social identities. The bottom line is that people want to be a part of something special. They want to connect to something larger than themselves that builds on a self-concept and creates distinctiveness in their own minds and in the minds of others.

The relationship works both ways. Not only do individuals gain from an enhanced self-concept, but also the resulting positivity broadens individuals' outlook. As we move from "me" to "we," our worldview and energy expands, allowing us to see more possibilities. A useful illustration of the power of belonging can be seen in the same press conference that was used to begin this book. The just-appointed president of Virginia Tech University, Timothy Sands, spoke about what drew him to the institution. He referenced the fact that Virginia Tech was a land-grant institution and anchored this part of the speech in the year 1862 with the Morrill Act and 1867, the year of the school's founding. He spoke about the mission and how Virginia Tech had taken a somewhat different path by consciously blending science, engineering, and the liberal arts—"Virginia Tech is the kind of institution you would create today for the 21st century."

Where he became most passionate was when he spoke to the motto *Ut Promsim* (That I May Serve) and how students at his new institution actually walked the talk. He was looking forward to "The Big Event" later in the spring at which faculty, students, and staff members did community service projects throughout the region (and later, in mid-April, he joined them as 7,806 participated in completing 878 jobs).

The structure of belonging creates a powerful bond and an energized sense of community. As such, it is a primary mechanism in developing the type of virtuousness that is fundamental to positive deviation (including benevolence, honoring, and flourishing as described in chapter 2).

Constancy of Purpose

A second dimension of a collective ambition useful for colleges and universities is constancy of purpose. Benjamin Disraeli, a British prime minister, once stated, "The secret to success is constancy of purpose," and nearly a century later the noted statistician W. Edwards Deming made "constancy of purpose" the first of his fourteen points in *Out of Crisis* (1982). The general idea Deming suggests is that organizations face two sets of problems: those of today and those of tomorrow. He believes that most managers have a tendency or perhaps obsession with the problems of the present: "It is easy to stay bound up in the tangles of the problems of today, becoming ever more efficient in them."[8]

We see this all the time. These are the individuals who spend all day responding to e-mails, taking calls, and sitting in meetings. They are working problems. They are attending to immediate issues, reacting to the person who is standing in the doorway or the urgent message, and, of course, believing that they are being decisive. But that leaves little time for the future—for planning it, for sticking to it. Structural advancement takes a backseat to structural oscillation.

The clear articulation of a desired state is incredibly useful for creating a future that demands attention and a framework that helps influence daily decisions. Indeed, "resolution" is all about a limited and purposeful set of actions rather than an unlimited and random set of reactions. One of the ways that institutions develop this "framing" ability is through model building that aligns mission, vision, values with strategic and unit plans as well as more focused action steps.

Fox Valley Technical College, for example, has its mission, vision, and values. But, in addition, they have what might be described as an institutional effectiveness model that aligns with strategic directions, college annual objectives, division plans, department plans, and, finally, individual performance plans.[9] Of course, the most important part of this exercise is the idea that every single individual in the institution has a specific and important role to play in helping the college advance.

The more pedestrian way to express the idea is for everyone to keep "their eyes on the prize." It is simply too easy to be distracted in a high-velocity environment. The result is often oscillation, a series of seemingly endless responses to irritants and minor issues that deplete individuals' and the institution's energy.

Institutional Legitimacy

The idea of "cascading vitality," explored in the previous chapter, suggests that virtuous processes produce energy and vitality. Moreover, an organization that is flourishing develops the potential to move beyond its immediate boundaries—that vitality is shared. But cascading vitality requires that the source of the enthusiasm can be articulated. It must be shaped into a narrative that exudes confidence and conveys legitimacy. Perhaps the people in higher education who know this best are the fundraisers. Their core document is a case statement that answers such questions such as "What is the need?," "How is your institution uniquely qualified to tackle this need?," and "What will be the benefits of your action?"

But the 2013 study *Million Dollar Ready: Assessing the Institutional Factors That Lead to Transformational Gifts* looks beyond the quality of the case statement to other, more foundational factors that help secure major gifts. Analyzing publicly announced million-dollar gifts from 2000 to 2012, the study yields a number of implications for colleges and universities who wish to strengthen their ability to attract million-dollar donations. The first of four implications is "Articulate a strong vision and donors will want to be a part of it." The study goes on: "Transformational philanthropy requires a transformational vision, and that vision must be articulated in a way that allows donors to see how students' lives will be changed."[10]

In the same way, the ability to express a distinctive and desired future state creates reciprocal energy and acts as an antidote to entropy (or the inevitable and steady deterioration of a closed system). A useful illustration of this concept is Portland State University (PSU). The institution was started for veterans after World War II and was seen as the local commuter school. It didn't have the prestige of the University of Oregon or Oregon State University, or as one longtime professor of urban studies and planning noted, "PSU had always been on the margins of Oregon's higher-ed trajectory." But a commission in the early 1990s worked with then-president Judith Ramaley to articulate a uniquely urban mission for the institution that still exists today: Let Knowledge Serve the City. The curriculum was revamped to reflect real-world issues in Portland.

The result has been a level of cooperation that is inspiring. The profile of Portland as a hip, green city cannot be separated from PSU as a nationally acclaimed leader in sustainability and community-based learning. That connectivity extends to a partnership with Oregon Health & Science University to build the largest academic structure in the state to house various shared programs as well as the "Urban Plaza," a public space on the campus that serves as a transit hub and a showcase for new innovations such as "Electric Avenue," which has charging stations for electric cars. With nearly thirty thousand students, PSU has grown to become the largest public university in Oregon.

Meaning or purpose at an institutional level must be well articulated and properly understood in order to convey legitimacy about a desired state. Without that, there is no discrepancy, no structural tension, and no possibility of significant advancement.

Distinctiveness

It follows that the ability of an organization to engage individuals around a preferred future requires that desired state to be distinctive. Indeed, being "compelling" strongly suggests that it is not simply a long-winded statement that is required by accreditors, stuck in a catalogue, and suitably punctuated with references to quality and excellence. Being able to describe, in a distinctive way, an institution's aspirations is an incredible opportunity to begin the process of breaking the bonds of inertia and building real momentum.

But an opportunity is just that—a favorable, appropriate, or advantageous combination of circumstances. Unfortunately, it would appear that most colleges or universities do not take advantage of that opportunity to describe a distinctive, desired state and, in turn, lose the opportunity to create structural tension. Certainly that is the case with most community colleges. An analysis conducted in *Noble Ambitions* finds that the vast majority of community colleges in a sample of more than two hundred institutions have remarkably undifferentiated visions. Examples include:

- DEF College is a dynamic, diverse environment where all are encouraged to become responsible community members, leaders, and world citizens.
- GHI College is committed to excellence in instructional programs, student services, service to community, and leadership in economic development and cultural enrichment in the region.
- VWX College will continue to be an active partner in building and maintaining the academic excellence and economic vitality of the diverse communities it serves.

The conclusion that followed: "A simple cut-and-paste exercise could be used to exchange the name of one college for another, and there is little evidence to suggest anyone would notice. The language does not enable any of the institutions mentioned to make the case for their being special."[11]

In contrast, there is the opportunity that is embraced. Returning to the example of Arizona State University, Michael Crow, ASU's president, spoke passionately at the 2013 Trusteeship Conference about the evolution of his institution's vision and design aspirations. He began by noting that too many institutions had developed generic identities and used a sled dog analogy in which it would seem that the primary exercise was simply to move up a place in line. But in order for ASU to pursue its own distinctive aspirations, its own unique identity, and then be able to achieve its ambitious goals, it needed to follow one overarching rule. He said, "We could do anything other than accept any model by which any other college or university operated as a core operating parameter for *our institution*."[12] The emphasis was on "our institution."

There is comfort in being part of the herd. Fewer bad things can happen. But, in contrast, great things are rarely going to happen too.

DESPERATELY SEEKING COMFORT

Earlier it was noted that being purpose-centered stands in contrast to seeking comfort and reacting to problems—advancement versus oscillation structures. And just as we have spent time exploring various dimensions of a search for meaning and purpose, it might be useful to also describe several dimensions of comfort. If discrepancy causes tension, it follows that no discrepancy will produce a tensionless state. Such a dynamic is a function of either of two conditions. In workshops Peter Senge illustrates these conditions by using a large rubber band.[13] In both instances you hold the rubber band between your thumbs in a vertical position. Your top thumb represents the desired state and your bottom thumb represents the actual state.

The first tensionless state occurs if you fail to extend your top thumb upward—that is, you fail to actually articulate a desired state that is sufficiently different from the present. No discrepancy. No tension. No need for resolution.

The ASUs and the PSUs are the exception, not the rule. Most institutions don't attempt distinctiveness. They, as Michael Crow noted, are content to stay in line, try to acquire enough resources to increase their reputation, and then sneak past a few of the other schools in a national ranking. One illustration of this dynamic can be seen in the language associated with community college visions discussed earlier. While some institutions in that dataset use the future tense of *will be, will become*, or other forward-leaning terms such as *aspires, envisions*, and *seeks*, many are content to use *is* or *will continue* in their vision statements.

Using the present tense when describing a desired state is the equivalent of a "staycation"—that is, "we were going to embark on a journey but decided that we are fine right about here." And *will continue* is the height of hubris—"we are fabulous and have decided to remain so." The rubber band is not being stretched when the desired state and the actual state are at the same level. There is no striving and struggling when the institution and individuals are unwilling or unable to identify a worthwhile goal.

A second source of structural and creative tension comes from getting clearer about the current reality or holding your top thumb high *and* extending the bottom thumb downward. Senge uses Martin Luther King's 1963 "I Have a Dream" speech as an illustration. While King's core vision was about freedom, he spent most of his life seeking to dramatize the current reality with marches that showed peaceful protesters being beaten by police, drenched by fire hoses, and being set upon by police dogs. It was important that the media be there. It was important that the rest of the nation could bear witness to a well-dressed, middle-aged black woman being arrested for not giving up her bus seat to a white man. Without that truth, without being precisely clear about what the current reality was, the vision would have lost its poignancy and power.

We also need to be honest and truthful about our current reality. A useful illustration is the current discussion on the Completion Agenda. The data suggest that far too many individuals who begin a certificate or degree program fail to complete their program. Indeed, according to Complete College America's groundbreaking report, *Time Is the Enemy* (2011), if you are an African American student going part-time to receive a two-year associate's degree, you have a 2.1 percent chance of completing in three years.

That's reality: higher education as an empty promise.

Now it is true that some legislators have used these numbers to beat us up. It is true that this becomes fodder for various anti-intellectual rants. And it is true that the call for various forms of accountability has been largely driven by these data. Unfortunately, it is also true that far too much time has been devoted to tiresome threat-rigidity responses that seek to blame the students for not being college ready, blame the state legislature for not allocating enough money, blame the administration for hiring too many administrators and not enough counselors, and so on.

What we don't do as much is be honest about the situation: We have systems and processes in place that are perfectly designed to enroll students but not particularly good at graduating them.

The approach we need to be taking is grounded in the same Socratic method that we expect students to use in the classroom. As an example, in 2014 the Education Trust conducted a study of "high-performing, fast-gaining" institutions in order to provoke discussion and action on college completion. The result was not a series of prescriptions but, rather, a "Top 10" set of questions that challenge colleges and universities to dramatize their own current reality:

Analysis 1: *How many students do we lose along the way?* This is a look at year-to-year retention rates.

Analysis 2: *But are those returning students actually sophomores?* This involves tracking the rate of second-year students who achieve sophomore standing.

Analysis 3: *Why aren't our students accumulating the credits they need to be on track?* This is analyzing the impact of course withdrawals.

Analysis 4: *What are some of the other reasons our students aren't accumulating the credits they need?* This is analyzing success rates in the twenty-five to thirty-five courses with the largest annual enrollment.

Analysis 5: *Who's struggling with math: only developmental students?* This is analyzing success rates in the first credit-bearing math course.

Analysis 6: *How many students who need remediation succeed at our institution?* This is digging into the data on developmental courses, especially math.

Analysis 7: *What is the role—or the lack thereof—of the major in student success?* This is analyzing the data on success for students in different fields.

Analysis 8: *How efficient are we in getting students to a degree without excess credits?* This is analyzing the data on units completed.

Analysis 9: *What pathways do our students take on their journey to a degree?* This is an analysis of transcripts.

Analysis 10: *How do the pieces of student success—or failure—fit together?* This is conducting a fuller analysis of student pathways.[14]

A final word about comfort is necessary. The two dynamics just described don't just happen. The inability to articulate a collective ambition is not circumstantial; the lack of truthfulness about current conditions is not incidental or anecdotal. It takes real people, doing real things (or not doing real things), to create the conditions that lead to inertia. Wayne Gretzky, the Great One of hockey fame, is reported to have uttered the now-famous line "I skate to where the puck will be." This is the kind of anticipatory judgment that is likely to create virtuous cycles of change in our colleges and universities. As such, we should have institutions that are thickly populated with Gretzkys skating hard to where the puck will be.

Unfortunately, too often our large, inclusive selection committees focus on "fit." We tend to hire people that validate our own worth and the decisions that were made in the past. "Fit" is what we are looking for when we ask questions about how many years the candidate has worked in institutions like our own. "Fit" is also seen in the career arc that someone has taken from job to job in a predictable path. We don't necessarily hire new leaders to take us to a different place and we also don't hire them to challenge "how we do things around here." We may talk enthusiastically about change but we prefer predictability. What we want is comfort but what we need are vision makers and truth tellers who do, at times, make us feel uncomfortable.

Richard Rush is the founding president of California State University at Channel Islands. The institution opened in 2002 as the twenty-third campus in the California State University System. The original campus consisted of state hospital buildings—low, adobe brick—updated with a consistent design element that blends with its seaside setting. Working with a core set of founding faculty members that came from all over the country, a design team saw the development of the new university as an opportunity to differentiate its mission. They wanted to break down traditional disciplinary silos and encourage faculty to work at the edge of their disciplines:

> Placing students at the center of the educational experience, California State University Channel Islands provides undergraduate and graduate education that facilitates learning within and across disciplines through integrative approaches, emphasizes experiential and service learning, and graduates students with multicultural and international perspectives.

The institution feels and acts different from others. It is extraordinarily collaborative. Some large part of the reason for that is because the president interviews every faculty hire. The key message he has is that the institution is serious about its "integrative approaches." Because of that, the reward structure is different. Publishing in narrow, scholarly journals does not carry much weight. And so, he gives each candidate a final opportunity to reflect on whether this is the right place for them. Because if it isn't, "do yourself and us a favor and please seriously consider rejecting this offer."[15]

STRIVING SUMMARY

Antoine de Saint Exupery, the celebrated French writer and poet, states: "If you want to build a ship, don't drum up people to collect wood and don't assign them tasks or work, but rather teach them to long for the endless immensity of the sea." Whether it is Fritz's description of a desired state, Senge's compelling shared vision, Crow's articulation of the New American, or even Frankl searching deep in the worst of all possible situations for dignity and hope, the core concept is the same: it is the worthwhile goal that creates meaning.

But it is also important to reiterate that the starting point for creating virtuous cycles or upward spirals of change in colleges and universities is a shift from individuals operating in the present to groups thinking about their collective future. It is the process of creating that is so compelling and so energizing, not just the goal itself. Taking responsibility for that process is really where momentum begins.

Yes, it can be uncomfortable. Longing and searching for something that is better places pressure on individuals and institutions; striving and struggling for it is often demanding work. But the labor has its rewards in being part of an effort, a shared exercise, in helping to create your own future. Choosing a destination and owning the journey is what can transform a heap of individuals into an organizational system, one that is capable of thriving in a high-velocity environment.

And as we noted in the opening chapter, if you are not gaining traction, you really aren't staying the same. You are losing ground.

NOTES

1. Viktor E. Frankl, *Man's Search for Meaning* (Boston: Beacon Press, 2006).

2. Ryan W. Quinn and Robert E. Quinn, *Lift: Becoming a Positive Force in Any Situation* (San Francisco: Berrett-Koehler, 2009), 59.

3. Robert Fritz, *The Path of Least Resistance for Managers* (San Francisco: Berrett-Koehler, 1999).

4. Ibid, 17.

5. All of the ideas behind this model can be seen at http://newamericanuniversity. asu.edu. Michael Crow has made numerous presentations as well. See, for example, www.youtube.com/watch?v=KW5Q74tGj28. Also see Michael M. Crow and William B. Dabars, *Designing the New American University* (Baltimore, MD: Johns Hopkins University Press, 2015).

6. Douglas A. Ready and Emily Truelove, "The Power of Collective Ambition," *Harvard Business Review* (December 2011).

7. See Daniel Seymour, *Noble Ambitions: Mission, Vision, and Values in American Community Colleges* (Washington, DC: American Association of Community Colleges, 2013).

8. W. Edwards Deming, *Out of the Crisis* (Cambridge: Massachusetts Institute of Technology, 1982).

9. See Fox Valley Technical College's Planning Alignment Model, www. nobleambitions.org/uploads/Fox_Valley_Technical_College_-_Planning_Alignment. pdf.

10. Johnson, Grossnickle, and Associates and Indiana University Lily Family School of Philanthropy, *Million Dollar Ready: Assessing the Institutional Factors that Lead to Transformational Gifts,* 2013, www.philanthropy.iupui.edu/ research-by-category/million-dollar-ready-report

11. Seymour, *Noble Ambitions,* 45–46.

12. From his speech at the 2013 Trusteeship Conference, www.youtube.com/ watch?v=8q5BXb9deik.

13. See Peter Senge's lecture on creative tension at www.youtube.com/ watch?v=wz337pj-oLE.

14. Joseph Yeado, Kati Haycock, Rob Johnstone, and Priyadarshini Chaplot, *Learning from High-Performing and Fast-Gaining Institutions* (Washington, DC: The Education Trust, 2014).

15. Personal conversation with Richard Rush (February 12, 2013).

Chapter 4

The War Canoe

Aligning People and Processes

Working in a college or university is a worthwhile endeavor. Many institutions have strong brand-name recognition. Some—Notre Dame University, Harvard University, Stanford University—are national brands with large, impassioned alumni that support their schools financially, as goodwill ambassadors, and as loud and loyal fans at sporting events. Smaller, private liberal arts colleges don't have these numbers but can, in many cases, inspire even more loyalty and a familial bond that turns into generations of prospective students. Land-grant universities, many of which have evolved into "college towns," because of their disproportionate impact on the local economy and culture, are seen as essential to the future of their regions. And community colleges—especially those in smaller cities and towns—are embraced as community assets with students running into their professors at the local grocery store.

There is also the common good. The vast majority of colleges and universities are nonprofit. They educate our first-responders, our teachers, and our scientists. They conduct basic and applied research. They partner with local industry and provide many valuable community-based services. Moreover, any study of "most respected professions" includes "professor" in the top ten along with doctors, nurses, and judges.

For all of these reasons, highly motivated people seek to join our colleges and universities. As mission-driven institutions, individuals feel a sense of pride being associated with organizations that contribute to society especially compared to those that are more focused on contributing to just a bottom line.

This is certainly true for staff members and administrators. But there is an additional motivator associated with being a college or university professor. UCLA's Higher Education Research Institute (HERI) conducts an annual faculty survey in which questions are asked about university priorities, stress factors, and other factors that relate to satisfaction of work-life. What is the most satisfying factor? Eighty-six percent indicated that they are highly satisfied or satisfied with "autonomy and independence." It trumps "competency of colleagues," "quality of students," and "salary and benefits." Moreover, "autonomy and independence" has remained at the head of the class for twenty years.[1,2]

So, colleges and universities hire highly motivated, independent-minded professionals who have a deep desire to make the world a better place. What could possibly go wrong?

Think of a barge.[3] Now think of hiring lots of people to move the barge in a purposeful direction to a new and better place (a future state that was described in the previous chapter). The student services people tend to cluster on one side of the barge. Another side might have individuals who are focused on the business aspects of the enterprise. Of course, there is a large and enthusiastic group of faculty members. There are administrators and trustees on our multisided vessel.

In order to create movement, everyone gets a paddle and, eager to make a difference, they produce an impressive volume of activity. There is plenty of splashing and lots of commotion, even huffing and puffing. But what about the barge? Where does it go?

Usually, it just stands there. That is because the forces described above often counteract each other. They push and pull the vessel, but without any coordination they aren't able to make any progress.

Now it might be argued that there is a flaw in our metaphor because not all paddles are created equal. That is true. The paddles that the board members, presidents, and other senior executives wield are indeed larger because of their greater influence. So what would happen if those with the larger paddles all gathered together on one side and decided to head off in a specific direction? Could the efforts of a relatively few people, executives to be sure, overcome the unaligned and random acts of many? No, they cannot. Try as they might—through policies and practices—their individual, personal visions will not result in any significant directional movement.

Our colleges and universities need a different type of vessel. We need a war canoe.

This chapter explores the metaphor of a war canoe for aligning people and processes to create more interdependency, more coordination, and more information flow. As the coupling becomes tighter, the opportunity is to replace the spinning and waffling associated with unaligned systems with a coherent, forward-leaning system capable of advancement. Momentum does not occur because of a series of lucky events; momentum is a direct result of choices and actions—that is, taking responsibility for creating virtuous cycles of change.

A METAPHOR FOR OUR TIMES

Good people get tired of paddling with no payoff. The return on their emotional investment is not there. Over time, they give up (barely breaking the surface with their oars) or they leave (taking their oars to another institution). New paddlers replace those who have moved on. It doesn't make much difference. Maybe there is a short burst of energy, but it is not sustainable. At best, those with the longer paddles, working in an isolated fashion, can only impact the speed with which the barge turns and twists, not its direction.

As we have discussed, this is one of the key challenges with loosely coupled systems. It is attractive to the individual entrepreneur because the institution offers legitimacy to their activities. The pigeonholes provide protection against controlling and, at times, overzealous administrators. But that autonomy comes at a significant price. Indeed, in the opening chapter Henry Mintzberg described the problems of coordination in professional bureaucracies. He states: "Unlike Machine Bureaucracies, Professional Bureaucracies are not integrated entities. They are collection of individuals who come together to draw on common resources and support services but otherwise want to be left alone. As long as the pigeonholing process works effectively, they can be."

But our high-velocity environment and the constant calls for holding colleges and universities accountable would suggest that the pigeonholing process has become increasingly problematic. The loose coupling results in the overuse of threat-rigidity tools that, in turn, create oscillating structures and the increasing potential for vicious cycles that pull institutions down.

The war canoe provides an alternative, advancing structure to the whirling and churning of the barge metaphor. Found in various forms throughout the world, the war canoe is generally a long, single-hulled vessel that is manned by many paddlers. The *waka taua*, as an example, is a 130-foot ocean-voyaging canoe used by the Maori people of New Zealand. As many as eighty tribesmen manned a waka in river travel, fishing, and, of course, fighting wars. The war canoe uses a slender prow to slice its way through the water. The pointed end aligns the vessel with its destination as leaders work hard to, in turn, align the occupants and their efforts with the chosen destination. There is also an elevated platform in the rear of the war canoe so that leadership can look out over the choppy, dark waters. Everyone chants. A rhythm begins to emerge as randomness is replaced by coordination. Arbitrary actions are supplanted by the energizing cadence of the canoe.

The lyrics of the song "War Canoe" by Rolf Harris provide a sense of the cohesion and spirit that develops:

All together
All together
Lean on the paddles
Lean on and lift out[4]

Finally, while the idea of fighting a war may be problematic to some, it must be reinforced that the external forces that are producing the blustery winds and surging tides for our vessel are neither insignificant nor benign. The "we-need-to-hold-them-accountable" crowd is not interested anymore in our lofty rhetoric or defensive maneuverings. "Demonstrating responsibility" is not for the faint of heart underneath such conditions. It will require vigorous action that is both spirit filled and intentionally executed. It may not be war but it certainly feels like war.

SENGE'S ARROWS

Within the context of systems thinking and organizational learning, Peter Senge uses a series of big and little arrows to describe the same idea as our nautical metaphors of barges and war canoes.[5] The large arrow in Figure 4.1 represents the purpose or direction of the organization. It is, in effect, the espoused future state. But an organization is made up of individuals and all of them have personal visions or their own little arrows.

The significance of the big arrow cannot be overstated. Robert Fritz, whose work has played such a significant role in the application of systems thinking to organizations, enumerates a series of laws associated with structure as initially described in the previous chapter. He suggests that creating a discrepancy between the current state and a future, desired state can and should produce structural tension, which, in turn, lays the groundwork for resolution—*momentum*. But what happens when the primary dynamic—the clear and meaningful articulation of a desired state—is missing in an organization? He states, "When a senior organizing principle is absent, the organization will oscillate. When a senior organizing principle is dominant, the organization will advance."[6] The big arrow is the higher-order organizing principle.

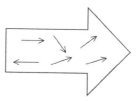

Figure 4.1   Unaligned Visions

When that organizing principle or vision is either absent or not shared, the result is an almost-daily set of mismatched encounters.

An unaligned team or institution is an emotional and energy drain. Sporadic initiatives, threat-induced responses, and even the occasional well-meaning effort do not result in any constancy of purpose. Like any investment, our expectation is that we will generate a nice return. We believe our work will pay off, which then increases the chances that we will engage in the further investment of our time and enthusiasm. When we don't perceive our efforts having a positive impact, the chance of disengagement—or disinvestment—greatly increases. The unaligned or incoherent institution tends to oscillate. The organization feels stuck, rocking back and forth, or running in place.

A lack of alignment is problematic enough, but now what happens when a lack of alignment is also accompanied by significant empowerment? According to Senge, "Empowering the individual when there is a relatively low level of alignment worsens the chaos and makes managing the team even more difficult." As shown in Figure 4.2, our big arrow begins to take quite a beating from the small, individual arrows that punch out harder in different directions.

Not only is any chance of forward momentum reduced, but also empowerment without alignment can result in violent swings and surges. The general malaise of an unaligned organization is replaced by one that is susceptible to heightened emotions, vehement disagreements, and provocative actions. A push becomes a shove.

New York University might be the modern definition of a multiversity with numerous colleges, campuses, and affiliations. And it would follow that such a sprawling enterprise would have numerous, energized stakeholders. But over the years most of the headlines have been about everything other than a shared sense of the future. There have been the strained efforts to redevelop a 1.9 million-square-foot area in Greenwich Village known as NYU 2013. There is the dubious distinction of being one of the most expensive institutions in the country—usually battling it out with Sarah Lawrence for the prized top spot—against a backdrop of national student debt surpassing $1 trillion. The president, John Sexton, has been on the top ten list of highest-paid presidents while at the same time enduring a series of no-confidence

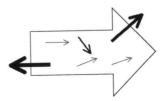

Figure 4.2 Unaligned (and Empowered) Visions

votes over the years. Two recent overwhelming votes of no-confidence brought to four the number of NYU schools or campuses whose faculty members have questioned his leadership.

While these incidences suggest a lack of alignment, the more recent headlines involving its new Abu Dhabi venture illustrates the challenge associated with empowered individuals. In May of 2014, the *New York Times* reported on the brutal working conditions for the roughly six thousand migrant construction workers building the campus in the capital city of the United Arab Emirates. The report detailed instances of beatings, arrests, deportations, and other abuses while at the same time quoting the president, who stated that the ambitious effort was "an opportunity to transform the university and, frankly, the world."

The story gained significant traction after it was revealed that a member of the university's Board of Trustees was also the chairman of Abu Dhabi's government-run Mubadala Development Company, which is charged with building the campus as well as being a policy advisor to the crown prince. Follow-up news articles in various newspapers identified the many Wall Street connections involved while the *Chronicle of Higher Education*, not to be outdone, ran an article listing the sixty-five-member board that concludes, "Members are predominantly wealthy, and their background skew heavily to finance and law."[7]

With such high-powered little arrows involved in the policy making of a university, it would suggest that the big arrow would need to be incredibly compelling and vigorously shared in order to prevent chaos and confusion. At NYU it appears that empowerment is trumping alignment and coherence.

This example stands in contrast to situations in which personal visions begin to align with a larger, organizational vision. The impact when the arrows—big and small—line up with each other is extraordinarily powerful (Figure 4.3). It is the war canoe. It involves synergistic collaboration with all the parts working together in a positive, reinforcing manner. No little arrows are misdirected. No "empowered" little arrows are punching out the back because they want to or simply can. Instead, we begin to see more coherence and synergy as interdependency, coordination, and information flow increases.

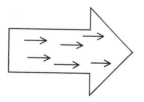

Figure 4.3   Aligned Visions

The powerful forces around this alignment include concepts that we have already discussed. For example, social identity is a strong bonding factor. A portion of an individual's self-image can come from the groups with which she or he identifies. Positivity and emotional contagion also come into play here. When describing upward spirals in her book on positivity, Barbara Fredricksen states:

> When you act on your sense of oneness with others and lend a helping hand, you externalize your positivity. It's moved from your own heart and mind into the space between you and another person. And, just like negativity, positivity is remarkably contagious. Once "out there," it spreads because people unconsciously mimic the emotional gestures and facial expressions of those around them. But that's only a small part of the story. Positivity also spreads because it sets off a chain of events that carry positive meaning for you and those around you.[8]

It is evident that something special can happen when individuals align with something larger than themselves: It helps to create the conditions under which structural advancement is possible and institutions begin to thrive.

ACHIEVING COMMITMENT

Getting our barge or random little arrows to develop more coherence is not an easy assignment. Senge begins his discussion on this topic by speaking to the issue of compliance. He suggests that compliance, in its various forms, has prevailed for a long time in many organizations:

Genuine compliance—Sees the benefits of the vision. Does everything expected and more.

Formal compliance—On the whole, sees the benefits of the vision. Does what's expected and no more.

Grudging compliance—Does not see the benefits of the vision. But, also, does not want to lose job. Does enough of what's expected because they have to, but also lets it be known that they are not really on board.

Noncompliance—Does not see benefits of vision and will not do what's expected.

Apathy—Neither for or against vision. No interest. No energy.[9]

Of course, while aspects of these different compliance levels apply to specific colleges or universities, and various units within them, *compliance* is not the preferred language of academe. Nor should it be. While it has been argued in these pages that more interdependency, more coordination, and more information flow is required in a high-velocity environment, the manner and means to achieve improved coherence need to be achieved in ways that do not provoke a threat-rigidity reaction.

What we are seeking is commitment. And there is a huge difference between compliance and commitment according to Senge:

> The committed person brings energy, passion, and excitement that cannot be generated if you are only compliant, even genuinely compliant. The committed person doesn't play by the 'rules of the game.' He is responsible for the game. If the rules of the game stand in the way of achieving the vision, he will find ways to change the rules. A group of people truly committed to a common vision is an awesome force. They can accomplish the seemingly impossible.[10]

How, exactly, might colleges and universities become more coherent, more aligned, and help create virtuous cycles through committed individuals? Several approaches are worth mentioning: developing situational awareness, shifting from discussion to dialogue, and creating a structure that spreads the authority to convene.

Situational Awareness

If a college or university and its many employees think only in terms of the parts and not the whole, centrifugal forces grab hold and refuse to let go. *Centrifugal* is Latin for "center fleeing" and is the tendency of an object following a curved path to fly outward. Centrifugal forces are critical to understand in our situation because spirals—the reinforcing loops that we are seeking to bring about responsibility-driven change in colleges and universities—are curved paths. How can we create momentum in our institutions without experiencing the center fleeing?

It requires a second force. Centripetal force is a "real" force that counteracts the tendency to fly outward, keeping it moving along its intended path. One way to think of this centripetal force is the idea of situational awareness, which involves being aware of what is happening around you in order to understand how information, events, and one's own actions will impact goals and objectives. In other words, it is the ability of the little arrows to be aware of where the big arrow is headed and to then make decisions that increase coherency.

Stanford University recently provided an illustration of situational awareness that appears to increase both coherency and commitment. In May of 2014 the institution announced that it would divest its $18.7 billion endowment of stock in coal-mining companies. The trustees began studying divestment after Fossil Free Stanford petitioned them to reevaluate their holdings of energy companies. After five months of study, an advisory panel that included students, faculty, staff, and alumni recommended that coal stocks be sold. Deborah DeCotis, chairwoman of the board's Special Committee on Investment Responsibility, stated in an interview that among the deciding factors, the panel noted that coal produces the most carbon per British thermal unit of any widely used fossil fuel, that practical alternatives to burning coal are available, and that the university was not dependent on coal or coal-derived products.[11]

Three days after the story was reported in the *New York Times*, Ivo Welch, a professor of finance and economics at UCLA, penned an op-ed under the banner, "Why Divestment Fails." He began:

> Tonight, the 20,000 students at Stanford will sleep more soundly. Earlier this week, a group called "Fossil Free Stanford" persuaded the university's endowment to divest its stock holdings from coal-mining companies. The world is a better place. Except that it won't be. Individual divestments, either as economic or symbolic pressure, have never succeeded in getting companies or countries to change.[12]

Having relieved himself of an initial burst of cynicism, Professor Welch went on to cite his own academic study showing divestment had no discernible effect on the valuation of companies that were being divested. Global equity markets, he noted, were so large that Stanford's endowment was only about five-hundredths of 1 percent of the world's capitalization. Returning to his earlier tenor, he added, "Even if Stanford divested itself fully of all its stock, both fossil and nonfossil, it would probably take the market less than an hour to absorb the shares."

But what Professor Welch failed to understand was that divestment wasn't an individual act. It wasn't a knee-jerk reaction to a bunch of sign-waving sophomores. Nobody caved in to political pressure or political correctness. The decision wasn't even the product of a faulty economic algorithm. It was, instead, Stanford being Stanford.

In a follow-up op-ed, Susan Weinstein, the chairwoman of Stanford's Advisory Panel on Investment Responsibility and Licensing, noted that the institution did not divest from coal to make a statement or with the expectation of solving climate change. She added that other institutions will, and should, evaluate these issues for themselves. Further, she noted that other efforts are clearly necessary to advance environmental sustainability, and that Stanford is deeply engaged in them:

> We are building a new energy system that will cut campus carbon emissions in half. Our proxy voting guidelines urge companies in which we invest to increase energy efficiency and reduce greenhouse gas emissions. And our faculty and

students continue to pursue one of the largest research programs in the country developing renewable energy solutions that can be put to work in the world.[13]

Again, it was just Stanford being "ever-so-situationally aware" Stanford and being committed as an institution to developing renewable energy solutions.

Discussion to Dialogue

A second way to encourage the alignment of people and processes into a war canoe or a coherent set of arrows is through dialogue. Having situational awareness is one thing. Being aware of what is going on around you needs to be a starting point. Being purpose-centered as an institution, as we have already seen, makes the exercise quite a bit easier. It effectively changes the unit of analysis from "me" to "us."

But in describing his arrows and alignment, Senge emphasizes dialogue as a means to expand team learning. He offers the following paradox: "How can a team of committed managers with individual IQs above 120 have a collective IQ of 63?" The same question might be asked of many of the colleges and universities already discussed in various stages of doom loops. And the opposite is true as well. Teams that perform at a higher level of effectiveness than one would predict based on the abilities of the individuals do exist. This is a particularly well-known phenomenon in sports where a team of fairly ordinary players can develop such incredible "team chemistry" that they are able to defeat a collection of superstars.

Our colleges and universities are full of teams. We have academic departments and business units. We have councils and committees; indeed, we have lots and lots and lots of committees. These entities engage in discussions all the time (discussion being the practice of presenting different views, often with the hope of solving a problem or resolving a question). As such, individuals feel compelled to argue and defend their point of view. Under the constraint of time, long-held beliefs are used to win the day and move on to the next topic. As the saying goes, there is often a good deal of heat without the benefit of light.

Dialogue, in contrast, attempts to go beyond any one individual's understanding. The word *dialogue* comes from the Greek *dialogos* with *dia* connoting "through" and *logos* connoting "the word," or more broadly, "the meaning." It is about the free flow of meaning, not winning or losing. If discussion often takes on the characteristics of a ping-pong match with the ball being hit back and forth, dialogue looks a bit more like a stream flowing between two banks. Senge references the work of David Bohm in deriving the following three basic conditions necessary for dialogue:

1. all participants must "suspend" assumptions, literally to hold them "as if suspended before us";
2. all participants must regard one another as colleagues;
3. there must be a "facilitator" who "holds the context" of dialogue.[14]

A fascinating illustration of this important theme in advancing alignment was detailed in a lengthy *New York Times* article that explored the question: Should Harvard Business School enter the business of online education and, if so, how?[15] A "discussion" of this topic would have all the necessary elements associated with empowerment without alignment. After all, two of Harvard B-School's most distinguished professors have come at the answer from very different viewpoints.

Michael Porter, widely regarded as the father of modern business strategy, believes that differentiation is the key competitive advantage and that all of an organization's activities should be mutually reinforcing. His answer to the question is "yes"—create online courses, but not in a way that undermines the school's existing strategy. And what is the school's existing strategy? Well, Harvard Business School is renowned for its big arrow, the case method, which has served as its pedagogical foundation since 1924.

The alternative model is championed by Clayton Christensen, who wrote the best-selling book *The Innovator's Dilemma: When New Technologies Cause Great Firms to Fail* (2000) and later *The Innovative University: Changing the DNA of Higher Education from the Inside Out* (2011). He suggests that the only way market leaders like Harvard Business School will survive "disruptive innovation" is by disrupting its existing business model itself. As we saw in our discussion of high-velocity environments in chapter 1, such proactive and preemptive disruption would include the development of MOOCs in the manner of other colleges and universities. But, of course, none of these institutions have the mantel of a nearly century-long pedigree, either.

The facilitator of the ensuing dialogue was the dean, Nitin Nohria, who was able to suspend advocacy and pursue, instead, a line of inquiry that centered on the idea that "We don't do lectures. Part of what had already convinced me that MOOCs are not for us is that for a hundred years our education has been social." The result of the productive conversations and deep dialogue will be HBX or Harvard Business School's "vision of business education, reimagined for the digital age."[16]

Instead of disrupting its traditional MBA and executive education programs, the new initiative will focus on an entirely new segment of business education: the pre-MBA. The program includes three online courses—accounting, analytics, and economics for managers—that are intended to give liberal arts students fluency in what it calls "the language of business."

Instead of pursuing an all-or-nothing approach, the path forward appears to be the invention of a digital architecture that simulates the B-School classroom dynamic without looking like a classroom using a combination of case studies, interactive technologies, and final exams.

This could have been empowered arrows all over again. It is only through dialogue and productive conversations that the HBX hybrid emerged and momentum more than likely will be maintained.

Convening Authority

Every regional accreditor has a requirement that the college or university has a chief executive officer with defined responsibilities. The Southern Association for Colleges and Schools, for example, states in its core requirements: "The institution has a chief executive officer (CEO) whose primary responsibility is to the institution and who is not the presiding officer of the board." The New England Association of Schools and Colleges states in a standard on organization and governance: "The chief executive officer through an appropriate administrative structure effectively manages the institution so as to fulfill its purposes and objectives and establishes the means to assess the effectiveness of the institution."

The primary challenge associated with this charge, as we have discussed, is that being CEO over a tightly coupled business organization with clear lines of authority and a hierarchical structure is one thing, but being a CEO of a loosely coupled college or university operating under shared governance principles is something else entirely. This would be a challenge to any CEO, but for years the job of "managing" these disparate entities has been further compromised by evolving job duties that place fund-raising at or near the top of the list of responsibilities.

If the CEO is the only one in the organizational structure with cross-functional responsibilities and she or he is intently focused on increasing the endowment or raising funds for a new football stadium, then how is the requisite dialogue supposed to take place? Who is convening and facilitating the larger, strategic conversations that need to take place?

At the same time, every regional accreditor has also committed to standards that reflect the requirement for demonstrating institutional effectiveness and continuous improvement. Northwest Commission on Colleges and Universities, for example, introduces standard 4 (Effectiveness and Improvement) with the following statement:

> The institution regularly and systematically collects data related to clearly defined indicators of achievement, analyzes those data, and formulates evidence-based evaluations of the achievement of core theme objectives. It

demonstrates clearly defined procedures for evaluating the integration and significance of institutional planning, the allocation of resources, and the application of capacity in its activities for achieving the intended outcomes of its programs and services and for achieving its core theme objectives. The institution disseminates assessment results to its constituencies and uses those results to effect improvement.[17]

This standard and others like it are taking a decidedly systems approach. No longer can an institution slide through accreditation by making effusive statements about "all" of its academic programs being excellent and then offering up several noteworthy examples. Instead, these standards involve being able to describe "how" a rigorous set of learning outcomes is developed and the results are then evaluated, improved, and aligned with an institutional mission. This is decidedly not loosely coupling stuff.

So, who is facilitating these conversations?

This conundrum is being solved more and more by the creation of new (or redesigned) organizational structures that are responsible for institutional effectiveness. While the term continues to evolve, one way to envision it is as an institution-wide process consisting of specific components, including the evaluation of all academic programs, administrative units, and support services; the assessment of student learning outcomes, and the data-driven support by the institutional research arm of a college or university.[18] This suggests an evolution from traditional institutional research that is focused on reporting data to external agencies (accountability) to one that also includes a powerful decision support system to drive continuous improvement within the institution (responsibility).

Inside Higher Ed recently conducted an interview with Paula Gill, Belmont University's Vice President of Institutional Effectiveness. Initially, she was asked about her job responsibilities and responded by stating that she was charged with evaluating the university's progress toward its performance objectives and seeking ways to improve services and processes that help student success. She added that over the past few years the university had engaged in a series of broad institutional planning exercises in order to define more precisely its strategic position and sharpen its focus on goals designed to enable it to fulfill its educational mission effectively.

Then she was asked about why the importance of institutional effectiveness had grown. She states:

The importance has grown in part because of the rapid change taking place in the world. We have seen industries and organizations disappear because they did not respond to the changing environment. Higher education institutions are becoming increasingly intentional about institutional effectiveness efforts to help their organizations meet the needs of the students, the needs of future employers, and the needs of their city, their state, and the world. . . . Like Belmont, many institutions are creating positions that are responsible for looking across the institution for opportunities for improvement and appropriate change. This is in part due to the fact that data-informed and people-centric decision making and change takes a lot of time. You must have the ability to see the big picture and the ability to dive deep into the details, moving from strategic to execution.[19]

In many institutions this function is being broadened even further to include responsibility for helping to facilitate the development of a strategic plan and monitoring its implementation. At others, the function includes that of the accreditation liaison officer. For our purposes, however, the key part of institutional effectiveness is not the precise nature of the job duties associated with the person in charge, but rather, to whom the position reports. In the past, and from a nonsystems perspective, the institutional research function reported to . . . whomever. It didn't matter because the parts were perceived as being interchangeable that results in upward spirals.

But in a system, structure really matters. In order to accomplish the goal of transitioning from a barge to a war canoe, resources need to be committed to aligning people and processes. As such, this "new and improved" institutional effectiveness function needs to report directly to the CEO and have "convening authority." It is this ability, in the absence of a distracted CEO, to facilitate dialogue across functional units that is of critical importance to the process of structural advancement.

ALIGNING SUMMARY

An incandescent light bulb diffuses light in all directions and can brighten up a single room, while a laser is so coherently focused that its light can reach the moon. The quality or state of cohering is defined as (1) a systematic or logical connection or consistency or (2) the integration of diverse elements, relationships, or values. When Senge's little arrows begin to line up within the larger arrow, they begin to exhibit coherency. When the rowers on a barge have the opportunity to work together as rowers on a war canoe, they also begin to concentrate their efforts in a coherent fashion. That coherency is just like the laser beam—it can take you a long, long way.

Exactly how does this coherency work with individuals and organizations to produce virtuous cycles of change? This entire chapter has shown that when things begin to align there is an additional factor in play. The sum is greater than the parts. The term that is often used in Positive Organizational Scholarship is "transcendent behavior." It is described as behavior that creates exceptional or extraordinary change. It is behavior that overrides a present set of circumstances. It is evidenced when people affect extraordinary change by exceeding demands, eliminating or overcoming constraints, and creating or seizing opportunities.

As you might imagine, a war canoe is not a place for apathy. It is full of individuals who are committed to something larger than themselves. Transcendent behavior abounds as the rhythm of the organization infects them: all together, all together.

NOTES

1. *Faculty Survey: 2010–11*, UCLA, Higher Education Research Institute, 2011.

2. Christina Leimer, "Stasis and Change: Faculty Satisfaction, Stress and University Priorities" (presented at AIR Forum, Kansas City, MO, June 2, 2006).

3. The barge and war canoe metaphor is developed in Daniel Seymour, "Tough Times: Strategic Planning as a War Canoe," *About Campus,* September–October 2011.

4. For a visual demonstration of a war canoe, see: http://compulsivetraveler.tv/videos/97-An-aggressive-ride-in-the-waka-the-war-canoe-.

5. Peter M. Senge, *The Fifth Discipline: The Art & Practice of the Learning Organization* (New York: Doubleday, 1990), 233–38.

6. Robert Fritz, *The Path of Least Resistance for Managers* (San Francisco: Berrett-Koehler, 1999), 145.

7. See Jack Stripling, "A Trustee's Connections May Complicate NYU-Abu Dhabi Labor Probe," *Chronicle of Higher Education,* May 29, 2014, http://chronicle.com/article/A-Trustee-s-Connections-May/146843/?cid=at&utm_source=at&utm_medium=en; Ian Wilhelm, "NYU's Abu Dhabi Controversy Draws Host of Twitter Reaction," *Chronicle of Higher Education,* May 30, 2014, http://chronicle.com/blogs/ticker/nyus-abu-dhabi-controversy-draws-host-of-twitter-reactions/78883?cid=pm&utm_source=pm&utm_medium=en; Matt J. Duffy, "NYU's Promise of Academic Freedom in Abu Dhabi Is 'Essentially Worthless,'" *Chronicle of Higher Education,* May 29, 2014, http://chronicle.com/blogs/worldwise/nyus-promise-of-academic-freedom-in-abu-dhabi-is-essentially-worthless/33859?cid=pm&utm_source=pm&utm_medium=en; Ariel Kaminer, "Fourth No Confidence Vote for the President of NYU," *New York Times,* May 10, 2013; and Andrew Ross Sorkin, "NYU Crisis in Aby Dhabi Stretches to Wall St.," *New York Times,* May 27, 2014.

8. Barbara L. Fredrickson, *Positivity* (New York: Three Rivers Press, 2009), 69.

9. Senge, *The Fifth Discipline,* 218–25.

10. Ibid., 221.

11. Michael Wines, "Stanford to Purge $18 Billion Endowment of Coal Stock," *New York Times,* May 6, 2014.

12. Ivo Welch, "Why Divestment Fails," *New York Times,* May 9, 2014.

13. Susan Weinstein, "Why Divestment Can Be Successful," *New York Times*, May 13, 2014.

14. Senge, *The Fifth Discipline*, 226.

15. Jerry Useem, "B-School, Disrupted," *New York Times*, June 1, 2014.

16. For an overview of HBX see, www.hbx.hbs.edu.

17. See Northwest Commission on Colleges and Universities, "Standard Four," www.nwccu.org/Standards%20and%20Policies/Standard%204/Standard%20Four.htm.

18. Ronald B. Head, "The Evolution of Institutional Effectiveness in the Community College," in Ronald B. Head (ed.), *Institutional Effectiveness, New Directions for Community Colleges* (San Francisco: Jossey-Bass, 2011).

19. Andrew Hibel, "Institutional Effectiveness and Your Campus," HigherEdJobs, 2014, www.higheredjobs.com/HigherEdCareers/interviews.cfm?ID=519&Title=Institutional%20Effectiveness%20and%20Your%20Campus.

Chapter 5

The Accumulators

Deciding What Assets You Want to Grow

Let's begin with bathtubs. The water that you use to take a bath—say, thirty-five gallons—is an accumulation. When you run the bathwater, you can visually see the water accumulating in the tub. The average amount of water used to take a shower is seven gallons per minute and, as such, a five-minute shower uses the same amount of water—thirty-five gallons. In many ways, the world can be divided into two types: bathtub thinkers and showerhead thinkers.[1]

Showerhead thinking focuses on flows. The water flows in through the showerhead and flows out through the drain. Most people couldn't tell you how much water is being used because it disappears. Everything—water, dirt, soap suds—goes somewhere else. Bathtub thinkers don't have this luxury. First, they need to be aware of the capacity of the tub and the rate of accumulation. If you begin to fill up the tub and then are distracted by an important phone call, the results could be disastrous. Showerhead thinkers don't have to be concerned with these details: just turn it on and enjoy.

It should also be noted that accumulations can be both negative and positive. The build-up of carbon dioxide in our atmosphere seen as the primary contributor to global warming is an accumulation. Our atmosphere has a limited capacity (like the tub) to convert carbon dioxide into oxygen and so the remainder begins to accumulate over time. In contrast, our discussion in chapter 2 on reinforcing loops began with the simple idea of interest being earned on a savings account. If there isn't any outflow (withdrawals), the interest begins to accumulate over time and, combined with the savings, creates a virtuous cycle of wealth.

Carbon dioxide accumulation in the atmosphere is a bad thing; wealth accumulation in your bank account is a good thing.

In many ways it follows that our focus in higher education has been on flows—showerhead thinking. John Henry Newman, in his classic work, *The Idea of a University* (1852), states, "The view taken of a University in these Discourses is the following—That it is a place of teaching *universal* knowledge." He goes on to speak about the "diffusion" and "extension" of knowledge. More than 150 years later, Richard Kahlenberg, an author and senior fellow at the Century Foundation, gave a convocation address for new students at Flagler College, a private four-year liberal arts college, at which he outlined five purposes of higher education:

1. To ensure that every student, no matter the wealth of her parents, has a chance to enjoy the American Dream.
2. To educate leaders in our democracy.
3. To advance learning and knowledge through faculty research and by giving students the opportunity to broaden their minds even when learning does not seem immediately relevant to their careers.
4. To teach students to interact with people different than themselves.
5. To help students find a passion—and even a purpose.[2]

While Kahlenberg's language is a bit more pedestrian than Newman's, the underlying structural dynamic is a flow that extends beyond the institution and into society. Indeed, the entire rhythm of a college or university is built on the rituals of a springtime commencement. We put on our academic regalia, march to "Pomp and Circumstance" (and Alice Cooper's "School's Out" at the recessional), as we recognize the graduates and launch them into their new lives. It is a natural progression, a normal and appropriate flow of energy, resources, and, as Cardinal Newman suggests, universal knowledge.

In this chapter, however, the emphasis is not on flow but on accumulation. Elizabeth Doty, a business consultant, has written extensively on the nature of upward spirals. As has been described earlier, just as a vicious cycle or downward spiral is a metaphor for decline, a virtuous cycle or upward spiral is a metaphor for growth. So, when she describes various principles for mobilizing an upward spiral, she begins with a simple question:

> The first step in building an upward spiral is to ask: What do we want to grow? The answer is usually some kind of asset that enables us to generate the results we want (an asset refers to an enabling resource, infrastructure, or stock—physical or intangible).[3]

Notice that this is not about results or an *effect*. This is about assets or the capabilities that we need to grow in order to *cause* something else to happen.

Given what we have seen about the demands that our stakeholders have for us, it is clear that there is and will be no shortage of expectations. But to shift from an accountability paradigm to a responsibility paradigm requires that we become more fully engaged in building our own capacity to produce results that will advance our collective ambitions and be responsive to stakeholder requirements.

THE ACCUMULATION AGENDA

The current national discussion known as the Completion Agenda provides a useful illustration of Showerhead Thinking and Bathtub Thinking. At the end of 2008, the College Board's Commission on Access, Admissions and Success in Higher Education issued its action agenda for increasing the proportion of Americans with college certificates and degrees. The commission's report, *Coming to Our Senses: Education and the American Future*, called for an increase in the proportion of the nation's young adults—those ages 25–34—who hold a two- or four-year college degree to 55 percent by 2025.

While pressure to increase the numbers of college graduates had been building for years, the real impetus for change came with President Obama's very first State of the Union Address: "By 2020, America will once again have the highest proportion of college graduates in the world." He went on to say, "In a global economy where the most valuable skill you can sell is your knowledge, a good education is no longer just a pathway to opportunity—it is a prerequisite."

Over the next several years, a flood of resources and focused attention on the issue resulted in new organizations and reports centered on completion. One such organization and one such report that captured the attention of colleges and universities and their stakeholders was Complete College America's 2011 seminal study, *Time Is the Enemy*.[4] The report tracks "the flow" of higher education students in thirty-three states. The summary data for one state, Arizona, is given in Table 5.1.

Most of our attention has historically been focused at the showerhead. For community colleges the issue has always been about access. It has been about being democracy's colleges and providing opportunity to as many people as possible. Four-year institutions have had a similar focus on inputs. Whether it is the selectivity of some institutions as a proxy for reputation and quality or the admissions staff needing to "hit the number" for the right size of a freshman class, the attention has been at the front of the flow. But as Complete College America and others began to connect the dots, concerns grew and quickly became a political firestorm.

Table 5.1   Arizona

Of Students Who Enroll in a Public College or University		100		
	Two-Year Public College		Four-Year Public College	
	Full-time	Part-time	Full-time	Part-time
Enroll	28	26	44	2
Return as sophomore	20	13	34	1
Graduate in 100% time	2	0	14	0
Graduate in 150% time	2	1	11	1
Graduate in 200% time	1	1	2	0
Total graduates	5	2	27	1
Graduate in four/eight years	7		28	

In Arizona, as is seen, forty-six out of one hundred higher education students attend a four-year institution and only twenty-eight (60 percent) graduate, not in four years or six years but fully eight years (200 percent) after initially enrolling. The numbers for community colleges are even worse. Out of fifty-four students only seven (13 percent) graduate a two-year program in four years (200 percent). Again, the attention has historically been on such metrics as the size of the freshmen class or the number of FTE (full-time equivalent) students. Little attention, however, was given to "throughput" or the ability to convert inputs into outputs. For community colleges nationwide the critical mantra that began to emerge was: "Access without success is just an empty promise."

Bathtub thinking sees the issue differently. Why are Arizona and other states only graduating thirty-five students out of every one hundred in twice the designated time? The answer to these "why" questions is seen in what is accumulating. One accumulation is part-time students, especially those who attend community colleges—"Part-time students rarely graduate—even when they have twice as much time." Graduation rates are also quite low for students who are African American, Hispanic, older, or poor.

While many of these accumulations begin to dissipate rather quickly by individuals dropping out, *Time Is the Enemy* also reported on the number of credits earned for those that ultimately do graduate. It should take thirty credits to receive a certificate but, on average, students take 68.5 credits; it should take sixty credits to receive an associate degree but, on average, students take 85.5 credits; and it should take 120 credits to receive a bachelor's degree but, on average, students take 136.5 credits. Students are wasting time by accumulating excess credits.

Perhaps the best example of an accumulator in higher education is remediation. A follow-up report in 2012 by Complete College America told it all: *Remediation: Higher Education's Bridge to Nowhere:*

The intentions were noble. It was hoped that remediation programs would be an academic bridge from poor high school preparation to college readiness— a grand idea inspired by our commitment to expand access to all who seek a college degree. Sadly, remediation has become instead higher education's "Bridge to Nowhere." This broken remedial bridge is travelled by some 1.7 million beginning students each year, most of whom will not reach their destination — graduation. It is estimated that states and students spent more than $3 billion on remedial courses last year with very little student success to show for it.[5]

With more than 50 percent of students entering two-year colleges and nearly 20 percent of those entering four-year universities being placed in remedial classes while fewer than one in ten graduate from community colleges within three years and a little more than a third complete a bachelor's degree in six years . . . we are going to need a bigger bathtub.

BATHTUBS AS ASSETS

So, the Completion Agenda is also really an Accumulation Agenda. In the illustration, the bathtub is an obvious liability. We would want to consciously design a system that reduces the number of noncollege-ready students flowing in, while also increasing the numbers flowing out (graduating) with the net effect of reducing accumulations. But if we think in terms of creating momentum in our colleges and universities, we need to invest in different types of bathtubs, those that are understood as assets that we want to grow as we pursue virtuous cycles of change.

One way to think about this critical kind of accumulation is using the idea and language of "core competence." In their classic 1990 *Harvard Business Review* article, C. K. Prahalad and Gary Hamel describe core competencies as particular strengths relative to other organizations in the industry that provide the fundamental basis for the provision of added value.[6] A core competency can be anything, but what it is not is a particular set of products or services. Your competitive advantage doesn't come from a successful product because any particular success can be copied. Instead, it should be derived from the collective learning in the organization that enables it to produce successful products or services over time.

When studying Walt Disney World—Parks and Resorts, for example, they concluded the organization had a portfolio of competencies, one of which was "storytelling." The parks weren't successful because of any particular attraction or ride but the foundational ability to tell engaging stories that were then manifested in those attractions and rides.

In general, developing core competencies, as practiced by many businesses, includes:

- *Core competencies* should provide sustainable competitive advantage within the areas of products, processes, and administrative execution of tasks.
- *Core competencies* have both a human and a technological element.
- To provide truly sustainable competitive advantage, *core competencies* should be kept firm-specific.
- Firms must concentrate their scarce resources on only a few—perhaps five or six—*core competencies.*[7]

While the idea of core competence comes from the business world, another way to think about the assets we want to grow in our colleges and universities comes from the nonprofit world. Many community-based organizations are small and fragile. Without a profit motive they often lack the kind of capital investment required to build robust organizations. The term *capacity building* has emerged in this sector to reflect this need. The concept, again, focuses on foundational issues.

Much like a house or any other structure needs a strong foundation on which to configure walls, floors, windows and roofs, capacity building seeks to ensure that the substructure is in place. As such, capacity building often deals not with the things you can see (the actual services being offered) but the things you don't often see. For example, Catholic Relief Services states that "capacity building is an ongoing process through which individuals, groups, organizations and societies enhance their ability to identify and meet development challenges." The key words used here are "enhance their ability." Meeting challenges is a short-term response; enhancing the ability to meet challenges is a longer-term view that requires investment.

In a study prepared by Venture Philanthropy Partners along with McKinsey & Company, a general framework has been offered as a means for developing the long-term health and effectiveness of nonprofit organizations. In a pyramid structure they place aspirations (mission, vision, overarching goals) at the top with strategy (coherent set of actions) just beneath it. But forming the base of the pyramid is:

Human Resources: The collective capabilities, experiences, potential and commitment of the organization's board, management team, staff, and volunteers.

Systems an Infrastructure: The organization's planning, decision making, knowledge management, and administrative systems, as well as the physical and technological assets that support the organization.

Organizational Structure: The combination of governance, organizational design, interfunctional coordination, and individual job descriptions that shapes the organization's legal and management structure.

Culture: The connective tissue that binds together the organization, including shared values and practices, behavior norms, and most important, the organization's orientation toward performance.[8]

Both "core competency" and "capacity building" reflect the same idea: foundational success is enhancing the capability to produce a successful product or service, which is then followed by operational success or the ability to deliver that product or service.

It should also be noted that asset growth is important to creating virtuous cycles in two general and important ways. The first is the idea of self-efficacy (beliefs about one's ability to accomplish a specific task), which was discussed in chapter 2. Self-efficacy is a widely used theoretical concept mainly due to the work of Albert Bandura, a Stanford University psychologist. Bandura identified four principal sources of self-efficacy: past performance, vicarious experience, verbal persuasion, and emotional cues. The first two of these sources, past performance and vicarious experience, have particular relevance to self-efficacy in organizations and with the notion of asset accumulation.

Past performance suggests that employees who have succeeded with job-related tasks are likely to have more confidence to complete similar tasks in the future (high self-efficacy). Not only is this the most important source of self-efficacy according to Bandura, but also it is a classic illustration of a reinforcing loop: Your belief in your ability to perform a task improves your performance on that task, which, in turn, increases your belief in your ability.

Vicarious experience suggests that seeing someone else succeed at a particular task tends to boost your self-efficacy. Individuals in organizations who are part of a conscious effort to build capacity or develop a specific set of core competencies will benefit from a sense of self-efficacy. As they are successful, and as they watch others be successful, their confidence and skills grow as the asset grows.

The flip side of the self-efficacy coin is resilience. Just because an individual or an organization gets increasingly better at growing a foundational asset doesn't mean that they are not subject to failures and setbacks. Stuff happens. But a characteristic of an organization that is "on a roll" is that disappointments don't have the weight to tip the teeter-totter into a downward spiral. There is just too much basic strength at the center of the organization. The accumulation of core competencies or the building of capacity provides that foundational strength.

DIMENSIONS OF DESIGN

How can we focus on the positive aspects of accumulation in our colleges and universities? What are the kinds of efforts that will enable us to identify and develop our foundational capabilities? The following are a series of design dimensions that are important to consider.

Culture of Discipline

Kay McClenney of the University of Texas has observed that the average community college has roughly 1,400 classes in its course catalog but less than twenty of those classes produce upward of 90 percent of the total enrollment. Vilfredo Pareto, an Italian economist, noticed roughly the same proportionality when he observed in 1916 that 20 percent of the pea pods in his garden contained 80 percent of the peas. Later, he applied the principle to land ownership and found that, surprisingly, 80 percent of the land in Italy was owned by 20 percent of the population. The Pareto Principle (also known as the "80-20 rule" and the "law of the vital few") is really about leverage. As systems and processes get larger and more complex, there is also a concomitant disbursement of energy and focus as we attempt to deal with all the known elements in the universe.

In *Good to Great* (2001), Jim Collins devotes a chapter to counteracting this disbursement by building a "culture of discipline." He notes that as companies grow larger and larger they begin to trip over their own success—too many new people, too many new customers, too many new orders, too many new products (or, in our case, courses). He says, "What was once great fun becomes an unwieldy ball of disorganized stuff."[9] In many ways he is describing the natural universe and centrifugal force—an outward force on a body rotating on its access. Connections and communications get weaker as the distance between the objects grows. A sense of purpose—the center of things—is often a casualty of this increasingly "unwieldy ball of disorganized stuff."

A culture of discipline, then, involves developing the ability to focus on the vital few or, in our case, those limited number of bathtubs that will provide us with the capability to advance the institution toward a compelling shared vision.

The Completion Agenda provides a useful illustration. One group that had emerged in the national discussion is Completion by Design, an initiative funded by the Bill & Melinda Gates Foundation. And one resource they developed is the document "Changing Course: A Guide to Increasing Student Completion in Community College."[10] While the problem associated with a lack of completers was described previously in terms of an accumulation

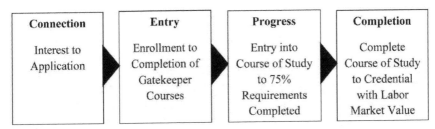

Figure 5.1   Stages of Student Progression

(liability), the solution to that problem might be viewed through an accumulation lens as well—in this case, the assets we want to grow. Figure 5.1 shows four different stages of student progression.

The graphic details loss points associated with each stage in the process as well as a series of momentum strategies: there are six for connection, five for entry, four for progress, and another four for completion, bringing the total to nineteen strategies. These strategies are well researched and well articulated. Taken together, they are a powerful, comprehensive approach to increasing student completion in community colleges.

But it should also be noted that the framework and all of its details sits on top of three critical assets.

1. *Leadership Focused on Completion*—Faculty, staff, administrators, and trustees must make student learning and completion their top priorities and undertake college-wide redesign to develop and sustain completion pathways.
2. *Student Engagement*—While engaging students in their coursework and through extracurricular activities is important, the foundational principle is engagement through every contact and every service.
3. *Student Data System*—From day 1 to completion there needs to be access to and use of disaggregated data on the effectiveness of the various momentum strategies on loss points.

If you were asked the question, "What assets do we want to grow in order to achieve the results of greater student learning and increased completion?" you might very well focus on these three because they undergird everything else. These are the vital few and it requires discipline to identify them, focus on them, invest in them, and grow them as organizational assets. Why? Because if we were to grow these assets we would be better able to implement effective strategies, which, in turn, would positively impact the goal of increasing completion rates.

Task Certainty

Another aspect of asset growth involves being able to establish clear, causal relationships. Researchers have found that one of the reasons that vicious cycles occur is because there is a lack of clarity between an action and a result.[11] When there is task uncertainty, feedback that is necessary for making positive adjustments is problematic. In contrast, being able to establish a strong and clear means/end connection is critical to producing engines of growth in organizations.

A useful example of task certainty as an important dimension of asset growth has been described by Neil Kreisel, the president of the Board of Directors of the Foundation for Santa Barbara City College, and Vanessa Patterson, the executive director. In an article in the *Chronicle of Higher Education,* they note a Century Foundation report stating that community colleges are at great risk of becoming "separate but unequal institutions in the higher education landscape."[12] But community colleges, as we have already discussed, receive the lowest amount of state funding per student of all institutional types.

It follows that an increase in private support would be of obvious great benefit. But they go on to point out that for each dollar given to a four-year college, only a cent or two goes to support community colleges. Moreover, the Century Foundation study found that the gain from private and group donations, grants, investment returns, and endowment income averaged $46, 324 per full-time student at private research institutions compared with $372 for community colleges. As Kreisel and Patterson state, "And yet we—particularly those of us with fund-raising responsibilities—could be doing so much more than we are to help close the parity gap and help our institutions thrive."

So, what does thriving at Santa Barbara City College look like? It is laser-focused on building the task-certain asset of community support. A 2013 winner of the Aspen Institute's Prize for Community College Excellence, the college's foundation oversees $45 million worth of net assets, which is well above those of most community colleges but still well below most four-year colleges. But the real goal is ten thousand. That is the number of donors it hopes to get involved in the 2014 Student Success Campaign—"Show Your Love"—which should bring in $2 million. The ten thousand represents community engagement, which is the real asset that the college needs to grow. It represents the core of future political and economic support.

In 2014, Villanova University announced a $600 million campaign—"For the Greater Great: The Villanova Campaign to Ignite Change." The upper echelon of Catholic universities is Notre Dame, Georgetown, and Boston. Each has a significantly larger endowment than Villanova. The consultant's study had suggested a working campaign goal of $500 million for Villanova.

And while raising that amount might have narrowed the gap between Villanova and "the big three," the real push for stretching to $600 million came from a different source—President Peter Donohue.

Father Peter, as most Villanovans call the president, graduated from Villanova in 1975, the son of an Irish immigrant and the first male in his family to attend college. Because of that, half of the endowment portion is to be used to bolster student financial aid. "There was this fear on my part that we were going to become this exclusive, expensive institution that was really going to struggle to create diversity," he said, not just racially but economically and geographically as well.[13]

While both these examples involve added resources, the real focus is on growing more task-certain assets—for example, community support and student diversity. Grow those assets and other resources are certain to follow.

Investment Mentality

There is a big difference between an expense and an investment. An expense simply involves the spending of money. Hopefully, the expense makes sense and a benefit is derived. But it is transactional. An investment, on the other hand, is intended to generate a return over the long haul. As such, an investment can be transformational. The assets we are interested in are investments that will produce a return for the institution.

Two recent surveys highlight the importance of an investment mentality with a longer-term horizon. The 2013 "Survey of College and University Presidents" conducted by the *Chronicle of Higher Education* and Pearsons asked CEOs to rank eighteen measures of success.[14] The number-one performance indicator was a balanced budget. Next was "strengthening the institution's reputation." Interestingly, "improved U.S. News rankings" scored last. We also know that a general resource/reputation reinforcing loop is fundamental to most of higher education. It would seem, therefore, that presidents understand that short-term fixes or gaming the rankings is not the answer. But if "strengthening the institution's reputation" can lead to more resources, the questions are, "How exactly do I do that?" and "Isn't that what I need to grow?"

Next, from interviews with more than thirty thousand graduates a new Gallup-Purdue Index measures the degree to which graduates have "great jobs," through successful and engaging careers, and if they are leading "great lives," by thriving in their overall well-being.[15] The *Great Jobs/Great Lives* study is an attempt to go beyond the standard college education outcome measures—job and graduate school placement and alumni salaries—by taking a holistic view of college graduates' lives. It found that the top two elements contributing to high levels of workplace success and personal satisfaction were a professor who made a student excited about learning and a professor who cared about them. That's great. But if "student interaction with faculty members and engaged learning" leads to more thriving, the questions remain, "How exactly do I do that?" and "Isn't that what I need to grow?"

We need to invest. Several examples are useful here. Knowledge management (KM) is a relatively new field. It is the process of identifying and leveraging the collective knowledge in an organization to help it succeed. The standard framework associated with the application of KM in an organization involves four core processes: knowledge creation, storage, transfer, and application. Since higher education is in the business of "knowledge" as a product it might also follow that it would be interested in "knowledge" as a process—that is, sharing knowledge to spur innovation, improve student services, or achieve operational excellence all with the idea of helping to achieve our collective ambition.

The Kentucky Community and Technical College System recently made this type of investment in order to integrate what had become disparate cultures, systems, and work processes. The fact was that critical information was stuck in silos and cubbyholes, making even the most basic and routine work tedious and frustrating. Investing in collaborative tools—in this case, SharePoint—can have significant long-term benefits.[16] Knowledge about how to make the college or university an effective and efficient organization, then, would seem to be an asset worth accumulating.

Joshua Wyner, the executive director of the Aspen Institute's Community College Excellence Program, recently provided another example of the nature of a long-term investment to fuel virtuous cycles. While it was easy to focus on the specific attributes of each cycle's finalists and winner, he observed that a common thread among the finalists was that all were "dedicated to continuous improvement."[17] As was noted earlier, every regional accreditor has moved toward a systems approach that looks at institutional effectiveness in terms of: having a mission, vision, and goals, developing a plan to meet those aspirations and linking the budget to the plan, having a comprehensive means to evaluate and assess the effectiveness of those efforts, and finally being able to demonstrate that changes are made based on that feedback.

Nothing about being dedicated to continuous improvement involves a tweak here or there. Instead, it involves the development of a comprehensive, integrated approach to administering the institution. The transition from loosely coupled systems to moderately coupled systems is, then, a long-term investment in systems thinking that can form the basis for . . . momentum.

Desired State

Chapter 3 discussed the importance of creating discrepancy in an organization. Homeostasis or a comfort-based worldview undermines the ability to create momentum. Instead, a desired state that differs significantly from the current state creates structural tension, which, in turn, catalyzes the institution forward through various resolution-seeking actions. It is necessary to address accumulating within this context.

First, it has been established that colleges and universities need to work hard to be distinctive. It follows that any assets that are targeted for growth need to be aligned with that unique vision. It isn't what you have in common with other institutions that creates specialness; it is what you do differently. As such, a set of vital few assets should not be randomly chosen or be generic in nature.

If an institution seeks to be known as a great undergraduate teaching college, for example, a capability that needs to be developed is one that narrowly and aggressively focuses on good practice in undergraduate education. A bathtub thinker would then suggest that there are only two ways to attain this desired state since merely "saying it does not make it so." One way is to hire great teachers. Since most college professors are, statistically, just average, that would mean a conscious investment in a rigorous methodology that ensures only the very best are recruited, hired, and retained. The other way to grow the asset is to build great teachers. And doing both would be best.

In an issue of *Washington Monthly*, Kevin Carey explored this precise means/end connection through the eyes of Hayley Bates.[18] At the time, Hayley was a typical American college student, except that to fulfill her wide-ranging course requirements, she enrolled simultaneously at two institutions of higher education. At one, a branch campus of the well-regarded University of Washington, she sat in the back of the classroom listening to lectures from her professors. The courses were straightforward and not particularly difficult. Because some of her professors posted the lectures online, she didn't feel she always had to make it to class.

At the other college, however, she described how things were harder. Her professor never seemed to make it easy. Instead, he was constantly posing questions and then challenging them to find the answers. She couldn't skip class because she was part of a group of students who were all doings hands-on research and wrestling with tricky problems together. And the other institution? Cascadia Community College.

Cascadia is located in Bothell, Washington, and is the newest community college in the state, having been built in 1994. From its inception, the administration and faculty decided to translate educational theory into practice. They began by adopting Arthur Chickering and Zelda Gamson's groundbreaking work, "Seven Principles for Good Practice in Undergraduate Education," and embedded active learning, collaborative learning, critical thinking, and communications in their strategic plan. They designed the classrooms such that students faced each other—student engagement was in; sage-on-a-stage was out. They hired talented faculty (almost 40 percent have PhDs) and once hired, new faculty worked with mentors in a learning and teaching academic setting that includes classroom observation and serious critiques. As Carey stated, "At Cascadia, good teaching—the expectation and the resources to learn—is part of the design."

What makes this story so powerful is the tight connection between the assets being grown and the desired state. Unlike other institutions, Cascadia doesn't have a disparate set of vaguely worded aspirations. Instead, they have enumerated a tightly linked collective ambition under the title—"Our Intention":

We strive for a place where . . . every individual is supported and engaged in lifelong learning. *(Our vision)*

We do this by . . . transforming lives through integrated education in a learning-centered community. *(Our mission)*

We stand for . . . a caring community, pluralism & cultural richness, collaboration, access, success, innovation, environmental sustainability, global awareness, responsiveness, creativity. *(Our values)*

We teach students how to . . .

   think creatively, critically, and reflectively
   learn actively
   interact in complex and diverse environments,
   communicate with clarity and originality. *(Our learning outcomes)*

We are committed to . . . increasing opportunities for academic-transfer education, strengthening collaborations to enhance professional-technical programs, being a national model for community college best practices, helping students complete their education. *(Our Strategic Directions 2012–2017)*

By the way, the data don't lie. Although Cascadia's enrollees don't quite measure up to the academic backgrounds of UW students, Cascadia graduates who then continue at UW earn better grades than their peers.

DECIDING SUMMARY

This chapter has been concerned with assets, which ones are important to a college or university and becoming much more focused and diligent about growing them. An anonymous story about a grandfather and his grandson puts it all in perspective.

One evening an old Cherokee told his grandson about a battle that goes on inside people. He said, "My son, the battle is between two wolves inside us all. One is

Evil. It is anger, envy, jealousy, sorrow, regret, greed, arrogance, self-pity, guilt, resentment, inferiority, lies, false pride, superiority, and ego.

"The other is Good. It is joy, peace, love, hope, serenity, humility, kindness, benevolence, empathy, generosity, truth, compassion, and faith."

The grandson thought about it for a minute and then asked his grandfather, "Which wolf wins?"

The old Cherokee simply replied, "The one you feed."

This story resonates with several themes throughout this chapter and this book. It obviously ties directly to our discussion regarding responsibility versus accountability. The wolf that wins is the one you *decide* to feed. It is a choice. The attributes of the good wolf align with the virtuousness orientation in chapter 2—extraordinary, benevolence, flourishing. The problem-solving orientation describes the attributes of the evil wolf—unethical, harmful, threat-rigidity.

But for this chapter the focus is really on the last line: the fact that the wolf that wins is "the one you feed." Feeding and growing is the language of virtuous cycles and momentum. These efforts are not random or reactive. They are not borne out of good intentions. "Deciding what assets to grow" involves the incredibly hard work of discovering and nourishing a set of core competences that are foundational to generative learning and advancing structures. Once these are in place, a college or university is in a position to leverage that strength across a broad set of initiatives that amplify that strength and fortify themselves against the bumps and bruises that will inevitably occur in high-velocity environments. The result is a more resilient institution that learns and grows,

The lesson: Find the good wolves and feed them.

NOTES

1. For a more detailed explanation of this concept, see Daniel H. Kim, *Systems Thinking Tools* (Williston, VT: Pegasus Communications, 2000), and Donella H. Meadows, *Thinking in Systems: A Primer* (White River Junction, VT: Chelsea Green Publications, 2008).

2. Richard Kahlenberg, "The Purposes of Higher Education," *Chronicle of Higher Education*, September 1, 2011, http://chronicle.com/blogs/innovations/the-purposes-of-higher-education/30258.

3. Elizabeth Doty, "The Upward Spiral, Bootstrapping Systemic Change," *The Systems Thinker*, March 2012.

4. *Time Is the Enemy* (Indianapolis: Complete College America, 2011), http://completecollege.org/docs/Time_Is_the_Enemy.pdf.

5. *Bridge to Nowhere* (Indianapolis: Complete College America, 2012), http://completecollege.org/docs/CCA-Remediation-final.pdf.

6. C. K. Prahalad and Gary Hamel, "The Core Competence of the Corporation," *Harvard Business Review*, May 1990.

7. Anders Drejer, *Strategic Management and Core Competencies: Theory and Application* (Westport, CT: Quorum Books, 2002).

8. "Effective Capacity Building in Nonprofit Organizations" (Reston, VA: Venture Philanthropy Partners, 2001), www.vppartners.org/sites/default/files/reports/full_rpt.pdf.

9. Jim Collins, *Good to Great* (New York: Harper Business, 2001).

10. Thad Nodine, Andrea Venezia, and Kathy Bracco, "Changing Course: A Guide to Increasing Student Completion in Community Colleges" (San Francisco: WestEd, 2011), http://knowledgecenter.completionbydesign.org/sites/default/files/changing_course_V1_fb_10032011.pdf.

11. Dana H. Lindsley, Daniel J. Brass, and James B. Thomas, "Efficacy-Performance Spirals: A Multilevel Perspective," *Academy of Management Review* 20, no. 3 (1995).

12. Neil Kreisel and Vanessa L. Patterson, "How Community Colleges Can Help Themselves," *Chronicle of Higher Education,* July 8, 2013, http://chronicle.com/article/How-Community-Colleges-Can/140121.

13. Don Troop, "To Enter the Pantheon of Great Catholic Colleges, Villanova Stretches for $600 Million," *Chronicle of Higher Education*, January 27, 2014, http://chronicle.com/article/To-Enter-the-Pantheon-of-Great/144177.

14. "What Presidents Think," *Chronicle of Higher Education*, 2013.

15. "Great Jobs, Great Lives: The 2014 Gallup-Purdue Index Report," Gallup, 2014, http://products.gallup.com/168857/gallup-purdue-index-inaugural-national-report.aspx.

16. See Jillinda J. Kidwell, Karen M. Vander Linde, and Sandra L. Johnson, "Applying Corporate Knowledge Management Practices in Higher Education," *Educause Quarterly* 4 (2000), and Microsoft Case Studies at www.microsoft.com/casestudies/Microsoft-SharePoint-Server-2013/Kentucky-Community-and-Technical-College-System/College-System-Brings-Its-Organizations-Together-with-Line-of-Business-Integration/710000002231.

17. Paul Fain, "Biting the Bullet on Completion," *Inside HigherEd*, February 20, 2013, www.insidehighered.com/news/2013/02/20/community-college-learns-boosting-retention-comes-cost.

18. Kevin Carey, "Built to Teach," *Washington Monthly*, June 2007, www.washingtonmonthly.com/features/2007/0709.careycascadia.html.

Chapter 6

Icebergs

Understanding What Lies Beneath the Surface

In 2012, on the occasion of the 100th anniversary of the sinking of the RMS *Titanic* on April 15, 1912, *Scientific American* republished an article, "What We Know about Icebergs." The article was originally published on April 27, 1912. It began:

> An iceberg is a fragment of a glacier. Inch by inch the huge river of ice which we call a glacier creeps toward the sea, and here its projecting end is broken off by the action of the waves. "Calving" is the technical name which has been given to this process of breaking bergs from glaciers. It is a process that occurs all the year around, but more frequently in summer than in winter, a process, moreover, that sets adrift thousands of huge ice masses during the course of a year.[1]

The shape of the underwater portion of an iceberg can be difficult to judge by looking at the portion above the surface (as many ships and their captains throughout history have unfortunately experienced). As such, the iceberg has become a particularly useful metaphor to describe a situation in which a small (and visible) problem belies a much larger (and invisible) problem—just the "tip of the iceberg."

Icebergs are particularly useful metaphors when engaged in systems thinking. Remember, a system is a group of interacting, interrelated, or interdependent components that form a complex and unified whole. We have established that a college or university meets the criteria associated with a system—that is, there must be a purpose, the parts need to be arranged in a specific way, and so on. Many systems, like a toaster or car, are made up of tangible or visible parts. Other systems have a mix of elements that are readily observable accompanied by another set that are linked but not easy to see or understand.

For example, a freshman at the Texas A&M University (sixty thousand students) has virtually no chance of having or developing a comprehensive understanding of how the university works. Even a tenured professor at Gettysburg College (2,500 students) would probably admit that they don't know much about financial aid processes or the college's deferred maintenance program. For the freshman, more is below the surface than above; for the professor, many important components of the system are not readily visible or understood as well.

Icebergs are also important because they remind us of the ever-present challenge of living in a high-velocity environment. As we have seen, political, economic, social, and technology factors make it difficult for colleges and universities to continue to rely on a slow, incremental adjustment methodology. Not only do the factors themselves seem to be more energized than in past decades, but also the interaction of these factors has created a powerful new dynamic. While the ideas in this book both can mitigate the chances that problems will occur and can inoculate institutions against a downward spiral, the fact remains that "stuff" will still happen.

This chapter acknowledges that fact.

If our goal is to shift the paradigm to becoming both more responsible and proactive, then when issues and challenges do present themselves, and they will, it is critical that we understand exactly what we are seeing (and not seeing). The considerable danger that colleges and universities face is getting locked into the type of oscillation structure—fighting one fire after another—that never allows us to generate momentum. This chapter begins with a closer look at the importance of the iceberg metaphor followed by a detailed analysis of what lies beneath the surface and how that knowledge can help colleges and universities create virtuous cycles.

ICEBERGS AHEAD

As was discussed in chapter 2, systems thinking is the conceptual basis for creating upward spirals of change. Systems thinking looks at the whole to see what connections exists between the parts. It is the opposite of reductionism, the idea that something is simply the sum of its individual parts. A collection of parts that do not connect is not a system. It is a heap[2]. The difference between the two is summarized in Table 6.1.

The implication throughout this book has been that even though colleges or universities are, undoubtedly, systems, they often behave in heap-like fashions. This is largely a function of their being operated as loosely coupled systems with, in particular, faculty members seeing themselves as independent, certified professionals who are arranged in "departments."

Table 6.1   Heap vs. System

A System	A Heap
Interconnecting parts functioning as a whole.	A collection.
Changes if pieces are taken away. If a system is cut in half, the result is not two smaller systems, but a damaged system that will probably not function. The arrangement of the pieces is crucial.	Essential properties are unchanged whether pieces are added or taken away. When a heap is halved, the result is two smaller heaps. The arrangement of the pieces is irrelevant.
The parts are connected and work together.	The parts are not connected and can function separately.
Its behavior depends on the total structure. Change the structure and the behavior changes.	Its behavior (if any) depends on it or on the number of pieces in the heap.

A new twist on the timeworn analogy of "managing faculty members is like herding cats" is provided by Rob Jenkins in "How Are Professors Like Cats: Let Me Count the Ways." He writes, "Like cats, professors tend to be highly intelligent, deeply self-actualized, and fiercely independent. They need to be stroked occasionally, but on their own terms and in their own good time. Mostly, they want to be left alone to do their own thing."[3] He then explains that the independent-mindedness of cats is hardly a negative trait in professors. Cats also have a certain moral integrity and are not easily manipulated (compared to dogs); again, he compares this favorably to professors. He observes, "Like cats, professors are naturally suspicious, not because they are cynical (although some are) but because they are highly sensitive to ulterior motives."

There is certainly truth to all of this. There is also truth to the idea that no one, cats and professors, likes to be "herded." But it must also be stated that this independence comes at a cost. Seeing each faculty member, each department, and every division as unique and special suggests that many of the skilled professionals in colleges and universities are narrowly focused on the parts, not the whole.

Enter the iceberg (Figure 6.1). This conceptual model used in systems thinking has four levels: events, patterns, structure, and mental models.[4]

We live in an event-focused world. Our ubiquitous electronic gadgets and twenty-four-hour news cycle combine to provide a steady stream of "breaking stories." At work we are subjected to meetings lined up like toy soldiers one after the other, while at the same time our e-mail inbox fills at a seemingly unstoppable rate. Our personal lives have gotten complicated, too. Social media and the expectations that go along with it have kept us connected in ways distance and time prevented in the past. Many of these intrusions seem

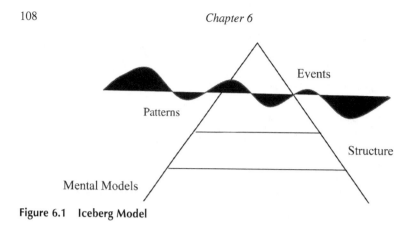

Figure 6.1 Iceberg Model

to require an immediate response. Stimulus is followed by response, with little tolerance for delay or careful consideration. This world, the world above the waves, is all about the parts, the pieces, the events.

But beneath the tip of the iceberg is an entire substructure that is fundamental to understanding what is causing those events to happen.

For example, the F that a student, Johnny, receives on a midterm exam is an event. Viewing the midterm and the student's grade in that context tends to provoke a reaction. The student may react by thinking that the exam was unfair; the professor may react by thinking that the student doesn't take the class seriously. But what if we look at events over time? Would it change anything if we knew that the student had "aced" the weekly quizzes leading up to the midterm? How about comparative data? Would it make any difference in how we perceive Johnny, if we knew that most students did very poorly on the midterm? Being able to see and understand patterns by linking individual events adds so much meaning to a situation. Most importantly, it enables, in this case, both student and professor to adapt rather than merely react, basing their responses on the additional information.

But being able to see and understand patterns does not necessarily provide the full picture. The next logical, "going deeper" question is "What is causing the patterns to emerge?" Patterns don't just happen. There is some structure in place that is causing those patterns to emerge. This is critical to systems thinking because it suggests that if the desire is to change events—what we see every day—we need to understand the patterns associated with those events and then create or design a different underlying structure. If, for example, our professor is aware and concerned that most students did poorly on the midterm, she or he may review the materials and the process used to prepare the students or may more closely analyze the nature of the exam itself. In either case, an opportunity exists to create a different outcome in the future by better understanding the structure, and then assess the learning that did or did not occur.

Mental models—the lowest level of understanding in the iceberg—are the beliefs, assumptions, and internal conversations we have about every aspect of ourselves, others, and situations. They are the shortcuts or rules of thumb that we use to simplify our lives. In contrast to events that occur in real time, mental models are built over a lifetime of experience. As might be imagined, this level is the most difficult to reveal, examine, or change. It requires one to be self-aware or reflective as a practitioner.

As an illustration, one professor may believe the purpose of an exam is to rank and sort the students. She teaches large sections of survey courses and, from her experience, many students are simply not "college ready." The fact that a substantial number of students performed poorly on her exam simply proves her theory. Another professor may believe the sole purpose of an exam is to decide what to do next. Given such a mental model, he is likely to see a pattern of failure in an entirely different light. Specifically, he is likely to observe the pattern of Johnny's grades and ask him if everything is okay, engaging him in a personal conversation. He is also likely to interpret a classroom of poor performances in terms of the structure—"Where is the disconnect between what and how I am teaching and their inability to demonstrate their learning?"

In summary, our beliefs influence how we design the structures that create patterns, which, in turn, manifest themselves in our daily lives as individual events—Johnny got an *F* on the midterm.

Event Management

We spoke in the first section of this book about structural advancement. Momentum and virtuous cycles in organizations are evident when success and positive gains are platforms for further successes and further gains. People engage in generative learning. But in organizations where inertia dominates, the underlying structure is one that oscillates—a period of advancement is followed by reversal. As you may recall, Fritz referred to this as the rocking-chair phenomenon in an illustration of adaptive learning.

But why does oscillation occur? What is it about most organizations and individuals that results in this insistent back-and-forth motion?

The key reason is that they are interpreting observable acts as independent events—a heap. As such, there is no history, no causality that needs consideration or explanation. There is no need to reflect or to withhold judgment. Instead, decisions need to be made. Events need to be managed. The dominant action mode is reactive. Enrollment is down: we need more marketing.

In many ways, the reaction to this scenario is understandable. Stacks of memos, phone calls, and e-mails lead to stress and time constraints. But revenues are based on FTE enrollment and this could become a significant problem. You and your colleagues are senior administrators and are expected to be decisive. After all, isn't that why you were hired? Spring semester enrollment begins in three weeks. But after this meeting, you have back-to-back meetings for the rest of the day. Something needs to be done: we need more marketing.

This is not a hypothetical example. The *Chronicle of Higher Education* did a 2013 survey of small colleges and comprehensive universities in which they asked whether they met their enrollment and revenue goals and what their responses might be in case of a shortfall. To no real surprise, making changes in enrollment-management practices and marketing strategies was the most popular fix. But when David Strauss, a principle with Art & Science Group, which does market research and strategic consulting for colleges, looked at the data, he was struck by how few actually questioned the "fundamentals" such as "How do professors at the college teach, and how does that need to change? What is it like to be a student there, and what could improve that experience? Perhaps most important, what are the outcomes?"[5]

Operating at the tip of the iceberg only allows one option—*react*. Your decision may be right but you are flying blind because you don't fully understand what is happening beneath the surface. You are not aware of enrollment patterns, program by program, over time. You probably don't know the dropout rates of gatekeeper courses or the grades being given in these classes. You may have missed that a new financial aid deadline caused so many problems in the trenches of student services. And you believe marketing at this college has always been weak. While all of these subsurface explanations may play a role in the observable event, exploring the true nature of the causal relationships and a collective understanding of what really is happening takes time.

A specific illustration of event management has been provided by Pasadena City College (PCC). The college's commencement speaker committee generated a list of eight potential graduations speakers for its 2014 graduation ceremonies. The events were managed as follows:

- A student trustee, and member of the committee, contacted PCC alumnus Dustin Lance Black, the Oscar-winning screenwriter of "Milk."
- Black replies, "What an honor!" and accepts six days later.
- The college president, deputy superintendent, and Board of Trustees' president soon discover that Black had a scandal in his past. The incident involved sexual images posted on websites. Black was found to be the victim and won a $100,000 lawsuit.

- The president informed the board that PCC could not take the risk and the student trustee had not been authorized to invite Black (later, it was found that the student was asked to extend the invitation because none of the other potential speakers expressed interest or availability).
- The president also informed the board that he and the deputy superintendent had selected a new commencement speaker, Pasadena public health director Eric Walsh.
- Four weeks after Black accepted and nearly two weeks after Walsh replaced him, the deputy superintendent finally sent an e-mail to Black's assistant: "I wish to inform you that Mr. Black will not need to rearrange his busy schedule to appear as commencement speaker."
- Black does not take the news well and sends an open letter published in the school newspaper.
- The college subsequently apologizes to Black for "an honest error" and says that the board has unanimously approved Walsh as the new speaker.
- PCC's LBGT activists began researching Walsh and listening to his online lectures. They discovered significant examples of sexism and homophobia—in 2006, Walsh said, "If God's plan was followed there would be no AIDS epidemic."
- The college announces that Walsh has withdrawn from commencement due to an "unforeseen scheduling conflict." The Pasadena city manager followed with an announcement placing Walsh on temporary paid administrative leave pending an investigation.
- A chastened board meets to express deep admiration for Black, apologizes for "any actions that may have caused hurt," and unanimously votes to reinvite him to speak.[6]

Subsequently, Robin Abcarian, who writes for the *Los Angeles Times*, detailed the tortured story and offered some advice to Pasadena City College's Class of 2014:

> As you close this chapter of your lives and begin to write the next one, always remember that if you do something that embarrasses you, your institution or a Hollywood heavy-weight, you should lie about it, blame someone else, pretend it was all a misunderstanding or call your lawyer. And by all means, never try to explain it in anything approaching plain English. Rather, water board the language until the words have lost their will to live. Then declare it's time to move on.[7]

Solutions designed at the event level tend to be short lived. The fixes fail. And as soon as one fire has been (temporally) extinguished, another one breaks out. Why? It is because the individuals don't take the time to understand the connections, the causes, and the belief systems. They simply react. And while the fix may bring some short-term symptomatic relief, the source of the problem is unattended with longer-term consequences.

Several months later, in August of 2014, the president of Pasadena City College announced his decision to retire.

Pattern Recognition

Event management fits the mode of oscillating structures and a threat-rigidity set of responses. The focus is only problem solving. But as we slip beneath the surface and begin to explore relationships and causality, our understanding increases and opportunities to create leverage emerge as well. The question that occurs most often at the tip of the iceberg is, "What happened?" The question that needs to occur in order to improve our understanding and ability to advance is, "What's been happening?"

The "What's been happening?" conversation took a serious turn in higher education twenty years ago when the Education Department began issuing proposed changes to the way accreditors operate. One of the regional accreditors, the Western Association of Schools and Colleges, responded by commissioning and distributing its own report—"Report on the Future of Self-Regulation in Higher Education." In it they called for continuous institutional assessment to create a "culture of evidence," rather than the traditional, periodic self-studies that colleges were going through.

Since then, the idea that higher education needed to provide evidence on a range of topics has gained significant ground. Institutional research offices were created or expanded as the need to report on "What's been happening?" dramatically increased. The logic and flow were understandable. If we created this culture of evidence, we could show that we were being accountable. The resulting data would indicate that we were compliant to minimum standards. We would be accredited.

But the real need is not the providing of evidence as if colleges and universities were being cross-examined in a court room. We should not be focused on providing proof of our innocence to those who want to hold us accountable. Instead, we have a responsibility to reflect on the trends and patterns that the information produces because it provides us, not them, with the means for continuous improvement. We need to shift from what's "on the surface" to "what's beneath the surface." The transition, as shown in Table 6.2, is from event management to pattern recognition and learning as an organization.

The Completion Agenda has helped to foster this "culture of inquiry." The emphasis on throughput has turned isolated data points and static reports into trend information and decision support systems. "Momentum points" that have been developed for performance funding also require the recognition

Table 6.2 On the Surface to Beneath the Surface

What?	
Culture of Evidence	Culture of Inquiry
Providing proof	Augmenting knowledge

Why?	
Accountability	Responsibility
Enforcing	Reflecting

How?	
Data	Information
The means of describing	The means of obtaining

Where?	
External	Internal
Compliance to minimum standards	Means to continuous improvement
An Accredited Organization	A Learning Organization

of patterns over time. Achieving the Dream initiative created by the Lumina Foundation is focused on tracking students' performance over time and identifying barriers to academic progress.

Without trend information and the ability to recognize patterns, the fallback option is usually management by anecdote. An issue emerges, someone offers an example of a student or a class or another data point, and with little time or inclination to explore further, a decision is rendered. The development and application of business intelligence (BI) and decision support systems have enabled some colleges and universities to overcome this tendency.

Loyola University Chicago is illustrative. With four campuses spread throughout the Chicago area, it has a total enrollment of sixteen thousand students with eighty-five master's programs and thirty-one doctoral degrees. The institution has evolved from simple columnar reports to more sophisticated analytics that allow people to visualize information through interactive charts and graphs. Conrad Vanek, the BI team leader, notes, "We tend to raise more questions than we can answer but thanks to the BI visualization capabilities, we now have the tools to investigate further, extrapolate knowledgeably, and detect anomalies in ways we could not easily do before."[8]

The key point here is that these type of emerging decision support systems provide the means to answering the "What's been happening?" question, which, in turn, enables the institution to take responsibility.

Structural Explanations

The next level of the iceberg explores causality: What are key causes and consequences of the trends we are observing? Another way to think about this level is in simple means/ends terms. If an institution looks at its reports and finds that an increasing number of students are not retained at the end of their freshman year, an underlying structure caused the pattern. Patterns don't just happen. Poor retention numbers are not circumstantial. Indeed, the institution has systems and processes in place operating in a precise fashion to produce those discouraging results. Events happen. But again, a *pattern* of poor results (or good results) is not an isolated or indiscriminant act or event. Thinking at the structural level means thinking in terms of causal connections. Moreover, thinking at this level is uniquely creative because by altering or designing a different structure, events and patterns can be changed.

A causal loop diagram is useful to illustrate the significance of structure. The economic problems of public colleges and universities were well documented in the opening chapter, and how they contribute to a high-velocity environment. The standard response for institutions has been to cut back on deferred maintenance and slash supply and travel budgets. On the instructional side, however, additional pressures to help close the budget gap occurred. The result has been twofold: (1) a larger percentage of classes being taught by adjunct instructors and (2) more online classes offered. While there is little doubt that some adjuncts are hired specifically for their applied skills, and it is also true that online classes give many students flexibility in scheduling their time, the fact is that a significant driving force is purely budgetary in nature.

This is a balancing loop (B), as shown in Figure 6.2. As the budget gap increases, the tendency is to rely on "a fix" of more adjuncts and online classes to reduce the gap.

Something else is going on, however. In addition to states disinvesting in higher education, legislatures have also moved toward more

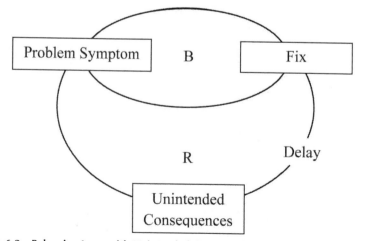

Figure 6.2   **Balancing Loop with Unintended Consequences**

performance-based funding with persistence/completion being a key performance indicator in many of those calculations. But one of the clear results from the Completion Agenda and the many research studies associated with retention is that student engagement is a strong predictor of student success. Students who feel connected to one or more faculty members are much more likely to persist.

The problem, of course, is that online and adjunct instructors are not available to provide that engagement. They come; they go. The result is *fewer* completions. If future state funding is based on institutions' ability to graduate students in a timely fashion, this unintended consequence is likely to decrease state funding, leading to decreased college budgets, leading to further reliance on online and adjunct instruction, and so the loop continues.

This is a "Fixes That Fail" systems archetype in which a problem symptom requires resolution. A solution is quickly implemented that alleviates the symptom (B), but the unintended consequence of the "fix" aggravates the root problem (R). Over time, the problem symptom returns to its previous state or quite often becomes worse. The delay part of this structure is critical because the side effect of the "fix" is not immediately obvious. The tendency in an event-management world is to not fully understand the true nature of cause-and-effect relationships because individuals (and institutions) are distracted by the next set of emergencies demanding their immediate attention.

Again, at the surface of the organization, we react. If we can dip below the surface, we see that events emerge from trends. An appreciation for these patterns allows us to anticipate and plan. As such, anticipating is an improvement over reacting, but we still are unlikely to be able to create the results we want. We really need to understand the organizational structure that, in turn, is responsible for producing those patterns. Because when we do understand the causality associated with the underlying structure, we are then able to intervene with redesigns that move us from oscillation and reactivity to advancement and thriving.

Mental Models

According to Peter Senge, mental models are "deeply ingrained assumptions, generalizations, or even pictures or images that influence how we understand the world and how we take action."[9] Our beliefs are at the very depths of the iceberg. While events (the tip) are specific and tangible, our mental models can be extremely general and intangible to the point that we may not even be consciously aware of them. Still, they are incredibly powerful because they provide the "rules of thumb" we use to negotiate everyday life—what we choose to eat, how we think about the homeless, where we go on vacations.

Our mental models are a long time in the making. We are exposed to a great deal of data throughout our lives. Obviously, we can't attend to all of it so we select only some and add meaning in order to make sense of things. Based on this meaning, we form conclusions and take actions. One reason mental models are so powerful is that they exhibit all the qualities of a reinforcing loop. Our belief system acts as a filter. Because of the meaning and conclusions we have assigned to previous events and the worldview that results, we become practiced at selecting only new data that conforms to that view. We conveniently miss or discount the rest. Our mental models are like sunglasses for the mind.

While mental models can be extremely useful shortcuts, they can also be quite harmful. The most problematic aspect of mental models is that they act to cut people off from the feedback necessary to learn and grow. Further, this limiting influence may not be random or circumstantial but associated with . . . smart people. Chris Argyris, the noted Harvard management professor, explored this idea in his classic *Harvard Business Review* article, "Teaching Smart People How to Learn." He begins by suggesting that most people define learning too narrowly as mere "problem solving," so they focus on identifying and correcting errors in the external environment. He coined the term single loop learning to describe this phenomenon; he states:

> Highly skilled professional are frequently very good at single-loop learning. After all, they have spent much of their lives acquiring academic credentials, mastering one or a number of intellectual disciplines, and applying those disciplines to solve real-world problems. But ironically, this very fact helps explain why professionals are often so bad at double loop learning.[10]

What is double loop learning? First, it should be obvious that single loop learning is closely aligned with our surface-level event management: a problem is presented and a solution is quickly rendered. But for our highly skilled professional, that would suggest that while solving problems is important, if learning is to persist they should be looking inward. They would need to reflect critically on their own behavior—"they must learn how the very way they go about defining and solving problems can be a source of problems in its own right."

This requires the ability to challenge one's own mental models. The problem is "smart people" are almost always successful at what they do and rarely experience failure. And because they have rarely failed, they have never learned how to learn from failure. It follows that whenever their single loop strategies go wrong, they become defensive, screen out criticism, and place the blame on everything and everyone else. The result is defensive reasoning in a closed loop. It encourages individuals to keep their mental models private and avoid testing them in an independent, objective fashion. Such reasoning is remarkably impervious to conflicting points of view and inevitably short-circuits real learning.

The challenge with defensive reasoning is the loss of the ability to have productive conversations. One way to analyze conversations is as a mix of advocacy and inquiry. Advocacy involves taking a position, while inquiry is a process of questioning, exploring, and suspending judgment. Too often, when we find ourselves facing a challenging situation, we increase advocacy and decrease inquiry.

A recent article on Brenau University provides an illustration. While many women's colleges have struggled financially, Brenau is running budget surpluses.[11] The *Chronicle of Higher Education* explored the methods being used by Ed Schrader, the president, and his trustees and administrators to produce a financially stable institution. At its core, Brenau is a women's college with a liberal arts emphasis, but it also offers weekend, online, and professional programs in business, occupational therapy, and other select fields. While its women's college has always lost money, the losses were especially pronounced in the last few years. It lost $3.6 million in the 2012 fiscal year and $4 million in the 2013 fiscal year. At the same time, the college's gross income increased significantly, doubling in the past decade from $23 million to $48 million with investments in both evening and weekend classes as well as online classes.

The key reason given for Brenau's "net surpluses" was that before Mr. Schrader entered the academic world as a geology professor, he worked in a more "cutthroat" environment: the mining industry. "We counted nuts and bolts, we dug for pennies and sold them for dimes," he said. He brought that same forensic accounting approach to Brenau and began to count, down to the penny, what it costs to graduate a business student, or a humanities student, or a nursing student. Moreover, they now know which academic units are strong revenue generators, by how much, and use that information to grow strategically while still preserving the core mission of being a women's college.

The comment section of the article produced two illustrations of mental models at work. First there was *MChag12*:

> How nice, from one business to another. Notice: not a word about actually learning in the classroom. Or faculty. No wonder no one has heard of the place. Why not just stop messing around and become for profit? You can add more on-line courses and up every fee you can. Brilliant.

This is a conversation stopper. The fact that Brenau University is still delivering on its core mission, while many other women's colleges are either defunct or endangered, does not seem to matter. The only thing that seems to matter to *MChag12* is the advocacy of beliefs around the commodification of the academy.

In contrast, *wchristie* made the following observation:

> What many faculty (and, indeed, many trustees) miss is that in contrast to for-profit businesses that operate to a single bottom, colleges (and other non-profits) operate to a double bottom line. The notion of operating to a double bottom line is not widely known or discussed, but it is crucial to effective college administration. In broad terms, it means that the financial bottom line (providing long-term financial stability) and the educational bottom line (maximizing educational quality in accordance with the mission) are equally important in decision making.

This statement resulted in productive conversations because it invited others to explore an interesting premise. What followed was a series of observations, comments, and questions by others around the challenges associated with finding the right balance required to sustain a college or university.

MISDIAGNOSES AND MISADVENTURES

An important caveat to all of this is that disturbances will happen. W. Edwards Deming devotes a sixty-page chapter in his class book *Out of the Crisis* (1986) to describe the two distinct origins of variation in a process. One is "special cause" and suggests an idiosyncratic origin. As such, the cause is something that has not been observed before and is nonquantifiable. The second is "common cause" and involves a usual, historical, and quantifiable variation that forms a natural pattern.[12]

So, when an event or episode occurs (the tip of the iceberg), the first question that needs to be asked is, "Is this a one-time event?" Obviously, a pattern-recognition exercise will help answer the question. If, indeed, it is a one-time event and we manage it with a one-time solution, we are just fine. But what happens if we misdiagnose the situation? What happens if the disturbance that we perceived as being an isolated instance actually involves common cause variation? The resulting misdiagnosis is what we typically see in a threat-rigidity, loosely coupled system. The misadventures end up being the organizational equivalent of the popular arcade game of whac-a-mole with each new disturbance demanding an aggressive response. But with little or no effort devoted to understanding the root cause by analyzing the patterns, structures, and beliefs below the surface, a new mole is certain to appear.

The resulting misadventures seem to dominate in loosely coupled systems because individuals don't have a systems view. Rather, they, have a parts view and can't see the connections and the underlying causality. Obviously, a rocking chair (oscillation) and a game of whac-a-mole are closely related analogies.

But there is another classic misdiagnosis. What happens when an isolated episode is misdiagnosed as having a common cause? Illustrations of this in colleges and universities and in society in general usually involve some variation on the theme of "that will never happen here again." A form that requires six or eight signatures didn't start that way. Something unfortunate happened and the universal answer was to add more layers of signatures to ensure a better outcome. Policies for policies' sake often have the same derivation and effect—inertia.

A recent story is illustrative.[13] A professor of business administration at Polk State University was arrested on charges related to accusations that he had forged the transcript and doctoral diploma from the University of South Florida used to get his job. The problem was that he was never a student there. A spokeswoman for Polk State said that the transcripts had been verified by college personnel, which was the college's policy at the time. In response to this case, however, the college announced that it would now use a third party to verify academic degrees before employment—"that will never happen here again."

In this contrasting scenario, momentum can become a victim of a tentative, overly cautious culture that is ruled by thick policies and procedures manuals with every negative event being interpreted as requiring a comprehensive, bullet-proof solution.

UNDERSTANDING SUMMARY

Meaningful change—the kind we are trying to accomplish through virtuous cycles—takes time. This chapter has shed light on the opposite scenario: the tendency for our institutions to become addicted to a reactive mode of operation. We "find and fix." We don't design. We don't build. We overvalue our own experience and use an increasingly narrow lens to make problems disappear—*management by anecdote.*

So, what would an organization look like that is more generative in nature, one that is always looking to create its own future? One way to think about this is to literally turn our iceberg on its head (Table 6.3). Once we do that, it becomes apparent that the most important aspect of daily life in an upward-trending organization—one that is "on a roll"—is a compelling shared vision.[14]

It is the constancy of purpose that comes from having the kind of vision discussed in chapter 3 that gives us the greatest leverage. From there, we develop a powerful set of beliefs about who we are as an organization and

Table 6.3   Creating Your Own Future

Level of Perspective	Action Mode
Vision	Generative
Mental models	Reflective
Structures	Creative
Patterns	Adaptive
Events	Reactive

how we want to treat each other. That, in turn, empowers individuals to create new, robust work processes and operational structures that can produce positive trends and patterns. From this perspective, an event is the least important part of the puzzle. Momentum is clearly not a coincidence. Its trajectory is the result of highly leveraged investments in a range of aspects of organizational life that can and will amplify learning and growth.

NOTES

1. "From the Archives, 1912: What We Know about Icebergs," *Scientific American*, April 10, 2012.

2. Adapted from Joseph O'Connor and Ian McDermott, *The Art of Systems Thinking* (London, UK: Thorsons, 1997).

3. Rob Jenkins, "How Are Professors Like Cats? Let Me Count the Ways," *Chronicle of Higher Education*, April 12, 2010, http://chronicle.com/article/How-Are-Professors-Like-Cats-/65032.

4. The iceberg metaphor is central to the application of systems thinking to organizational issues. See, for example, Virginia Anderson and Lauren Johnson, *Systems Thinking Basics* (Waltham, MA: Pegasus Communications, 1997), and Daniel H. Kim, *Introduction to Systems Thinking* (Waltham, MA: Pegasus Communications, 1999).

5. Scott Carlson, "If Enrollment Falls Short, Cutting or Adding Program Is No Quick Fix," *Chronicle of Higher Education,* October 18, 2013, http://chronicle.com/blogs/bottomline/if-enrollment-falls-short-cutting-or-adding-programs-is-no-quick-fix/?cid=at&utm_source=at&utm_medium=en.

6. The sources for this narrative include Scott Jaschik, "Commencement Flip-Flops," *Inside Higher Ed,* May 5, 2014, www.insidehighered.com/news/2014/05/05/commencement-speakers-changing-rutgers-and-pasadena-city-college; Nick DeSantis, "Pasadena City College Blames 'Errors' for Commencement Speaker Dispute," *Chronicle of Higher Education*, April 22, 2014, http://chronicle.com/blogs/ticker/pasadena-city-college-blames-errors-for-commencement-speaker-dispute/76355; and Jason Song, "College Chief to Receive Payout," *Los Angeles Times*, August 15, 2014.

7. Robin Abcarian, "PCC Graduates, Take Note," *Los Angeles Times*, May 2, 2014, www.latimes.com/local/la-me-abcarian-pcc-20140502-story.html#page=1.

8. See "Loyola University Chicago Fulfills Its Charter with WebFOCUS," Information Builders, www.informationbuilders.com/applications/loyola.

9. Peter Senge, *The Fifth Discipline* (New York: Doubleday, 1990).

10. Chris Argyris, "Teaching Smart People How to Learn," *Harvard Business Review*, May 1991.

11. This example is unusual because Brenau College shared all of its financial data. See Scott Carlson, "Accounting for Success," *Chronicle of Higher Education*, February 3, 2014, http://chronicle.com/article/Accounting-for-Success/144351.

12. See W. Edwards Deming, *Out of the Chaos* (Cambridge: Massachusetts Institute of Technology Center for Advanced Engineering, 1986). Also, Daniel Seymour devotes two chapters to this subject in *Once Upon a Campus: Lessons for Improving Quality and Productivity in Higher Education* (Phoenix: Oryx Press, 1995).

13. See Charles Huckabee, "Professor in Florida Is Accused of Forging His Doctoral Credentials," *Chronicle of Higher Education*, May 22, 2014, http://chronicle.com/blogs/ticker/professor-in-florida-is-accused-of-forging-his-doctoral-credentials/78247.

14. Adapted from Kim, *Introduction to Systems Thinking*.

Chapter 7

Bootstrapping

Managing the Angle of Approach

The idea is really a simple one. In almost any situation, too little of a good thing really means that nothing changes, while too much of a good thing can lead to unforeseen problems. When it comes to matters of force, the same principle applies. Resupplying the international space station, for example, requires that enough rocket "boost" be applied to gain escape velocity. But if we apply too much force, the vehicle will overshoot earth's orbit and fly off into the cold, dark cosmos. We need to apply just the right amount of force to be successful.

Organizational change is quite similar. Too little dynamism and not enough energy exists to create a sense of progress. Things feel the same. We bump along. But too much disruption introduces doubt and anxiety. Things feel too different. We lose our bearings and fear the worst. This phenomenon—too little or too much—plays a critical role in creating virtuous cycles of change in colleges and universities.

Elizabeth Doty (cited in chapter 5) is a consultant who uses systems thinking to support organizational learning and has done a lot of work in this area. She often begins by distinguishing between two prototypical models of change: grassroots change and heroic change.[1] Change at the grassroots level relies on many small-scale efforts and, through ripple effects, gradually wins converts until a new way replaces the old. While this approach has the benefit of allowing creative energy to emerge through local efforts, such change efforts often "fall back to earth" because there is little ability to engage system constraints—that is, addressing structural barriers is usually beyond the responsibility of frontline workers or even mid-level managers.

In contrast, the key challenge associated with change that is heroic in nature usually involves implementation. Such high-level changes often tend to bulldoze past opposition. This presents a problem later on when the heroes come to realize they need broad, committed support to make their vision come alive.

What we really need to do is find the sweet spot between these two extremes. The advice is not unlike that given by the inventor Daedalus to his son Icarus in Greek mythology. Upon building bird wings made of wax and string, he warned Icarus to fly at medium altitude. If he flew too high, the sun would melt the wax of his wings, and if he flew too low the sea would dampen his feathers.

The sweet spot or medium altitude described by Doty involves bootstrapping change. The term *bootstrapping* means starting a self-sustaining process that can proceed without external input. This alternative approach prompts us to engage various limits and opposition at a manageable angle: "It is not straight up, nor is it entirely sideways. Like a spiral staircase, it grows an asset stepwise, in increments that fit our resources at any given time, This does not mean we lower our sights; it simply means we only go as fast as we can go and keep it real."[2]

The result is a series of reciprocal actions. Each success provides the platform for future successes. This intentionality activates higher levels of aspiration, commitment, and then action. The sweet spot allows us to send the message that the status quo is unacceptable while at the same time seeking to view opposition as part of the process.

Since too many of our institutions swing back and forth between too little change followed by bursts of too much change, it is important to spend some time in the beginning of this chapter describing these opposing phenomena. Attention then shifts to the hard work of managing the angle of approach. Advancement, rather than oscillation, is not a matter of good luck or benign exogenous factors. It is a matter of choices that enable institutions to demonstrate they are capable of designing robust systems that meet the expectations of their stakeholders. Simply, that means in a responsibility-driven paradigm being able to manage change effectively.

SMALL BALL

It must first be acknowledged that evidence suggests small changes *can* make big differences. The concept of choice architecture was developed by Richard Thaler and Cass Sunstein in their book, *Nudge: Improving Decisions about Health, Wealth, and Happiness* (2008). Choice architecture describes the way decisions may (and can) be influenced by how the choices are presented. Their work focuses on the alteration of people's behavior by introducing a simple, easy option—a mere nudge—in order to evoke a beneficial behavior. The methods that they describe are then applied to complex situations such as school choice, prescription drugs, environmentalism, and investments.

The popular book by Malcolm Gladwell, *The Tipping Point: How Little Things Make a Big Difference* (2000), uses an epidemic model to discuss a similar phenomenon. His idea is that the best way to understand such things as the emergence of fashion trends, the ebb and flow of crime waves, or the rise of teenage smoking is to view these trends as epidemics—"Ideas and products and messages and behaviors spread just like viruses do."[3]

Moreover, he organizes his arguments around three rules of epidemics: the Law of the Few, the Stickiness Factor, and the Power of Context. The first rule, the Law of the Few, centers on the idea that certain kinds of people—connectors, mavens, and salesmen—are critical to spreading information. The Stickiness Factor suggests that a contagious message is made memorable in specific ways, while the Power of Context states that epidemics are sensitive to the conditions and circumstances of the times and places in which they occur. Taken together, his straightforward thesis is that sometimes big changes follow from small events.

Other illustrations of this concept occur in both systems thinking and chaos theory. Systems thinkers such as Peter Senge remind us of the importance of root cause analysis and leverage. That is, we are often surrounded by symptoms or events we react to, resulting in crisis management. But as was detailed in the previous chapter, the fundamental source of problems too often goes unexamined. An intervention at the foundational level, however, can result in tremendous leverage—a relatively small effort (the use of a long lever and a properly placed fulcrum) producing a large effect.

In chaos theory, the butterfly effect (a term coined by the mathematician Edward Lorenz) is derived from the idea that a seemingly minor event (a butterfly flapping its wings) could trigger a significant event (a hurricane's formation) through an extended series of interrelated, causal steps. Again, the fundamental idea is that disproportional and significant impacts can be derived from relatively modest origins.

But several challenges are associated with "playing small ball" in higher education and they are related to Gladwell's notion of context and the importance of the immediate surroundings. First, we have established that colleges and universities are inherently conservative structures in light of their role in knowledge preservation. Individuals, especially academics, self-select into higher education accordingly. They obviously prefer the norms, the culture, and the mores of academic life to other professional endeavors—starting a small business, working for a major corporation, enlisting in the military, and so on.

Status quo bias is a well-documented phenomenon in which there is a strong tendency to go along with the status quo or the current state of affairs based on the idea that any change introduces risk and the potential of loss. This cognitive bias is exhibited by people in many situations. But does this bias—the tendency to stick with the current situation—occur more frequently at a start-up company or a liberal arts college? Would we expect loss aversion and other such factors to play a role in the work-life of a university professor or a business executive? A classic study of college professors and status quo bias might suggest that inertia is a greater factor in the academy:

> In one study conducted in the late 1980s, participants in TIAA-CREF, the pension plan of many college professors, the median number of changes in the asset allocation of the lifetime of a professor was, believe it or not, zero. In other words, over the course of their careers, more than half of the participants made exactly no changes to the way their contributions were being allocated.[4]

Also, it is reasonable to believe that the organizational structure of colleges and universities—our much-discussed notion of loosely coupled systems—also plays an important contextual role. Loose coupling infers that the parts of the enterprise are not tightly connected to each other. Without this important connectivity, it is hard to image how grassroots change could be consistently effective. This type of change involves ripple effects or the ability to convert small-scale efforts into increasingly larger rings of consequence and amplification. The nudge or spark that sets off a series of actions in other more connected contexts never gets the oxygen necessary to catalyze change in higher education. Viruses don't spread and the epidemic model founders when isolated and when structural barriers prevent creative energy to emerge and spread.

City College of San Francisco's (CCSF) accreditation crisis serves as an illustration of the challenges associated with relying too much on grassroots change in higher education. After CCSF submitted a self-evaluation report in 2011 to its regional accreditor, Accrediting Commission for Community and Junior Colleges (ACCJC), a site visit team issued a devastating evaluation in July 2012. That generated an ACCJC action letter that gave CCSF until March 2013 to show cause as well as submit a closure report—that is, show cause why its accreditation should not be withdrawn while also describing how it plans to cease operations. Another evaluation team conducted an onsite visit after the show cause report was submitted and in July 2013 ACCJC issued its decision—"After careful consideration, the Commission acted to terminate accreditation effective July 31, 2014."

If they weren't engaged before, the decision to revoke accreditation at one of the largest community colleges in the country energized all possible (and even remote) stakeholders. The California Community College Chancellor's Office appointed a special trustee to manage the daily affairs of the institution. The city attorney of San Francisco filed a lawsuit against ACCJC claiming political bias, improper procedures, and conflicts of interest. The California Federation of Teachers pushed a federal panel to cut off recognition of ACCJC. Both chambers of California's legislature passed resolutions that called for the commission to give CCSF more time, while Rep. Nancy Pelosi, the top Democrat in the U.S. House of Representatives, went directly to the Department of Education seeking similar relief—an extension.

One reporter called the skirmish between the ACCJC, CCSF, and the college's supporters "a highly politicized game of chicken."[5]

As of June 2014, ACCJC, besieged by the political and legal onslaught, decided to rewrite the rule book to allow the institution up to two more years to meet its standards by creating an entirely new accreditation status: restoration.

But, drama aside, accreditation is an open-book exam. In 1988 CCSF was placed on warning: "The Commission is concerned about the insufficient response to recommendations of previous accreditation teams." A comprehensive evaluation in 2006 issued eight recommendations involving multiple standards and resulted in an action letter that the college complete a focused midterm report that addressed financial planning and stability. The action letter of July 2013 initiating the ensuing game of chicken stated that the college had failed to implement the eight recommendations from the 2006 evaluation team (five were partially addressed while three were completely unaddressed) and concluded: "The 2012 evaluation team has repeated much of the content and intent of the 2006 evaluation team's recommendations as annotated in this action letter."

Finally, at the request of the Chancellor's Office, the state's independent Fiscal Crisis and Management Assistance Team (FCMAT) was asked to review and evaluate CCSF's fiscal condition and issued a fifty-six-page report in July 2013. Some of the findings highlighted in the executive summary include:

- CCSF has not developed a plan to fund significant liabilities and obligations such as retiree health benefits, adequate reserves, and worker's compensation costs.
- The college has used temporary one-time measures to mitigate its operating deficits, thus deferring difficult decisions to the future.
- CCSF has significantly more regular full-time employees than comparison districts.
- CCSF has almost twice the number of tenured faculty as the two largest comparison districts.
- CCSF is the third lowest of the comparison districts in productivity (FTES per section average).[6]

FCMAT's report concludes with: "Past decisions have reduced the management team to spectators rather than organization leaders," which parallels the comments made earlier by ACCJC that cited a profound lack of board oversight and administrative leadership.

Against this backdrop, the college's response has been a "Roadmap to Success" of *350 tasks* that includes targeted marketing efforts, upgrades to the network firewall, and purchasing a document scanner.

The question is not whether CCSF will survive. It probably will. Politicians and legal maneuvering have created the necessary bulwark against default. And there are also a lot of people within the institution who really are making good-faith efforts to ensure survival. The real question is whether CCSF can thrive. That is a much more difficult question to answer because CCSF has been playing small ball for decades, relying on narrow, special-interest-driven, grassroots efforts to deal with issues that remain foundational to the fiscal health of the institution.

Thus, there is little sense of any larger coherence. Pettiness and small-mindedness dominate, while the larger, more critical issues that could lead to structural advancement are ignored. There is a lack of positivity or the perception that people are willing to work together, to make tough choices, or to commit to a better future. Instead, an outside observer gets the feeling of a "rear guard action" that has only been willing to do just enough to make the immediate problems go away.

HEROES AND DISRUPTORS

While grassroots change presents a certain set of challenges for growth in higher education, heroic change has a different, but no less weighty, set of problems. This model of change is the intermingling of two concepts: big personalities and big ideas. The stereotypical image of a hero is someone who rides in from someplace else to save the day. There is certainly a sense of initial relief in such instances. Salvation is uplifting. Pain and suffering cease as answers to the most intractable problems are provided. It is an enticing scenario and it is understandable why individuals in dysfunctional or underperforming organizations would hope to be rescued.

But Jim Collins paints a different picture. In his book *Good to Great* (2001) he notes the following about leadership:

> We were surprised, shocked really, to discover the type of leadership required for turning a good company into a great one. Compared to high-profile leaders with big personalities who make headlines and become celebrities, the good-to-great leaders seem to have come from Mars. Self-effacing, quiet, reserved, even

shy—these leaders are a paradoxical blend of humility and professional will. They are more like Lincoln and Socrates than Patton or Caesar.[7]

It does follow that this type of change and this type of leadership could present longer-term problems. Sustainable change requires the building of various assets (as noted in chapter 5). Investments are made in personnel and the development of more rigorous processes. Too often, heroic efforts require bursts of energy that are not sustainable over the extended arc of organizational life. Like a sprinter, heroes often experience shortness of breath and tightness of muscles as they exceed their capacity to maintain a certain pace.

In one article, "My Alma Mater, the Cautionary Tale," Elizabeth Kennen laments the fact that Loyola University had offered early retirement packages to faculty and staff after facing a $7.5 million budget deficit. To be fair, much of the current crisis can be associated with the devastating impact of Hurricane Katrina in 2005. But she also details the decisions made a decade earlier when then-university president Bernard Knoth led a massive facelift of the institution's physical plant in a very short period of time. She notes:

> At the beginning of his presidency, Knoth noted that he wanted the school to resemble his previous employer, Georgetown University. But he overlooked the fact that Loyola has a much lower rate of donation from its alumni—which is the usual source for these large-scale renovation projects, like the one my current employer, Fordham University, has undertaken for its law school. He also overlooked the fact that the university was, despite years of recruiting outside the area, still chiefly a commuter-based institution with a middle-of-the-middle-class student population.[8]

She goes on to describe the extent of the budget-busting beautification plans that were meant to completely transform the campus including the brick sidewalks (inspired by Georgetown's) in a city with a water table that made them a terrible, high-maintenance idea. In this case, the inspirational *Field of Dreams* logic of "If you build it, they will come" led to a super-sized, ego-driven, personal vision that was well beyond the circumstances of the institution to realize.

Big ideas—the notion of a silver bullet—seem to suffer similar challenges. A useful example of this is Total Quality Management (TQM). As noted elsewhere in this book, TQM had a solid history of helping to improve performance in organizations through a focus on the end user, process design, and feedback mechanisms. But when many of the tools were introduced to higher education in the 1990s, they were packaged together as a program— "Quality at Main Street University." Mass trainings were conducted (often by industry consultants), T-shirts and coffee mugs were issued, and a new day in efficiency and effectiveness was proclaimed.

But the champions forgot to check with the culture. With any frontal assault on a culture, the culture will win. TQM (and its capital letters) was labeled a fad and the academy quickly responded to expunge it from the academic corpus. Twenty years later, however, the principles of continuous quality improvement (without the capital letters) are fully operationalized at many institutions in the form of all six regional accreditation's significant emphasis on "institutional effectiveness."

Perhaps the best illustration of the heroic change's leadership/idea intersection is the current fascination with "disruption." Disruptive innovation, as coined by Clayton Christensen, occurs when a technological advancement takes root initially at the bottom of a market and then relentlessly moves up market, eventually replacing the established competitors. Transistor radios, pocket calculators, and cell phones are used as examples of how this near-ravenous march takes place.

In recent years, the "disrupt or be disrupted" mantra has reached into every aspect of American life, including K–12 and health care, with consultants ready to dispense disruption advice and conferences popping up across the nation. The "gospel of disruption," as Jill Lepore describes it in a June 2014 article in the *New Yorker*, has driven the fascination with massive open online courses (MOOCs) in higher education and has now even cracked the academic program level with USC announcing an Academy for Arts, Technology and the Business of Innovation funded by music-industry leaders Jimmy Iovine and Dr. Dre.[9] The announcement states, "The degree is in disruption."

The question is not whether certain areas or certain industries could use a healthy dose of disruption: they can. The question for us is whether the gospel of disruption and its disciples will make the same all-or-nothing, high-profile, frontal assault on academe that resulted in the immune-system reaction that took place with TQM. In a 2013 special edition of the *Chronicle of Higher Education* titled "Shaking Up the Status Quo (and Why It's So Hard to Do)," the editors present a series of "big ideas" that include competency-based education, nonlinear paths through college, and new flexible calendars. But the challenge—to the point of disconnect—is in evidence when juxtaposing two key articles in the special edition.

The first article summarizes the results of a *Chronicle* survey of college president and faculty members. One question asks about the positive and negative impacts of seven innovations: hybrid courses that have both face-to-face and online components, adaptive learning to personalize education, technology that increases interactions among students, competency-based education, free or open resources, prior learning assessment, and MOOCs. Perhaps not surprisingly, the two extreme results are that nearly 80 percent of presidents saw hybrid courses as having a positive impact in the future, while about two out of three faculty members believed that MOOCs would have a negative impact. But when it came to driving change, presidents and faculty members were on the same page: politicians were often the ones pushing the agenda when faculty members, instead, should be driving change.[10]

Turn the page and the next article was contributed by the aforementioned Clayton Christensen and a coauthor, who begin, "As disruptive innovation has crept into higher education in the form of online learning, traditional colleges are beginning to feel the pinch."[11] They then go on to identify two paths to "survive" disruption and use the furniture giant IKEA as their key example for others to follow.

But remember that this zero-sum-game approach to change was what vaulted the University of Virginia into the national headlines, as described in chapter 1. While Teresa Sullivan, UVA's president, was a self-described "incrementalist," the Board of Visitors decided the institution needed a focus on strategic dynamism and sought to replace the president with a "bold, strategic, visionary leader." While the disruption-inspired, corporate-heavy board saw an existential threat, the reinstated president confidently stated, "Being an incrementalist does not mean that I lack vision."[12]

The University of North Texas–Dallas (UNT–Dallas) provides a similar lesson for those who insist on flying a bit too close to the sun. Founded in 2000 as a small extension of UNT, their president, John Ellis Price, convened a group of business, civic, education, and philanthropic leaders in 2011 that included Dallas Mavericks owner Mark Cuban, Dallas Mayor Mike Rawlings, and Harvard professor and author Clayton Christensen. The "21st Century Commission" was facilitated by Bain & Company, who provided a multiyear pro bono partnership to develop a strategic vision for creating a national model of best practices for emerging universities. According to a Bain & Company's news release:

> The Commission will oversee the development of a University strategy to build upon and implement UNT Dallas' first strategic plan—Vision 2020—with the overarching goal of providing high quality education at a lower cost than traditional universities, thus improving access to a large segment of the state's population that has been traditionally underrepresented in higher education, particularly in greater Dallas.[13]

While this heroic vision was certainly admirable, the "dream team's" message never made it to the faculty. In 2012, the first annual faculty survey was administered. When asked whether UNT–Dallas was a good place to work, 58 percent either disagreed or strongly disagreed. And when asked "Do you agree that the University environment is guided by the following core values?," the clear loser was "transparency of actions" with 46 percent in the most extreme category of strongly disagree. In 2013, John Ellis Price, who the *Chronicle of Higher Education* called "a champion of disruptive innovation," stepped down—"It's an appropriate time for me to move on to my next challenge." In 2013 and 2014, the "annual" faculty surveys were not administered.

One of the biggest challenges associated with heroic change is that it has the potential to violate a near-universal precept: under-promise and over-deliver. The notion was originally formulated by Tom Peters and Robert Waterman in their classic book *In Search of Excellence* (1982) when they pronounced it as the "formula for success" in business. Specifically, many businesses fail because they consistently promise more than they can actually deliver. While the promises may get them a lot of new business, the lack of actual results won't bring them return business, which is what ultimately counts.

If our high-velocity environment is indeed resulting in situations where colleges and universities do not have the luxury of standing still, many more of them will necessarily be losing ground. As vicious cycles head downward, the inclination is to embrace the business equivalent of a turn-around artist— someone who can put the brakes on an impending doom loop. And pressure will be to make some pretty serious promises.

Another challenge is that heroic change—both people and ideas—make for great targets. The ranks of ex-CEOs in higher education are littered with those who conducted a frontal assault on the pace of change. New administrators are especially vulnerable because they are always viewed with suspicion among some faculty and staff as threats to the status quo. Finding the right angle of approach is thus a balancing act between engaging the "go-gos," who just want to get going, energizing the "go-buts," who need to have confidence in the changes being proposed, and acknowledging the "no-gos," who find extraordinary comfort in the safety and security of the status quo.

The final cautionary note associated with "going big" is that most such initiatives are resource intensive. Colleges and universities are obviously egalitarian and there is a considered belief in the equality of people, programs, and so on. In a resource-rich environment that presents no problem. But in the seemingly new normal of budget constraints, that tends to exert a great deal of pressure on such basic beliefs. Consequently, one of the biggest challenges in higher education now is the exercise of allocating "scarce" resources. In the past, new growth would be funded by new money, which was above and beyond everyone's base budget. If your department didn't receive new money, at least you were confident that you wouldn't lose money. No more. In such an environment, heroic change and its price tag must come from existing, not new, resources—a zero sum game.

BOOTING UP

The etymology of bootstrapping goes back at least to the nineteenth century when a tab or loop at the top of a boot was used to help pull boots on. Bootstrap as a metaphor generally means to better oneself by one's own unaided effort. A more modern application began in the 1950s with the pressing of a "bootstrap button" on a computer that caused a hardwired program to read a bootstrap program, which, in turn, caused it to read more program instructions. The process involved an internal chain of events. In effect, the computer "pulled itself up by its bootstraps," hence the term to "boot the computer."

Booting up our colleges and universities stands in stark contrast to the deafening calls for holding higher education accountable, which tend to generate defensive reasoning and knee-jerk reactions. Booting up is about demonstrating responsibility. But it isn't a simple matter of owning the change; it must be implemented in ways that bring about thriving. The change needs to be measured and self-sustaining. The trajectory must be planned and purposeful. Too much angle and the effort stalls; too little angle and lift-off is never achieved.

There are a number of useful ideas to keep in mind when attempting to manage the angle of approach; among them are Weber's Law, Trim Tabs, Springboard Effects, and Task Experience.

Weber's Law

First, it is important to remember that an upward spiral is the accumulation of changes as the system iterates over time. Each success provides a platform for future successes. But that assumes that the changes are discernible to individuals. It turns out that the ability to notice a difference (or change) is not an arbitrary concept and was originally investigated by Ernst Weber, a nineteenth-century physiologist. Weber's Law states that being able to detect a "just noticeable difference" (JND) is a function of a certain constant times the intensity of the stimulus. For example, if you are subjected to loud sound over a period of time (the constant), the sound needs to change significantly in order for you to recognize a difference. If the sound, however, is spoken as a whisper, it will take a relatively small amount of change to recognize the difference.

This area of psychophysics—also known as difference limen and differential threshold—has numerous uses in a broad range of telecommunications, artificial intelligence, and other applications under signal-detection theory. Manufacturers and marketers have a particular interest in JND because of its relevance for product improvement. Businesses would want to meet or exceed the consumer's differential threshold—that is, they would want consumers to easily perceive any improvements made to the original product or service.

The implications for creating responsibility-driven momentum in colleges and universities are twofold. First is the importance of the "constant" in the Weber's Law. Being able to discern a change is necessary both to escape the pull of inertia in institutions and to provide the platform for advancement and positive adjustment. But it should be obvious that JND is relative and context bound. A small, religiously affiliated, liberal arts college is the equivalent of a whisper: it does not take much change for it to be noticed. In contrast, a state university with a broad mission, located in a major city, might produce the decibel equivalent of a marching band: it takes a significant amount of sound (change) to be heard.

A second, closely related implication should also be mentioned. A manufacturer or marketer is careful not to exceed the just noticeable difference level because such investments can turn out to be wasteful or extravagant. For colleges and universities, this suggests there can be negative effects from trying to do too much. A current colloquialism says, "Go big or go home." The implication is that taking big risks will be rewarded. That certainly stokes the bravado of some and might be true under some circumstances when the risk is probably worth it. For example, in some of the doom loops we have seen in this book, people are caught in destructive patterns that are so self-reinforcing that individuals cannot see a way forward. In such instances, the chance of overreach is probably worth trying to put the brakes on the downward trajectory.

But the evidence suggests that when attempting to manage the angle of approach to change in college and universities, the truer statement might be "Go big *and* go home." Too much, too fast, too different is giving ammunition to those who are heavily invested in protecting their own turf.

Trim Tabs

It is important to return to a topic discussed earlier: the idea that "some" little things can make big differences. Buckminster Fuller, one of the previous century's greatest thinkers, used to love to invoke the power of the trim tab. A trim tab is a small rudder that is attached to a much larger rudder on vessels, including those of the size of the QE2. Moving the miniature trim tab builds a low pressure that pulls the large rudder around. What is important to reinforce here is that change efforts need to be analyzed in terms of causality. As such, it is not merely the size of the initial change that is necessary to understand but the longer-term consequences that those changes seek to manifest. It is all about leverage.

In an *Inside Higher Ed* article, "Higher Education Can't Wait," the authors describe such a highly leveraged situation. In looking at student costs, they suggest that conventional wisdom focuses on high tuition costs but misses a related problem that is often overlooked: time to degree. Taking five or six years to graduate adds an extra 25 to 50 percent in tuition costs along with the associated college-related fees and the opportunity cost of not working. They then cite data that "bottleneck courses," that is, courses where student demand outstrips available seats, play a large role in delaying degree completion:

> To put it in human terms, a student who needs Biology 201 to graduate—when a seat in Biology 201 isn't available until next year—is wasting time and money. That dynamic is why "access to courses" consistently ranks as the biggest complaint about higher education, according to Noel-Levitz annual student satisfaction survey. The fix is relatively straightforward: offer those bottleneck courses more often. Just 5 to 10 percent of courses are responsible for the vast majority of bottlenecks, so colleges and universities can address the shortages quickly. For instance, they can ensure that their most valuable resources—professors— are teaching the right mix of course to prevent bottlenecks, rather than spending limited resources on course offerings that are not needed (15–20 percent of a typical school's schedule."[14]

A 2013 study by the Campaign for College Opportunity looked at what this prolonged period to obtain a college degree costs students in the California State University system. Cal State students spend a median of 4.7 years to graduate and earn 135 credits. Collectively, these students spend 22,126 more years in college and more than $220 million extra in tuition, fees, and room and board, compared with a four-year graduate. The report concludes, "Reducing average credits to degree by one percent (the equivalent of one credit), from 135 to 134, frees up $20 million in state expenditures at CSU which potentially provide enrollment to more than 3,200 additional full-time students."[15]

The angle of approach, therefore, must be seen within the context of leverage. Any small changes that result in little or no consequential benefit should be seen as small ball distractions. Other smaller changes—the trim tab kind—that have highly leveraged consequences can often vault us into a momentum-producing sweet spot because of their longer-term, disproportionate impact.

Springboard Effects

Another factor to consider as we pursue structural advancement is that every success provides the platform for future successes. Research suggests that there is a springboard effect in which individuals become accustomed to new levels of well-being. For example, the entering college student who does well in her first semester may define herself as being a more successful person than she was in high school. The student acquires a new and higher well-being baseline that not only resists erosion but also provides a potential springboard to even higher levels of ego development.[16]

A similar phenomenon occurs in groups and organizations. Indeed, Rossabeth Moss Kanter examines in great detail the idea of winning streaks in her book, *Confidence* (2004):

> Winning streaks are empowering. People feel in control of their game, and, in turn, they are more likely to be handed control. An expectation of continued winning gives decision makers and resource allocators confidence that people can handle responsibility, deserve to know the facts, attract the best talent, benefit from training, pulling together as a group without depending excessively on stars—and produce those wins. This confidence means that winners get the power of continuity and self-determination.[17]

Winning is contagious. Once a win has been accomplished, forces are set in motion that favor more wins. The impossible doesn't seem so impossible any more. As successes accumulate, new challenges are tackled, added resources and creativity flow, and more ambitious goals are set.

Endicott College has been on an extended winning streak. Back in the 1980s, the institution—then a two-year women's college—was in serious trouble with a shrinking enrollment, no endowment, an operating deficit, and deteriorating buildings. The unionized faculty and the administration were locked in a destructive pattern of finger-pointing. Keeping lawyers busy, the college's faculty members filed many grievances a year, citing alleged contract violations and other complaints. Richard E. Wylie, the college's president since 1987, helped secure the first success: earning four-year status in 1988. Then came Paint Day. It was staged at the height of the financial crisis as a way to get its employees to pitch in on badly needed maintenance. "Impact bargaining"—talks held outside the formal contract-negotiation process—quickly followed as a way to build trust. Each step was a springboard for future community building.

The college, which went coed in 1994, now receives more than four thousand applications for the six hundred seats in each entering class. Its financial picture and buildings are both in good shape. A total of just two faculty grievances were filed over the next sixteen years. And in 2013, Endicott College was recognized as one the *Chronicle's* "Great Colleges to Work For."[18] They still do Paint Day each year, not so much as a scheduled maintenance task, but as a matter of tradition and team building.

The bottom line is that booting up is just as much about the qualitative aspects of change as the quantitative. Yes, being careful about "just noticeable difference" and the heroes and disruptors who shoot for the moon is important. But what also matters a great deal is simply to generate successes that provide the energy, work ethic, and confidence to learn and grow—or provide success to the successful. As Kantor writes, "Success is neither magic nor dumb luck; it stems from a great deal of consistent hard work to perfect each detail. It is even a little mundane. Win, go back to work, win again."[19]

Task Experience

A final factor in managing the angle of approach is task experience. Research suggests that success or failure on early, initial tasks may be particularly important.[20] As such, the angle of approach needs to be calibrated with the experience individuals have with the area or idea that we are seeking to bootstrap. Without task experience, individuals are not quite certain what efforts need to be made and what success looks like. The outcome is that initial results—good or bad—serve to provide the context for moving forward. Moreover, early task performance provides individuals with hypotheses about themselves and serves as a filter for subsequent feedback. We end up seeing what we expect to see.

For our purposes, this suggests that attempting to initiate virtuous cycles or upward spirals of change without an experience base is especially tricky. A failure under conditions when a group has had multiple successes can be absorbed and interpreted as a minor setback. With no task experience, that same failure can easily lead to incorrect attributions and/or faulty adjustments from which a change initiative may not recover.

Judging from the headlines during 2014, it might seem that Mitch Daniels, the former governor of Ohio and new president of Purdue University, is reinventing not only his institution but also all of higher education:

- "Mitch Daniels Reinvents the American University," wrote the editorial board of the *Chicago Tribune* on August 15.
- "Mitch Daniels Battles the Campus Bureaucracy," commented a July 28 blog on Reason.com.
- "Mitch Daniels, Now University President, Spurs Rethinking on Value of a Degree," was how the *Wall Street Journal* put it on July 25.

But in an extensive review of Daniels' first eighteen months on campus, Eric Kelderman came to a far different conclusion. He writes in the *Chronicle of Higher Education*: "But the headlines and conference appearances obscure the reality of Mr. Daniels' presidency: Far from being a disruptive force, he has doubled down on many of the most traditional aspects of a major research university."[21]

The centerpiece of Daniels' plan, "Purdue Moves," is built on leveraging the institution's strengths. Most importantly, he has shown a talent for attracting big money. In the 2013–2014 fiscal year, grants and contracts for sponsored research increased by nearly 22 percent, with most of the growth coming from corporate and foundation awards. Purdue announced a three-year degree program in five majors and a deal to give students price breaks on textbooks through Amazon, and has frozen tuition in order to make the institution more affordable.

It would seem that Daniels' real talent is dialogue, not disruption. It is about finding out what works, doing a lot more of it, and then communicating the success of those efforts. As Patricia Hart, chair of the University Senate, says, "President Daniels is an incredibly talented communicator. He's been very good at telling Purdue's story."[22]

MANAGING SUMMARY

In past decades, the smart money would be placed on the status quo. A few incremental changes were enough. Comfort-driven individuals would have been able to tolerate the every-so-often program discontinuance or the launch of a few low-key, administrative-driven initiatives. Many more CEOs have been sent packing for being too aggressive than for being too circumspect (with the University of Virginia being the obvious exception). After all, when did you last hear of a president or chancellor receiving a vote of no-confidence from the faculty for doing too little? But that was then.

Today, the high-velocity environment described in the beginning of this book and the hectoring calls to disrupt higher education might influence some to take a significantly more aggressive approach. New presidents and chancellors are on the job for fewer and fewer years and need to make their mark quickly. Boards are stacked with corporate types who often view higher education as anachronistic and in desperate need of bold action in a post-incrementalist world. Other stakeholders—alumni, donors, legislators, community groups—seem disinclined to be patient and/or trust that needed changes will happen at an acceptable pace.

It is as if we have one foot on the dock that represents the grassroots change of the past and the other foot on today's ship of heroic change.

This chapter counsels an alternate methodology. It calls for *change at the speed of context*. Being lazy or inattentive to the churn of a dynamic environment will simply bring more calls for accountability; being of a mercurial mind-set will cause an institution to lurch back and forth as big bets are placed, as wins are followed by losses. Momentum is a long-term strategy. It is a measured approach to change.

Each success becomes part of the foundation that enables the institution to aim higher, to move higher. It is that arc or trajectory that creates the narrative of being a special place and catalyzes virtuous cycles of change.

NOTES

1. See Elizabeth Doty, "The Upward Spiral: Bootstrapping Systemic Change," *Systems Thinker*, March 2012, and the video "An Introduction to the Upward Spiral," www.youtube.com/watch?v=YnpnKBPEqJE.

2. Doty, "The Upward Spiral."

3. Malcolm Gladwell, *The Tipping Point: How Little Things Can Make a Big Difference* (New York: Back Bay Books, 2002).

4. Richard H. Thaler and Cass R. Suinstein, *Nudge: Improving Decisions about Health, Wealth, and Happiness* (London: Penguin Books, 2009).

5. Paul Fain, "Fight over San Francisco's Community College Heats Up Again," *Inside Higher Ed*, May 30, 2014, www.insidehighered.com/news/2014/05/30/fight-over-san-franciscos-community-college-heats-again.

6. "California Community College Chancellor's Office: City College of San Francisco," Fiscal Crisis and Management Assistance Team, July 26, 2013, www.ccsf.edu/BOT/Special%20Meeting%20Notices/2012/Sept_2012/Sep18/FCMAT%209_14_2012.pdf.

7. Jim Collins, *Good to Great* (New York: Harper Business, 2001).

8. Elizabeth Keenan, "My Alma Mater, the Cautionary Tale," *Chronicle of Higher Education*, June 12, 2014, https://chroniclevitae.com/news/545-my-alma-mater-the-cautionary-tale.

9. Jill Lepore, "The Disruption Machine," *New Yorker*, June 23, 2014.

10. Jeffrey Selingo, "Presidents and Professors Largely Agree on Who Should Lead Innovation," *Chronicle of Higher Education*, September 30, 2013, http://chronicle.com/article/PresidentsProfessors/141893.

11. Clayton M. Christensen and Michael B. Horn, "How Disruption Can Help Colleges Thrive," *Chronicle of Higher Education*, September 30, 2013, http://chronicle.com/article/How-Disruption-Can-Help-/141873.

12. Andrew Rice, "How Not to Fire a President," *New York Times,* September 16, 2012, http://query.nytimes.com/gst/fullpage.html?res=9F06E1DA143EF935A2575AC0A9649D8B63&module=Search&mabReward=relbias%3Ar%2C%7B%222%22%3A%22RI%3A14%22%7D&module=Search&mabReward=relbias%3Ar%2C%7B%222%22%3A%22RI%3A14%22%7D.

13. See the Bain & Company website, "University of North Texas at Dallas and Bain & Company in $1 Million, Multi-year Pro Bono Partnership to Develop Strategic Vision for Universities of the 21st Century," October 4, 2011, www.bain.com/about/press/press-releases/university_north_texas_and_bain_partnership.aspx.

14. Gene Hickok and Tom Shaver, "Higher Education Can't Wait," *Inside Higher Ed*, April 26, 2013, www.insidehighered.com/views/2013/04/26/colleges-cant-wait-systemic-reform-must-make-changes-now-essay.

15. "Prolonged Degree Completion in California Costs Students and State," *Chronicle of Higher Education*, July 1, 2014, http://chronicle.com/blogs/ticker/prolonged-degree-completion-in-california-costs-students-and-state/80933.

16. See Michael Cochran, "Creating Upward Spirals of Positive Well-Being: A Psychological Approach," Proquest Dissertations and Theses (3400971), 2009.

17. Rosabeth Moss Kanter, *Confidence: How Winning Streaks & Losing Streaks Begin & End* (New York: Crown Business, 2004).

18. Adapted from Peter Schmidt, "Administrators and Professor Find Listening Is a Survival Skill," *Chronicle of Higher Education,* August 5, 2012, http://chronicle.com/article/AdministratorsProfessors/133307.

19. Moss Kanter, *Confidence*, 62

20. Dana H. Lindsley, Daniel J. Brass, and James B. Thomas, "Efficacy-Performance Spirals: A Multilevel Approach," *Academy of Management Review* 20, no. 3 (1995).

21. Eric Kelderman, "Mitch Daniels Isn't Rebuilding Purdue's Engine, He's Tuning It," *Chronicle of Higher Education*, August 26, 2014, http://chronicle.com/article/Mitch-Daniels-Isnt-Rebuilding/148483.

22. Ibid.

Chapter 8

Peripheral Vision

Sharing Knowledge about
How a System Works

In the human eye, the term *fovea* refers to the "pit" in the retina, which allows for the maximum acuity of vision. It is the center of gaze or the thing you are looking directly at. The receptor cells are packed densely at the center of the retina, which allows you to distinguish color and texture. Humans are especially well adapted to foveal vision. In contrast, anything that you are not directly looking at is peripheral vision. While we lose a lot of detail in our periphery, we are, nonetheless, good at detecting motion outside our center of gaze.

The distinction between foveal and peripheral vision is useful because it mimics what happens in organizations under the conditions of vicious and virtuous cycles. As has been described, a vicious cycle is a reinforcing loop that is characterized by deterioration and decline. As these "losing streaks" take hold, a set of negative attitudes and behaviors emerge. Individuals begin to feel powerless. A lack of initiative quickly follows. Criticism and fault-finding becomes standard as trust and confidence erodes. Relationships are strained, communication decreases, and isolation increases.

As a doom loop begins to feed on itself, individuals disinvest and people begin to feel they are on their own. The net effect of this deepening pathology is that individuals within the organization end up with "tunnel vision." Whether it is because they choose to disengage or whether they are increasingly cut off from necessary information, the result is they lose the ability to see the bigger picture. Their organizational life gets smaller and smaller.

Life in an organization that is experiencing an upward spiral of change—a virtuous cycle—looks quite different. A sense of belonging in organizations establishes a feeling of community. This leads to trust and the belief in a shared vision. Information in a doom loop is often seen as a weapon to protect oneself or advance one's position at the expense of others. Not so when an institution is upward trending. Information in a thriving scenario is something to be experienced and shared because it helps everyone do a better job. And with such shared knowledge, the field of vision is expanded. It becomes easier to make sense of things. It is also easier to make effective decisions because context is known and consequences are understood. Finally, it should be obvious that the sharing of knowledge and its concomitant reduction of uncertainty tends to reinforce trust and enhance even more communication.

Elizabeth Doty pulls these together within the framework of systems thinking by stating, "Systems thinkers believe that if people have a shared picture of how a system works, they can shift things for the better."[1] The logic to the statement is pretty straightforward. If a system is a set of interrelated parts, as we have seen, then making piecemeal changes is not particularly effective. Moreover, the changes, as we have seen, tend to be reactive and often lead to oscillation as unintended consequences amplify any misguided quick fixes. Without having a picture of how the "system" works, then, individuals can do little other than to attempt solutions and hope for the best.

But a different future is possible once knowledge about a system is shared. Under such conditions, work processes are made explicit and causality is established. That information acts to broaden the vision of every person within the system. And while such information doesn't automatically make anything better, it does enable those involved to take action whatever the circumstances. Collective understanding becomes the catalyst for change.

This chapter explores three different methods for developing peripheral vision in our colleges and universities. The first is appreciating and communicating the nature of our extended processes. Most in higher education are familiar with the basic matriculation process from admissions to graduation. Far fewer have much understanding and appreciation for the extended process; that is, what happens *before* we admit students and what happens *after* we graduate them. Both of these perspectives are important because they can enlighten and energize an institution and counter the negative, entropy-producing effects of a closed system.

Next, within our colleges and universities it is critical that we develop methods for moving from our historical loosely coupled system to one with more interdependency, more coordination, and more information flow, as described in chapter 2. This moderately coupled system is focused on breaking down the barriers between entrenched, balkanized units so that we can see and appreciate the whole rather than fixating on the parts.

Finally, there is the necessity to develop models that create visual schemas that can actually describe the system. Systems thinkers use models as a way to enumerate essential elements within organizations and to study their relationships. On a smaller scale, causal loop diagrams can be used to analyze specific challenges within an organization; on a larger scale, however, the resulting models can be used to explain how the parts fit together and the nature of their "connectedness."

Together, these efforts address a singular truth: if you want to create momentum through spiral dynamics in your college or university, you will need a lot of people knowing a lot of things about how the system works.

EXTENDED PROCESSES

A system is a set of interacting or interdependent components forming an integrated whole. As we have discussed, a college or university is such a system, with many of the interacting components coming together to form work processes. The simplest process has three parts: input-transformation-output. The input is the raw materials being provided. This supply is then converted to add value and is handed off as output.

A student comes to a class with a certain foundation of knowledge, skills, and abilities and the professor attempts to build on that base such that a predetermined set of student learning outcomes is achieved. Of course this simple structure gets quickly complicated by, for example, multiple sources of inputs. Our student didn't acquire his or her foundation from just having taken a prerequisite course. Co-curricular activities, for example, are known to create their own learning opportunities. The institution (the system) is populated by hundreds of these work processes that seek to add value.

But if we were to spend all our time focusing on just these processes, we would, in effect, be viewing our institution as a closed system. The result would be a limited worldview and a decrease in energy (or entropy). An enhanced vision (Figure 8.1) looks at these "truncated processes" in terms of "extended processes" that stretch beyond the traditional domain of the institution and reflect an open systems perspective.

On the input side this is often discussed in terms of "working upstream." This aspect of increasing our peripheral vision is important because our input is, by definition, someone else's output. By shifting our view upstream it

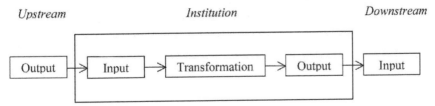

Figure 8.1   Extended I-O Model

allows us to articulate our requirements and to actively engage our upstream stakeholders in productive dialogue. In the same way, when we begin "working downstream" we enhance our potential to learn and grow as an organization by adapting to our downstream stakeholders' feedback. The net effect from both of these activities is to reduce the chance of tunnel vision and increase the opportunity to create virtuous cycles.

Working Upstream

In industry, an entire new discipline has evolved around the fundamental idea of working upstream. Instead of viewing the company as an isolated entity responding to immediate challenges, "supply chain management" is designed to provide an integrated approach to the extended processes of the organization. While some managers traditionally focus on functional units, the role of a supply chain manager is to view the entire process as a comprehensive whole and coordinate the flow of goods and materials. Active engagement comes from a unit being specific about its input requirements and then working with the supplier to overcome any challenges in meeting those requirements. This idea of being intentional about managing the system, and not just the parts, has revolutionized business and produced much more effective and efficient outcomes by looking at entire (extended) work processes, especially on the input side.

This idea doesn't come naturally to higher education. Historically, we have had a tendency to publish our entrance requirements and, if we are lucky, more people apply than we have spaces in our freshman class. As we have seen, some institutions reject 90 percent of those that seek admission. But the unfortunate reality is that most colleges and universities are in quite a different situation. A large number of their students are not college ready and are simply not prepared to do the work that is expected of them. The time devoted to assessing and then remediating weakness is time not devoted to "adding value" in our process model. We are finding and fixing; we are not discovering and developing.

But the challenge is even greater than that. It isn't just a matter of the time and resources required to improve the quality on the input side of the equation; the real problem is that those individuals—faculty, staff, and administrators—who do the finding and fixing feel as though they have no control over the situation. Yes, the need is there but, for many, that is not how they saw their professional lives playing out. The thriving and flourishing that is a part of a virtuous cycle is replaced by a feeling of victimhood that is more associated with a downward arc. This loss of control is debilitating to individuals. The only thing they feel they can do is complain about how poorly students are prepared for college-level work.

In 2012, Complete College America issued a clarion call that described remediation as higher education's *bridge to nowhere*—"This broken remedial bridge is travelled by some 1.7 million beginning students each year, most of whom will not reach their destination — graduation. It is estimated that states and students spent more than $3 billion on remedial courses last year with very little student success to show for it."[2]

One state that has tackled this head-on is Colorado. The state estimates that 74 percent of all jobs will require a college degree by 2020 but fewer than 30 percent of Colorado's students who place into remedial courses earned bachelor's degrees in six years. That represents a huge roadblock to the stated goal: two-thirds of the state's residents between the ages of twenty-five and thirty-four to hold a high-quality credential. In recent years, however, all the stakeholders have made remediation a priority. For example, the state's community colleges have worked to focus remedial coursework such that students can complete remedial work and "gateway" courses in math and English in just one year. Moreover, in the past students at four-year institutions were required to complete remedial coursework at a community college. No longer. Students who have "limited academic deficiencies" can now take credit-bearing gateway classes that feature supplemental academic instruction—tutoring, peer-study sessions, and extra class time at some universities.

At Metropolitan State University of Denver, they have coupled this "co-requisite" model with new placement methods developed by faculty members. The methods are aimed at identifying students who are likely to succeed in college-level courses through different cutoff scores and the use of supplementary assessments. Additional efforts involve new state-mandated standards for K–12 that are better aligned with college placement requirements as well as the expansion of such federal programs as GEAR UP, which takes early remediation into the middle schools. The state's annual progress report shows that they are making headway with a 3 percent drop in the need for remediation.[3]

Another illustration of developing an upstream perspective is occurring at the University of Buffalo. The school became aware of a study that found that simply providing students with information about the Free Application for Federal Student Aid (FAFSA) didn't increase the form-completion rates. So, beginning in 2011, a professor in the Graduate School of Education developed a volunteer network of undergraduate and graduate students from the university to work with graduating seniors and their parents at fifteen public schools and five charter schools.

The one-on-one time serves two purposes: first, it eliminates a potential roadblock especially for those families with little knowledge of higher education processes, and second, it frees up high school counselors to work on other important tasks. It is working. Understanding the extended process and aggressively engaging upstream has led to a 61 percent increase in the number of students completing the FAFSA.[4]

The list of upstream interventions that broaden the view of individuals in colleges and universities is beginning to gain significant traction. Whether it is summer bridge programs, dual credit (or dual enrollment), mandatory orientations, or other "pathway" endeavors, there is a guiding principle involved: Being able to visualize the extended progress provides information about what is needed to be successful:

- West Los Angeles College has begun offering classes in cooperation with Brotherhood Crusade, a local nonprofit to individuals who have expressed an interest in going to college but need help in adjusting to college life. The two-credit course, which is partially funded by the city of Los Angeles, focuses on explaining what is required to be successful and then providing them with a preliminary set of tools.[5]
- At the new Norwalk Early College Academy in Norwalk, Connecticut, high-school-aged students simultaneously take secondary and community college classes while working with a private employer who provides mentors and summer internships. "The goal was to smooth the transition from school to career, and to develop an innovative model that would get people from high school to their community college degree," says Stanley Litow, vice president of corporate citizenship at IBM, which led the design of the Pathways in Technology (P-TECH) model.[6]

Moving the field of vision upstream also allows the institution and its employees to invoke another principle that is core to all of process management: preventing failure rather than trying to correct defects. This is done through two efforts. First, it is critical to be intentional in our role as a customer—that is, someone who uses or benefits from someone else's output—to state our requirements in clear, concise language. Next, it is our responsibility to engage our upstream partners in dialogue concerning those requirements and how we intend to support their efforts to meet those requirements. As part of that relationship, we have an obligation to provide them with timely and actionable feedback.

Whether you use the metaphor of working upstream or that of links in chain, the idea is to develop and share knowledge about how the system works. Ultimately, this is critical to our efforts to establish momentum because it changes the dynamic of the system from one that is passive and reactive to one that is engaging and energizing. The spiral turns upward.

Working Downstream

In addition to supply chain management, the world of commerce has developed a second, related cure for tunnel vision—value chain analysis. The concept was first introduced in Michael Porters' classic 1985 book, *Competitive Advantage: Creating and Sustaining Superior Performance*, and again reflects the idea that products pass through the activities in a chain, gaining value at each stage. Every person in an organization does essentially the same thing—he or she transforms input into output. The organization becomes a highly complex interrelationship of individuals adding value through a task or series of tasks and then handing their work product off to others to add even more value.

The problem is that most people, in most organizations, have a pretty myopic view of how the essential work of the organization gets done. They are placed in a job with duties that pertain narrowly to their immediate surroundings. Their view is limited to their work partners, who act as either internal suppliers or customers, as well as a supervisor who manages the activities being performed. Value chain analysis tends to start at the other end of the extended process—the customer or end user. By evaluating the customer's needs and tracking back to all the internal processes, the processes can be modified in order to maximize value. As such, each and every step in the process or chain is analyzed from the point of view of whether and how it adds value through the lens of the end user.

For colleges and universities, working downstream provides another important source of energy that can be used to change the trajectory of institutions. Examples of spiral dynamics through positive adjustment comes from the following: Pennsylvania State University, University of Arizona, and with a new Gallup-Purdue Index.

Penn State's College of Liberal Arts uses a longitudinal methodology to answer the question, "Can a department place its Ph.D.'s in good career tracks, either academic or nonacademic?"[7] They have been tracking PhD placements across sixteen graduate programs since 1996 and now have records on nearly sixteen hundred of their PhDs. They track both a student's initial placement (in six types of career paths) and subsequent moves, and update the data annually. While these "where are they now" data do not adequately measure the value of a PhD in the humanities, they do provide insight into the extended process that can form the basis for dialogue centered around another question, "How will we know if we are successful?"

Similarly, the University of Arizona has been tracking students since 2007 in their Arizona Pathways to Life Success initiative. In addition to suggesting a connection between early financial behaviors and becoming self-sufficient, the findings are beginning to show how young adults' lives are taking shape.[8]

The Gallup-Purdue Index, a study introduced in chapter 5 is an online survey supported by the Lumina Foundation and Purdue University. The survey is to be conducted with a new cohort of thirty thousand graduates each year over five years, eventually surveying more than 150,000 people. It assesses the well-being of graduates in terms of not only their finances, but also issues related to their sense of purpose, their social lives, their connectedness to community, and their physical health. Harold Hartley of the Council of Independent Colleges has noted, "The thing that I think is of particular value of the survey is that it is looking at outcomes of college that are different from the outcomes that we typically look at—like did you get a job, what is your salary, and those kind of things." And that provides the feedback to make the positive adjustments within the institutions, or as the executive director of Gallup Education, Brandon Busteed, says, "We have a formula here for something that alters life and career trajectory. These are pretty specific things that we can think about how we move the needle."[9]

Another critical way to improve peripheral vision is by taking our role as a supplier more seriously. When we work upstream, our role is as a customer and our efforts need to be focused on making our requirements clear, working with suppliers to overcome any obstacles, and providing feedback on how the handoffs are working. That relationship building is critical when we work downstream as well. Indeed, working hard to develop strong partnerships has the benefit of providing a constant flow of energy and enthusiasm.

For example, Austin College recently announced a partnership giving its liberal arts students (as well as faculty and staff) a broader view that, in effect, articulates "next steps." Its "Gateways Initiative" links the college to more than a half-dozen law, medicine, health care, and accounting graduate programs across the country that offer perks to Austin College graduates such as research projects, summer study, dual degree opportunities, and preferred admission. Texas Tech University has agreed to the most extensive partnership so far—its law school and business administration college, as well as its master's program in accounting, all count themselves among the college's partners.

Austin's president, Marjorie Hass, believes her institution is responding to a real need: "Families increasingly are looking for a clear understanding of what opportunities the college degree will make possible for their children, and we want to be able to demonstrate, in a variety of ways, the kind of launching pad that we can be." She goes on to add, "By formalizing these partnerships, it really helps students see from the beginning that there's a road map to the profession." She isn't alone. Richard Ekman, president of the Council of Independent Colleges, states, "There is this public view these days that if you study the liberal arts, it's not pointing you toward a career path. So to make it explicit is a good thing."[10]

Another liberal arts institution has taken a similar expansive view. Clark University in Worchester, Massachusetts, describes itself as a liberal arts research university by marrying a liberal education with an applied education. In a recent interview, the president of Clark, David Angel, explained he believes a classic liberal education—critical thinking, good writing skills, and rigor of analysis in the major—was a powerful platform for life, career, and citizenship. But he went on the note that being able to "put that knowledge to work in the world" needed additional attention—"So I think most colleges and universities would say that their students are well educated at the point of graduation. Question is, do they have the skills that are needed to take that education and add value to the organizations that they're going to join after graduation?"[11]

Perhaps the best practitioner of "downstream thinking" in higher education has been community colleges. Advisory councils associated with workforce programs can, if done well, be a tremendous source of everything from equipment donations to adjunct faculty and, most importantly, to information about job skills used to develop student learning outcomes. The idea is to embrace aggressively the role of supplier in the extended process by both seeking out requirements and generating feedback on how well graduates are meeting those requirements. Apprenticeship programs are also illustrations of increased connectedness as well as dual admissions programs that allow students to be accepted at a four-year institution but take their general education classes at a community college.

Jeffrey Selingo has spoken to the issue of tunnel vision in a *Chronicle of Higher Education* article: "Many colleges continue to think that the bulk of their work is focused on just one moment in their students' lives, typically starting when they are 18 years old and ending when they are 22. During that time, institutions still treat them as they always have, welcoming them for orientation and wishing them well at commencement and saying, 'Our work is done.'"[12]

That vision is too narrow and it has a profoundly negative impact on the ability of colleges and universities to learn and grow. It ultimately has the same effect as any closed system by starving it of the energy needed to remain vital.

BREAK DOWN BARRIERS

W. Edwards Deming mentioned in earlier chapters, offers fourteen key principles for management to follow for significantly improving the effectiveness of a business or organization. One key point is: *Break down barriers between departments. People in research, design, sales, and production must work as a team, to foresee problems of production and in use that may be encountered with the product or service.* This idea has been discussed in many forms by management book authors and organizational design experts.

The key challenge is most individuals within functional units want to do a good job, but they are often cut off from developing close relationships with other units that act as their "internal" suppliers or customers. Different cultures evolve representing "how we do things around here." Moreover, different reward structures and office politics work to reinforce these standard operating procedures. The resulting "silo effect" creates individual units that may perform well while the organization as a whole never really thrives.

Not only does this same challenge exist in our colleges and universities, but also the silos in higher education may well be even more formidable (with some evidence to suggest that the situation has gotten worse). First, we have individualistic rather than collectivist cultures. It begins with our fascination with "sides of the house." We have the business side of the house versus the rest. This makes it difficult to even discuss the fact that we are really a double bottom-line organization. Yes, we should be focused on students and student learning but we also need to be fiscally viable.

We then have the student services side of the house versus the rest. The challenge here, of course, is recognizing and appreciating that this "side" contributes not just to student health and well-being but also to broader aspects of student success. This is followed by the instruction side. Disciplines, organized as departments, play their role in further fracturing the organization into subunits and specialties along with lower-division, upper-division, and the graduate division, which sits alongside the research and grants enterprise. We also need various institutes and centers to support our specializations and initiatives.

Finally, there is our smallest unit—the ubiquitous *Schedule of Classes* with hundreds and thousands of one- to six-unit classes.

We are divided into bits and pieces and often seem like a heap masquerading as a system.

Has this inherent challenge gotten better or worse? One major shift in terms of interconnectedness has been the promise of interdisciplinary programs and work. The idea of difference-based collaboration and "intersectionality" has been introduced in various disciplines and institutions as a way to overcome the seemingly forced separation of academics.[13] Efforts to overcome the most extreme and negative aspects of compartmentalization, however, haven't necessarily been easy.

North Carolina State University is one of a number of institutions that has focused on hiring professors to work on topics that cross disciplines and departments. The goal according to Laura Severin, an English professor and special assistant to the provost who helps lead NC State's interdisciplinary hiring efforts, is to allow faculty members with interests in more than one field to work together to tackle real-world problems. But the barriers are not to be taken lightly. "Our whole structure is a thousand years old, of dividing people into departments and disciplines, is working at cross purposes to that endeavor," she notes.[14]

These noteworthy efforts, however, may be more than offset by two other new and significant balkanizing forces—technology and stratification. Distributed learning provides incredible benefits to individuals. It allows access to those who are challenged by geography and creates flexibility in people's schedules, both for faculty members and for students. But the research is also clear that the more actively engaged students are—with college faculty and staff, with other students, and with the subject matter they study—the more likely they are to stick with their studies, to learn, and to attain their academic goals.

This double-edged sword of convenience versus engagement extends to faculty members as well. The technology allows them to teach from their offices or their homes, which can be of great convenience. But there is no chance they will bump into a student in the cafeteria or chat with an administrator or colleague about something that necessities any sort of collective inquiry. Those conversations simply don't happen. It is virtually impossible to be an active participant in the development and implementation of a compelling, shared vision when little in the enterprise is . . . shared.

The other force working against any efforts to extend our view and engage each other in collaborative dialogue is the increased stratification within our institutions. The social and economic inequality that we discussed in chapter 1 is present within the academy. In a December 2013 *Chronicle of Higher Education* article that drew an eye-popping 177 comments. Jeffrey J. Williams, a professor at Carnegie Mellon University, described the stratification as follows:

> Rather than a horizontal community of scholars, or even a pyramid with reasonable steps of rank, the American university has adopted its own harsh class structure: the mass of the contingent (and other workers) struggling at the bottom, tenure-stream professors in the middle class speaking for the university's intellectual values and productions, and superstar faculty and administrators in the upper class setting its directions and taking the greatest rewards.[15]

Williams goes on to suggest that higher education is not even really a pyramid at all but "a large, pancake-shaped bottom tier barely above level, a visible middle layer above it, and finally a barely visible aerie rising above them." While dramatic in his description, it is hard to argue with the numbers.

The number of private-college presidents who earn more than $1 million has risen steadily, from seven in 2004 to forty-two in 2011. Their counterparts at public institutions have also grown from just one who exceeded $1 million in 2006 to nine in 2013. But the CEOs are not the only ones who are well compensated. Indeed, some doctors, investment officers, and even coaches earn far more than CEOs with Mike Krzyzewski, the head coach for men's basketball at Duke University, leading the pack in 2013 with a total compensation of $9.6 million.

And that large, pancake-shaped bottom tier? In a report released by the Democratic staff of the House Committee on Education and the Workforce titled "The Just-In-Time Professor," it was noted that adjuncts made up 20 percent of all higher education faculty in 1970. Today, they represent half. The impact of this just-in-time exercise isn't limited to an assault on the professional ambitions of academics. Most importantly, the increasing dependence on inexpensive, part-timers is also bad for students. According to the report, students who took more courses taught by adjuncts "experienced lower graduation rates, lower grade point averages, and fewer transfers from two-year to four-year colleges, compared to other students."[16]

At the same time, the shift to a multi-tiered labor system both undermines core academic values including that of shared governance. In another recent study of more than one hundred research universities, it was found that about two-thirds had faculty senates that were off-limits to adjunct instructors, which seemingly would serve to increase the isolation of a large part of the academic workforce.[17]

These barriers are debilitating and the resulting atomization serves to undermine any effort to build coherence and momentum. As Parker Palmer has so eloquently stated:

> A classic method of maintaining institutional status quo is to create a system that isolates people from one another, keeping the sparks of change from jumping from one person to the next and preventing a critical mass of change agents from forming. In every case of that sort that I can think of, the separation imposed upon people soon gets reinforced by personal choice: people who live under structural isolation eventually internationalize the desire for isolation because of the negative stereotypes and mutual fears that come from not knowing one another.[18]

Simply put, structural advancement cannot occur in the face of structural isolation.

It does not have to be this way. For every situation described above there are powerful examples of colleges and universities that have worked hard to overcome our reductionist tendencies. At Ohio Northern University, admissions counselors and financial aid staff members have been cross-trained to do each other's jobs. The result is an "enrollment team" who create a seamless entry for students and their families. Campus leadership programs, like the one at Howard Community College, place a cross-section of faculty, staff, and administrators together to develop new skills that improve trust and openness. Otterbein University seeks to stimulate a year-long discussion of a common book by exploring it in classes, residence halls, and co-curricular programming. The common reading experience involves all incoming first-year students, faculty, many staff members, and student leaders.

More illustrations include Stanford University's joint major that fuses disciplines that might seem disconnected—computer science and the humanities— reflecting the growing role of computer science in far-flung sectors of society. Valencia College has made substantial efforts to engage adjuncts. Campus-wide and department-specific orientation programs have been developed at Valencia, along with an extensive array of professional-development opportunities, and the chance to become "associate faculty," a designation that comes with a pay increase. Service events such as Virginia Tech's "Big Event" described earlier are opportunities to nurture a sense of institutional purpose.

Finally, the new collaboration between Cornell University and the Technion-Israel Institute of Technology in New York City is purposefully being designed with "office zones." The dean insisted on an open plan because "we want this building to support and encourage collaboration across very different groups of people who might normally be siloed in different places across a university."[19]

The bottom line is that every effort, large and small, needs to be made to overcome the individualistic and energy-draining nature of our colleges and universities. We focus inward. We slice and dice. But the promise of collaboration can be a powerful antidote to our loosely coupled systems. Peter Block in *Community* (2008) refers to it as "the structure of belonging" and it has a huge impact on an institution's ability to create emotional contagion and virtuous cycles of change.

MODEL BUILDING

Most people are familiar with story about the six blind men who lived in a village visited by an elephant. They had no idea what an elephant was, and so they decided to touch the animal to find out.

"It's like a pillar," said the man who touched the elephant's leg.
"No, it's more like a fan," said the man who touched its ear.
"It's like a spear," said the man who touched its tusk.
"Wrong! It's like the branch of a tree," said the man who touched the trunk.
"I think it's like a rope," said the man who touched the tail.

Of course, the story is really about the fact that, though each man was partly right, all of them missed the whole—the elephant.

So far our work to find a cure for tunnel vision has been limited to a linear exercise. By articulating a process (input-transformation-output) and then extending it from far upstream to far downstream, we broaden our view and provide energy necessary for building momentum in colleges and universities. Also, breaking down barriers within the institution increases the likelihood that knowledge about how the system works will be shared. But peripheral vision doesn't simply mean being able to expand one's view along a horizon, it means detecting information outside our "center of gaze."

A third approach available to colleges and universities is model building. A model is a simplification of reality. As such, it is an abstraction of something that is inherently more complex and requires the "modeler" to make a series of assumptions that may or may not impact the predictive value of the model. Models are extremely useful in science because they allow for simulations and experimentation such as with the current focus on climate change and global warming models.

The modeling process is also useful in studying organizations, especially when using visual schemas to, as an example, understand systems and the underlying work processes. In effect, the idea is to capture the complexities of the institution (our elephant) so that individuals are not forced to make important decisions based on their foveal vision (the ear, the leg, the tail). By being able to see a simplification of the reality within which they work, there is a much greater chance they will understand and appreciate their role in pursuing a compelling shared vision.

A useful illustration in higher education is the "5-column model" developed by James Nichols in 1990 aimed at connecting institutional effectiveness with the assessment of student learning outcomes.[20] The basic elements are: (1) the mission/goals of the program or unit, (2) the intended outcomes/objects, (3) the means of assessment or criteria for success, (4) the summary data, and (5) the use of results. Over the years, many institutions—for example, Southwestern University, Clark Atlanta University, Chaffey College, Moorpark College, and North Central Texas College—have taken this basic framework or model and adapted it to their particular situation as regional accreditors pressed for the development of student learning outcomes.

A more dynamic approach that seeks to "close the loop" (in accreditation jargon) has been offered by the author. The model (Figure 8.2) is based on a reinforcing systems loop diagram that bridges the gap between institutional research, strategic planning, and continuous improvement. In this model, the Figure 8.2 begins with a longer-term loop that contains elements associated with mission, vision, and planning that is linked to a shorter-term loop that allocates resources and collects data on the success of the planning and decision making. The model is "reinforcing" because the bottom part of the figure-eight (shorter-term) is designed to deliver on the promise of the upper

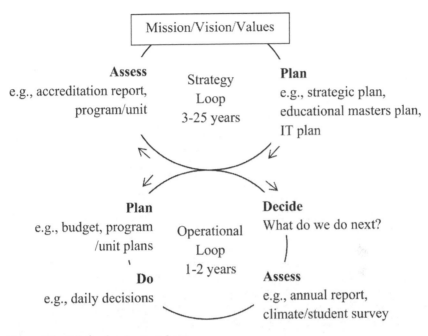

Figure 8.2 Reinforcing Systems Loop

part of the figure-eight (longer-term) which, in turn, provides the feedback necessary to adapt and grow the collective ambition of the institution.[21]

Virginia Highlands Community College, among others, has used this approach to develop its model, which is described in its *Institutional Effectiveness Handbook*. Again, part of the reinforcing loop is focused on developing a mission-driven, strategic plan, while the second part is focused on plan implementation, assessment, and then using the results to inform future direction setting.[22]

Numerous institutions have developed similar institutional effectiveness models that are variations on the basic Plan-Do-Assess-Decide model presented in chapter 3. The University of Scranton, for example, has a planning and institutional effectiveness model with a core hierarchical structure linking mission and vision with a strategic plan (five-year cycle), tactical plans (three-year cycle), and academic and administrative program/unit plans (annual cycle). The model is informed by an environmental scan. Importantly, it factors in accreditation (so it is not a separate quality assurance exercise) and creates a continuous improvement dynamic by adding various feedback loops.[23]

But perhaps one of the most comprehensive attempts to describe "how the system works" is contained in the University of Texas's (UT) *Handbook for Institutional Effectiveness*. The material developed by UT begins by mapping the paradigm shift from an institution focused on accountability to one that is focused on advancement. That broad shift is reflected in a series of other transformations: from status quo to continuous improvement, from external focus to internal focus, from reporting to feedback loops, from compliance to commitment, and so on. This initial effort sets the context for a discussion of the development of assessment plans, which, in turn, is set within the context of an institutional effective cycle.

Finally, UT includes a table that enumerates the responsibilities of all those involved from faculty and staff to administrators, to the institution, and to the students. It begins with:

Faculty and staff will be able to:

- Develop curricula or programs that align with department and university goals
- Streamline curriculum/program development
- Determine student or program areas of strength and weakness
- Illustrate course or program value to the university
- Provide evidence-based feedback to colleagues and students
- Contribute to creating a disciplined culture of excellence.[24]

The value of such models in colleges or universities is their ability to shift the center of gaze associated with an individual's immediate job responsibilities. We spend most of our professional lives staring at the parts. We can describe our part of the elephant in exacting detail. But we struggle to understand how those parts interact to form a fully functioning elephant. And without that more comprehensive knowledge, it becomes nearly impossible to come together and improve the effectiveness of the enterprise. The exercise, then, is to first engage in model building to explain—simply and graphically—how large portions of the institution are supposed to interact. Next, it is important to use every opportunity to describe the bigger picture to people so that they feel part of something larger than themselves and so that they can work collaboratively on substantive issues that will help the organization flourish.

SHARING SUMMARY

In an accountability-based environment, colleges and universities are hugely susceptible to negative forces, both intermittent and sustained. We are susceptible because our inherent tendency is to limit our field of vision. We have seen ourselves as standalone entities. Our receptor cells have been densely packed and focused on who we are and what we do rather than how we connect to others. And when we are attacked, as we surely are, our threat-rigidity instincts kick in.

At times it feels as though we are trying to maintain gated communities like those described by Edward Blakely and Mary Gail Snyder in their book *Fortress America: Gated Communities in the United States* (1999). In a chapter titled "Forting Up," they begin, "The setting of boundaries is always a political act. Boundaries determine membership: someone must be inside and someone outside. Boundaries also create and delineate space to facilitate then activities and purpose of political, economic, and social life."[25]

This chapter has been about "unforting" our colleges and universities. Manning our ramparts won't make change go away. Invoking our specialness will not deter our critics. Within the academy, reinforcing our divisions won't inoculate us from the disturbances created by a high-velocity environment. Instead, we need to embrace the bigger picture. Every individual in an organization has a view. Those who have entry-level jobs are necessarily going to have a narrower view, while those in senior leadership positions will have a more expansive view. But the lesson here is that everyone needs to have a broader horizon. Each person needs more interdependency, more information flow.

Having tunnel vision doesn't actually change the landscape; it just limits our ability to see what's coming and make the positive adjustments inherent in upward spirals that ultimately create momentum.

NOTES

1. Elizabeth Doty, "The Upward Spiral: Bootstrapping Systematic Change," *Systems Thinker*, March 2012.

2. *Remediation: Higher Education's Bridge to Nowhere* (Indianapolis: Complete College America, 2012).

3. Adapted from Paul Fain, "Early Success for Colorado's Broad Set of Remedial Reforms," *Inside Higher Ed*, June 19, 2014, www.insidehighered.com/news/2014/06/19/early success-colorados-broad-set-remedial-reforms.

4. Ben Gose, "Clearing a Path to College through the Fafsa Wilderness," *Chronicle of Higher Education*, May 27, 2014, http://chronicle.com/article/Clearing-a-Path-to-College/146721.

5. Jason Song, "Bridging the Gap to College Life," *Los Angeles Times*, August 3, 2014.

6. Ronald Brownstein, "Work/Study That Works," *Los Angeles Times*, August 29, 2014.

7. Susan Welch and Christopher P. Long, "Where They Are Now," *Chronicle of Higher Education*, February 10, 2014, http://chronicle.com/article/Where-They-Are-Now/144627.

8. Beckie Supiano, "2 Years On, 2 in 3 Graduates Aren't Self-Sufficient," *Chronicle of Higher Education*, June 6, 2014, http://chronicle.com/article/2-Years-On-Two-Thirds-of-This/146813.

9. Scott Carlson, "A Caring Professor: The Key, All Too Rare, in How Graduates Thrive," *Chronicle of Higher Education*, May 16, 2014, http://chronicle.com/article/A-Caring-Professor-May-Be-Key/146409.

10. Allie Grasgreen, "Austin College Partnerships Give Liberal Arts Students Leg Up in Grad School," *Inside Higher Ed*, March 4, 2014, www.insidehighered.com/news/2014/03/04/austin-college-partnerships-give-liberal-arts-students-leg-grad-school.

11. Interview conducted by Dan Berrett with David Angel published in the *Chronicle of Higher Education*, June 23, 2014; see video at http://chronicle.com/article/Clark-U-Seeks-to-Define/147229.

12. Jeffrey Selingo, "Colleges' Role Shouldn't End at Graduation," *Chronicle of Higher Education*, September 9, 2013, http://chronicle.com/article/Colleges-Role-Shouldnt-End/141463.

13. Leslie Niiro, "Breaking Down the Barriers between the Humanities and the Sciences," *Chronicle of Higher Education*, March 3, 2014, http://chronicle.com/blogs/future/2014/03/03/breaking-down-barriers-between-the-humanities-and-the-sciences.

14. Benjamin Mueller, "Hiring That Crosses Disciplines Can Create New Tensions," *Chronicle of Higher Education,* February 24, 2014, http://chronicle.com/article/Hiring-That-Crosses/144895.

15. Jeffrey J. Williams, "The Great Stratification," *Chronicle of Higher Education*, December 2, 2013, http://chronicle.com/article/The-Great-Stratification/143285.

16. "The New College Campus," *New York Times*, February 17, 2014.

17. Peter Schmidt, "University Adjuncts Are Often Denied a Share of Shared Governance, Study Finds," *Chronicle of Higher Education*, November 11, 2013, http://chronicle.com/article/University-Adjuncts-Are-Often/142917.

18. Parker Palmer, *The Courage to Teach: Exploring the Inner Landscape of a Teacher's Life* (San Francisco: Jossey Bass, 2007), 128.

19. Avi Wolfman-Arent, "How to Plan the Campus of the Future? Try Not To," *Chronicle of Higher Education*, August 1, 2014, http://chronicle.com/article/How-Do-You-Plan-the-Campus-of/147803.

20. See James O. Nichols and Karen W. Nichols, *Roadmap for Improvement of Student Learning and Support Services through Assessment* (New York: Agathon Press, 2005).

21. See Daniel Seymour, "Link Planning, Improvement, and IR" and "Link Planning, Improvement, and IR: Los Angeles City College," in *New Directions for Institutional Research: Strategic Planning and Institutional Research* (Hoboken, NJ: John Wiley & Sons, 2003).

22. The Virginia Highlands Community College examples can be seen at www.vhcc.edu/Modules/ShowDocument.aspx?documentid=838.

23. See www.scranton.edu/pir/planning/Planning%20Model_new_2011.pdf.

24. See www.utexas.edu/provost/planning/assessment/iapa/resources/pdfs/Handbook%20for%20IE.pdf.

25. Edward J. Blakely and May Gail Snyder, *Fortress America: Gated Communities in the Unites States* (Washington, DC: The Brookings Institute Press, 1999), 1.

Chapter 9

The Examined Life

Embracing Feedback to Learn and Grow

Is a college or university a learning organization? We certainly spend a lot of time thinking and talking about learning. Each of our many academic disciplines is focused on learning as the means to advance knowledge and humankind. We are inspired by philosophers, poets, and scientists, who speak eloquently on the subject: "Live as if you were to die tomorrow. Learn as if you were to live forever," said Mahatma Gandhi. "Tell me and I forget, teach me and I may remember, involve me and I learn," stated Benjamin Franklin, while Victor Hugo proclaimed, "To learn to read is to light a fire; every syllable that is spelled out is a spark."

Even Dr. Seuss is an advocate for learning: "The more that you read, the more things you will know. The more that you learn, the more places you'll go."

We have discussed the nature and role of learning from John Henry Newman's Discourse VI, "Knowledge Viewed in Relation to Leaning," in his 1850 treatise *The Idea of a University* to our very current dialogue on student learning outcomes as catalyzed by higher education's regional accrediting agencies. Our mottos expound on it—Fordham University's *Sapientia at Doctrina* (Wisdom and Learning) and Queens College's Discimus ut Serviamus (We Learn in Order to Serve)—and our institutional mission statements weigh heavy with language and thoughts about learning.

But do we, as organizations, learn?

While the concept of organizational learning took seed in the 1970s, it became popularized by Peter Senge's book, *The Fifth Discipline*, in 1990. Senge began his groundbreaking work by stating, unequivocally, that his intention was to destroy the illusion that "the world is created of separate, unrelated forces." Once we give up this illusion, according to Senge, we are then able to build "learning organizations" that are characterized as organizations where people continually expand their capacity to create the results they truly desire. Senge organizes his book into disciplines of the learning organization—systems thinking, personal mastery, mental models, building shared vision, and team learning—many of which we have discussed in other parts of this book.

This chapter takes a more narrow focus on the notion of organizational learning by honing in on a key element of exactly how we can expand the capacity of colleges and universities to create their own futures. Chris Argyris, the Harvard University professor and noted author on the subject of learning organizations, has stated that the better organizations are at learning, the more likely they will be able to detect and correct errors. Errors are defined as "a mismatch between plan or intention and what actually happened when either is implemented."[1]

Learning, within this admittedly narrow context, is not something we teach others to do or wax poetically about in our mission statements; it is a competence that needs to be developed by an organization. It is the ability to develop insights into what creates mismatches or errors and how to begin to correct them. Unfortunately, higher education in this country doesn't appear to be particularly eager to shine a bright light on its mismatches. In May of 2013, McKinsey & Co. released a wide-ranging study of almost five thousand college graduates, most of whom finished college between 2009 and 2012. The study, "Voice of the Graduate," begins by stating:

> The gap between higher education's undeniable value and the concerns of many recent graduates nonetheless should become the impetus for change. In a sense, the "voice of the graduate" revealed in this survey amounts to a cry for help— an urgent call to deepen the relevance of higher education to employment and entrepreneurship so that the promise of higher education is fulfilled.[2]

The results of the study include the following: (1) students largely believe they are overqualified for the jobs they find themselves in after graduation, (2) many students also feel unprepared for the world of work—the transition from campus to office is anything but seamless, and (3) half of graduates express regrets, saying they would pick a different major or school if they had to do it all over again. "This should be an alarming call to action for all of us," says Andre Dua, a director at McKinsey and lead author of the study. There is no evidence to suggest that his "call to action" was even heard, let alone acted on.

The essence of this chapter is timeless and goes back to Socrates's observation, "The unexamined life is not worth living." Indeed, an unexamined organization is unaware of mismatches and the gaps between its intentions and the results of its actions. At best it is working hard to maintain the status quo; at worst it is susceptible to the pull of a downward spiral. In contrast, the "examined life" is one in which organizations continuously build on their own capacity to detect and correct errors and, with that, are presented with countless opportunities to thrive.

Indeed, positive adjustments that are at the core of virtuous cycles are simply not possible without timely and accurate feedback.

ACCUMULATION AND AMPLIFICATION

As has been described, virtuous cycles or upward spirals of change that lead to momentum in organizations have many different elements. They require purpose or a compelling shared vision as well as the ability to align actions. They also require decisions about what to grow and the size of the investments to be made. An expansive view is needed such that new energy can help fuel an upward trajectory.

On a personal level, this energy can be described in terms of positive well-being. First, there is the upward spiral itself—"A sequence of events in which over the span of three or more cycles of reciprocal causation, deviation-amplifying feedback, and accumulation and compounding processes result in the balance of outcomes tipping toward desirable outcomes." Next, the terms can be defined as follows:

Reciprocal causation: Feedback processes in which elements in a system influence each other either simultaneously or alternatively.
Deviation-amplifying feedback processes: Reciprocal feedback processes in which an insignificant initial kick is amplified and deviations build up and diverge from the initial condition, resulting in an effect much larger than the initial kick.
Accumulation and compounding processes: Outcomes can accumulate in human experience in the same way that money can be accumulated; outcomes can also compound—due to reciprocal causation and deviation-amplifying feedback processes—in the same way that money in an interest-bearing bank account will earn compound interest over time.[3]

These are the processes manifested in a psychological broadening where one positive emotion leads to an increased receptiveness to subsequent pleasure or meaningful events, which, in turn, leads to further increases in positive as well as additional emotions. As this process continues over time, it can trigger an "upward spiral" in which people build psychological resilience and enhanced emotional well-being.

This technical explanation is more easily understood in the language of winning streaks and losing streaks described elsewhere in this book. In *Confidence* (2004), Rosabeth Moss Kanter explains how success "accumulates" over time. She notes that in the middle of winning cycles, people naturally gravitate toward behaving in ways that support confidence:

- *Responsibility*—People want to share information and take responsibility; they have nothing to hide. They seek feedback and self-improvement. Because they feel committed, they communicate more often and make higher-quality decisions. They set high aspirations and respect each other for meeting high standards. They avoid excuses and try self-scrutiny before blaming others.
- *Collaboration*—People want to work together. Mutual attraction is high, interpersonal bonds are strong, and relationships are multifaceted because people take the time to know one another in a variety of settings. People are willing to help others and give them a chance to excel. They feel a sense of belonging that makes them more amenable to taking directions from others.
- *Initiative*—People feel that what they do matters, that they can make a difference in outcomes, so they offer ideas and suggestions. Expectations of success produce the energy to put in extra effort, to keep going under pressure. People take initiative, and initiative results in improvements and innovations.[4]

It is important to remember that feedback, by itself, is a necessary but insufficient condition to cause upward cycles of change. As we discussed in chapter 2, feedback is fundamental in systems—no feedback, no system. But there are two different types of feedback. One is balancing feedback, which occurs when changes in a system are fed back and act to dampen the original change. Balancing processes can be thought of as "The Great Stabilizers" because they resist change in one direction by producing change in another. The result is goal-seeking behavior and a sense of constancy.

The other form of feedback is reinforcing and can be thought of as "The Engines of Growth and Collapse." The reinforcing dynamic occurs because change in one direction produces even more change in that same direction. There is an amplifying effect as things get better and better (virtuous cycles) or worse and worse (vicious cycles).[5]

If we review the upward spiral concepts that have already been described, such as cascading vitality, emotional contagion, empowerment, confidence, and others, they all begin with this same reinforcing dynamic that embraces and celebrates feedback as the engine for learning and growth.

LEARNING DISABILITIES IN HIGHER EDUCATION

At the very core of the examined life of our institutions is the asking and answering of one straightforward question: *How will we know if we are successful?* This is one of the fundamental questions associated with a broad view of institutional effectiveness as described in chapter 3:

Noble Ambition—Why do we exist? What do we want to create? What do we believe?
Strategic Intent—How are we going to get there?
Key Performance Indicators—How will we know if we are successful?
Discrepancy—What do we do now? What needs to change?

It is the question that can make manifest the mismatch or gap that is the impetus for organizational learning—error detection and correction. It is also part of the process that is so inherent to who we are. The process of asking and answering questions to stimulate critical thinking and illuminate ideas is what we do every single day in our courses and classrooms.

The Socratic Method has been fundamental to the process of learning for centuries; and yet, the incessant and strident calls for "holding higher education accountable" are a direct result of our unwillingness or inability to answer this same fundamental question. As we have noted, if we don't ask and answer questions about our own value, outcomes, and successes, someone else in a high-velocity environment will be more than happy to take a shot. Whether it is a magazine's special issue on higher education, federal mandates, or state legislatures who believe they need to manage colleges and universities, the result is the same: the abdication of our responsibility to learn and grow as institutions.

So, what are barriers that we have erected as institutions that stifle our own learning? What are our learning disabilities?

Delay and Inaccuracy

One key attribute associated with loosely coupled systems is a delay in the transmission of information. The lack of connectedness means that information that could help establish the nature of a causal relationship is not available when it would be easiest to see the effects. Instead, intervening variables, lack of focus, and a need to fight the next fire confuses the picture. The added problem is that delay also enhances the chance that any resulting feedback will be inaccurate. We simply do not pay attention to the details when the distance between cause and effect is played out over an extended period of time. Moreover, it becomes extremely difficult to understand and correct any unintended consequences when specific consequences are not examined in the context of specific actions because of intervening months or years.

Another way to think of this learning disability is in terms of the first law in Senge's *Fifth Discipline* (1990)—"Today's problems come from yesterday's 'solutions.'" This law suggests the existence of unintended consequences to even the most well-researched and effectively implemented strategy. But when we introduce "delay" into this equation, the ability to establish the nature of that causation becomes more challenging.

One professor described his frustration at "moving at the speed of academe" in an article in which he compared his world with that of a former student. The student had become the chief executive of a successful fitness and wellness company and stated that if he had an idea on Friday, they implemented it on Monday. The professor shared his frustration at being at the opposite end of that continuum. He described the juxtaposition of being charged with preparing the next generation of entrepreneurs and innovators with his institution's culture of time-consuming, unhurried progress when it comes to curriculum, personnel, and governance in the following way:

> As a professor, I often feel that I live a divided life. On the one side of the divide I am engaged with students in and out of class, sharing with them information from a rapidly changing world, hoping to keep them up to date and informed so that they might somehow use this information to follow and achieve their dreams. On the other side of the divide, I face a world consumed with sluggishness, personified by committees and committee structures at the department, college, and university levels.[6]

When feedback is delayed or inaccurate, individuals within the organization are likely to continue to employ inappropriate strategies, as we saw earlier in chapter 6, when describing the "fixes that fail" systems archetype. The faulty quick fix goes undetected because a delay occurs between the fix and a brewing, unobserved, and unintended consequence as we shuffle from committee meeting to committee meeting.

It Ain't Easy

In the previous chapter we spoke to the idea of value chain analysis: when the various activities in the organization can be seen in terms of their ability to add value to a product in the eyes of end users. While this metaphor provides a useful way to encourage us to engage in peripheral vision—especially downstream to society, graduate schools, and employers—it oversimplifies the issue when it comes to students and the basic purpose of our enterprises.

We are, like it or not, in the service industry. In a manufacturing sector, it is easy to visualize the flow of materials from suppliers through a manufacturer's facility and then into a distribution channel and on to the final end user. But the service industry is different. When we purchase a service, the customer is both a supplier to the individual or organization who is providing that service as well as a recipient of the service itself. This is where it gets tricky for us because as "co-producers of learning," the student can greatly affect the learning that occurs by being prepared, by being engaged, and by being inspired to learn. Measuring success—"How will we know if we are successful?"—in this kind of environment is problematic.

An illustration has been provided in an article written by a professor at Davidson College titled, "Measuring Success Is Not Easy." Erland Stevens, a chemistry professor at Davidson College, reflects on his efforts (with other staff and faculty members) to deliver their first MOOC, a course in medicinal chemistry. He begins by stating that evaluating success in education of any type is difficult, and MOOCs are no exception. The mountains of (often messy) data from online student activity—page views, time of engagement with videos, and discussion board interactions—create assessment challenges. As he notes, every time a student clicks within the platform, that interaction is recorded. Despite the opportunities posed by these plentiful sets of data, MOOC assessments are often reduced to simply reporting how many students finished the course. He states, "Even the idea of 'finishing' a MOCC is not a simple concept. How does one define finished—students who passed the course, took the last test, or viewed content during the end of the course?"[7]

The problem here is not so much that what we do—and how we measure success—is difficult. The problem is more that complexity is too often used to short-circuit other, necessary, productive conversations. For example, for many years efforts to advance assessment were marginalized by faculty members who argued such efforts were a violation of academic freedom. Later the argument shifted to the "commodification" of higher education and then finally to direct challenges associated with answering the question, "What do I want my students to be able to do and how will I know it?"

The vacuum created by our unwillingness to tackle the issue (other than the dismissive response that "I have a syllabus and give grades") in a more responsible fashion is now being filled by hyperactive state legislatures and political pundits' perceived need to hold us accountable. What we do is not easy. But the alternative to not fully embracing the complexity is to empower others to impose overly simplistic solutions on us.

Source of Embarrassment

A primary learning disability for individuals in general, and members of the academy in particular, is that feedback can be a source of discomfort and embarrassment. It is understood that individuals (and organizations) work hard to project an image of themselves to the world around them. They want to be perceived in a positive light with all the appropriate modifiers—a *great* teacher, an *excellent* university. And they have every right to believe that is so. A professor is defined as "one that professes, avows, or declares." There is nothing unequivocal about that. Our higher education system is often described as the best in the world, demonstrated by the hundreds of thousands of international students trying to gain entrance.

Feedback puts that self-image in jeopardy.

There are two ways to avoid the problem. The first is to dismiss or mini-mize the need for reflection in the first place. This learning disability is best illustrated in the debate over student evaluations. Many of the arguments associated with this disability were summarized in an article, "The Unneces-sary Agony of Student Evaluations." At first the author (and professor) revis-its the argument that student evaluations have emerged from the "alarming" shift in American higher education toward consumerism. This private enter-prise model of educational management is further advanced by the notion of "student as customer" even though students come and go, and professors generally remain, as well as the observation that as evaluators, students are amateurs. And then there is the following:

> In Europe generally, where universities are mostly free (though increasingly less so) and very difficult to get into, students are regarded not as consumers but as subjects needing either training or enlightenment. The life of the mind is valued and nurtured, or alternatively, technical skills are passed on, depending on what kind of institution you go to. Grades are nowhere near as inflated and student evaluations are regarded as formalities, like a form filled out for bureaucrats. Value is place not on how students regard their professors but how professors regard their colleagues.[8]

Apparently, if you are engaged in "the life of the mind," accepting feed-back from students is both unbecoming and unproductive.

A second way to minimize any potential embarrassment is illustrated by W. Somerset Maugham: "People ask for criticism, but they only want praise." A humorous higher education twist has been offered on this idea—"Do you want feedback or validation?"—by Allison Vaillancourt, an administrator at the University of Arizona. A university policy was not working as intended, and so a small group of individuals got together to craft a draft revision. One individual volunteered to write a first draft. After receiving the draft, she agreed that significant improvement had occurred but went on to provide detailed suggestion about how to make it better. Her ideas were not appre-ciated and prompted a prickly "reply to all" message explaining why the author's original ideas were smart and her suggestions were . . . ridiculous.

The good news is that the summary rejection of the feedback (as criticism, not praise) encouraged Ms. Vaillancourt to develop the following numbering system so that we might be clearer about our intentions when we ask for feedback:

Category One: "I seriously need your advice on this. Rip it up if you have to; I really want this to be good."
Category Two: "Does this make sense? Will others understand it?"
Category Three: "Please review for accuracy and typos."
Category Four: "This is my cover-my-back request. Please read this so I can claim I asked for your input."
Category Five: "Please marvel at my brilliance and use this request as an opportunity to praise me. Do not, under any circumstances, suggest improvements because this is perfect as it is."[9]

Funny as it is, this categorization comes pretty close to reflecting a stark reality and a reason why our organizational lives in academe go unexamined.

Attribution Error

Even if we are successful at generating robust feedback, there is another barrier to effective learning in college and universities—attribution error. Feedback exists along a broad range, from "Yes, this action really was successful and we need to leverage that approach," to "No, this didn't work out at all and we need to discontinue this effort." Again, the question is whether a mismatch exists between what we intended and what actually happened. Having mechanisms in place to identify gaps is the key to organizational learning and the ability to fuel cycles of innovation and growth. But identifying an opportunity to make a positive adjustment and actually implementing it are two very different things. Really making the positive adjustment is a function of accurate attribution; that is, assigning the "effect"—whether good or bad—to the proper "cause."

One pervasive attribution error found in individuals, groups, and organizations is the tendency to attribute successes to internal causes and failures to external causes.[10]

Perhaps the most obvious illustration in higher education is enrollment growth. Trustees, presidents, and other senior administrators have a tendency to use trend data showing a growing student body in their communications—speeches, convocations, websites, and press releases. The inference is these executives developed new, market-driven programs resulting in graduates who are swept up by industry. Then, a comprehensive plan was put in place to communicate the success of these strategic initiatives to cohorts of eager highs school students and their parents. The reputation of the institution is on the rise due to these efforts and it makes sense that more and more students and their families would see Main Street University as the answer to their aspirations.

And when enrollment begins to fall? More often than not, the cause is attributed to a downward economic cycle (the example is reversed for community colleges because of their counter-cyclical nature) or state budget cuts or even a series of idiosyncratic events such as a scandal in the press.

The fact is accurate attribution is critical to both the sustaining of momentum in virtuous cycles and the ability to put the brakes on vicious cycles. In the case of enrollment growth, certainly situations occur in which an institution has, over a period of time, done a lot of things right: developed excellent programs, hired top-notch faculty members, engaged their students, and worked aggressively upstream to build a presence in their community. By understanding which of those efforts have been most or least effective, the institution is contributing to its own self-efficacy. It is building capacity to make positive adjustments.

In turn, there are instances as well where enrollment decline (especially among tuition-driven institutions) feeds a doom loop of budget cuts, layoffs, and plummeting morale. The inability or unwillingness to make accurate judgments about the cause undermines self-efficacy by questioning whether individuals within the institution have the capacity to be honest with themselves and engage in tough interventions.

Smart People

The most important learning disability in higher education was introduced in the earlier discussion of mental models in chapter 6—Chris Argyris's *Harvard Business Review* classic, "Teaching Smart People to Learn."[11] Each of us has witnessed this disability: You are attending a regular meeting of the senior executive team at your institution. A serious, messy issue has surfaced over recent months and you have been asked to research the problem and make a presentation. You asked institutional research to run some numbers, you interviewed the key players involved (including those at the front lines), and you have conducted an online search for best practices identified at other institutions. The presentation is structured so that you can spend some initial time on "problem identification" and enumerating the available trend data.

Within a few minutes, however, a colleague seated across the table slips you a piece of paper that begins with the words, "We should. . . ." Not long after another colleague interrupts to just "toss out an idea." Before you know it— and before you have even presented all the background information—a cascade of brilliant solutions is being offered by a roomful of eager, smart people.

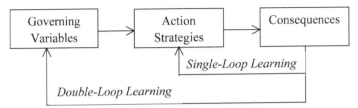

Figure 9.1   Single-Loop v Double-Learning Learning

According to Argyris, most people define *learning* too narrowly as mere problem solving. Coining the terms *single loop* and *double loop* learning, he captures this critical distinction in a simple model (Figure 9.1).

Upon the detection of an error, most people look for another operational strategy that will work within the same goal-structure and rule-boundaries. This is "single loop learning." Like a thermostat, this is a simple feedback loop, where outcomes cause adjustment of behaviors. It is generally in operation when goals, beliefs, values, and strategies are taken for granted and accepted without any critical reflection. "Double loop learning" is a form of higher-order learning because it challenges the assumptions unexamined in the single loop model

Highly skilled professionals are frequently good at single loop learning. Argyris states, "After all, they have spent much of their lives acquiring academic credentials, mastering one or a number of intellectual disciplines, and applying those disciplines to solve real-world problems." The result is that they are successful and, in turn, they begin to overvalue their own experience. They believe they are good at problem solving (How else do they explain their title of dean or deputy chancellor?) and are often determined to demonstrate that ability in public. But because they have failed so rarely, they never learned how to learn from failure. So, whenever their single loop strategies go wrong, they become defensive, screen out criticism, and place the blame on everyone and everything else.

This final point, the blame game, provides the basis for a disappointing but illuminating illustration played out in the comment section of the article "Can Universities Use Data to Fix What Ails the Lecture?"[12] The use of a program, LectureTools, designed to collect data on how students are reacting to lectures is examined in the article. A dispassionate introduction notes that large lecture classes are probably here to stay, especially at public universities, because of the need to be cost conscious. On the other hand, this new "culture of accountability" requires supporting students in their efforts to complete a certificate or degree. The article notes that lack of engagement is generally seen as a major cause of students falling behind and dropping out. The final element in the article's background is the degree to which professors face pressure to use technology to measure classroom experiences.

Within this broad context, the article introduces Perry J. Samson, a professor of atmospheric science at the University of Michigan, whose idea was to "invent a system that could spur his colleagues to squeeze data out of the thin air of the lecture hall—data they might use to become better teachers." LectureTools involves getting everyone on the same page in a large lecture hall by having students follow along with the professor's slides on their laptops and mobile devices. Among other features, students can take notes in the margins of the slides, they can respond to questions professors build into the lecture, and they can click a button that says, "I'm confused." At the end of each class, LectureTools sends an e-mail message with a summary of the participation data—how many students logged in, who took notes, which slides were flagged as unhelpful—all with the idea of tweaking the lecture on the basis of student feedback.

The article goes on to describe the positive aspects of "data-driven teaching" as well as the challenges associated with using LectureTools. One of Professor Samson's colleagues is featured as he tries to apply the program in a class. The president of the Association of American Universities is quoted as well as the provost at Michigan, Martha Pollack: "I still think there is an enormous amount of data that you can capture and analyze without turning classrooms into controlled laboratories." She added, "My goal is not to ensure that every single faculty member changes the way they teach. My goal is to have a group of people who are excited about innovation and who are trying out new sorts of things."

The proposed new thing, "Can Universities Use Data to Fix What Ails the Lecture?," is really just a subset of a larger question, "Should universities use feedback to improve student learning?" The answer is . . . yes. Next question: "Now, how do we go about doing it?" That should be the examined life of the academy and yet a remarkable 250 (and still counting) comments seem to suggest otherwise. A handful of the comments were thoughtful and attempted to explore the challenge of engaging students in a lecture hall setting and the viability of using LectureTools and other methods to generate student feedback.

But that view was overwhelmed by an avalanche of finger-pointing and misdirection:

Blame the student—"It's not the teaching, it's the taught."
Blame the faculty—"Technology is not the solution for faculty members who can't be bothered to put a little thought and effort into their teaching."
Blame the technology—"A fool with a tool is still a fool."
Blame the facilities—"I was in large lecture classes as a freshman and decided to buy the notes rather than attend class."
Blame the administration—"Large lecture halls are significant cash cows for universities, the giant lecture hall will never go away."
Blame the data—"There are more negatives than positives from data-driven instruction."

Unfortunately, while student learning should remain the paramount concern, the single loop, everyone-but-me response by many shut down the ability of others to have a productive conversation. Few took the opportunity to reason and reflect; most saw the topic as an opportunity to spew rhetoric and seek out others to confirm their own wisdom.

GERUNDS AND BEYOND

There is every reason to believe that colleges and universities are particularly challenged when it comes to embracing feedback as a means to learn and grow. That does not mean it doesn't happen. It only means that it isn't part of the culture of higher education. We have a professional population that is dominated by individuals who themselves are products of higher learning. But as we have seen, a room full of smart people with PhDs may very well have acquired a learning disability by being unwilling or unable to challenge their own thinking.

But the disease itself need not be terminal. Many individuals and institutions have developed methods for living an examined life. The generic phrase *embracing feedback* can be disaggregated to reveal a number of gerund-driven approaches that have proven to be successful at overcoming higher education's learning disabilities and, in turn, drive upward spirals. They include: leveraging, nudging, applying, listening, tightening, and closing.

Leveraging

Leveraging is the act of using something to maximum advantage. A survey of senior academic affairs officers found that 84 percent of their institutions had common learning goals for students, up from 74 percent four years ago. But the report from the National Institute for Learning Outcome Assessment found that the "prime driver" for assessment efforts was unchanged from the last survey: pressure from regional and specialized accreditation agencies.[13] Pressure? Being accredited is mandatory in order for an institution's students to receive federal financial aid. So, if you have to do it, why not take advantage of feedback from your peers to learn and grow?

In June 2012 Lebanon Valley College was placed on warning by its accreditor because it had no good mechanisms for assessing student learning. The story of how Lebanon Valley responded is described in an article with a subheading that begins, "An Accreditor's Warning Forced Lebanon Valley to Take a Hard Look. . . ." Forced? Later in the article it was noted that after a year or so of wrangling, "something else, too, appears to have happened along the way. Many of those most closely involved in Lebanon Valley's fight to retain accreditation say the college managed to recover its soul in the process. . ... The warning from Middle State forced a rare level of self-analysis, and the picture was not always pretty."[14]

Feedback is the gift that keeps on giving.

Nudging

Feedback in higher education is too often viewed in a zero-sum-game context: if you acquiesce to feedback it is because something is wrong and needs to be fixed. Feedback is not about blaming or fixing; it is about nudging. There is a saying in the process-improvement literature that says it best: "Once you declare something perfect, you lose the opportunity to improve it." That is why the language and tools associated with institutional effectiveness models and continuous improvement are so critical to building momentum in colleges and universities. It doesn't matter where you start because the purpose is not to rank and sort but to provide the information required to make necessary adjustments.

Maria Shine Stewart makes this point in a 2013 essay on performance evaluations: "Evaluations should nudge growth, not beat up or coddle." She enumerates a series of best practices designed to "help nudge growth, activate potential, and genuinely reduce deficits."[15] Similarly, Sanford Shugart, the president of Valencia College, a winner of the Aspen Prize for Community College Excellence, has offered a detailed look at the completion agenda in an article, "Moving the needle on college completion, thoughtfully," in which he begins by zeroing in on a simple imperative: "measure for improvement."[16] The examined life of a college or university is an exercise in progress, in seeking ways to get better and better, not in identifying winners and losers.

Applying

We often tell our students (and our children) that they need to apply themselves, meaning to work hard or spend a significant amount of time on something. In a related fashion, we need to be applying feedback in a consistent way in order to maximize learning. The first way to do this is by developing a mind-set that every significant event or critical process needs an evaluative component. The U.S. Army has developed such an approach—the after action review (AAR)—which now has become known and adopted by other organizations. Simply put, it is a structured review or de-briefing process for analyzing *what* happened, *why* it happened, and *how* it can be done better by the participants and those responsible.

Another way that feedback needs to be applied is through consistency over time. Comparative data are particularly useful for pointing out deviations from a norm—for example, "What is our six-year graduation rate compared to a set of peer institutions?" In contrast, longitudinal data are useful in another way—to identify trends (a key component of "The Iceberg" that answers the question, "What's been happening?"). Applying feedback consistently over time is critical to learning and the development of virtuous cycles. And yet, how many times do colleges and universities conduct a campus climate survey for a year or two (perhaps as part of accreditation) and then walk away? As organizations, we need to apply feedback in a more consistent way.

Listening

The most important precursor to a doom loop is denial. And the best way to actualize denial is by not listening. There are two illustrations of this idea (and its antidote) from colleges that have already been discussed. One is Houston Community College (in chapter 2). It was a ripped-from-the-headlines example of an institution that had lost the trust of the community. All of the dynamics of a downward spiral were present. But it was also noted that there had been "four or five years of relative calm" before the latest upheavals. During that time (under stable leadership), the institution implemented an annual comprehensive climate survey. What was unique about the survey was that senior leaders met after the survey results were in, analyzed the feedback, and identified a series of action steps to address the identified challenges. The actions steps were released at the same time the survey results were made available—here is what we are hearing and here is what we plan to do about it. And they did.

The first year's response rate was low. Few people believed. Then the results were communicated and changes were made. The second year's response rate was higher. Maybe they really are listening? More changes happened. The response rate soared in the third year. The following year saw key administrators leave under difficult circumstances. Doubt crept back in. The survey wasn't done that year. The institution stopped listening.[17]

Endicott College (chapter 7) was identified as an institution that has been on a roll after years of challenges. Richard Wylie, the college president, noted the early pattern, "I would bring my lawyer in. The union would bring its lawyer in." Eventually they moved to impact bargaining with talks held outside the formal contract-negotiation processes. A long list of structured listening devices followed. Some involved monthly campus forums and campus-wide planning meetings while others, like the annual Paint Day, became community building sessions. And, as mentioned, in 2012 was recognized for its collaborative governance in the Chronicle of Higher Education's Great Place to Work For survey. The institution started listening.

Tightening

Another important element of efforts to create thriving institutions is by tightening up feedback loops. It is obvious that more and better feedback is critical to organizational learning. But it has also been noted that one of the most problematic aspects of loosely coupled systems is the information lag. Our divisions and departments, our stratifications and categorizations, create barriers to timely feedback that connects cause and effect. Our standards, practices and culture also contribute to this disconnect.

A good illustration occurs every day in college courses. If the main purpose of an exam is to decide what to do next, rather than to merely rank and sort the students, then just giving a midterm and final exam (especially in semester-long course of fourteen to sixteen weeks) is waiting too long before being able to make adjustments. Fortunately, a host of systems have been made available recently to provide faculty, students, and counselors with early alerts and kudos that effectively tighten up the feedback loops. University of Texas, El Paso, is using Zoom In to engage students; Davidson County Community College has adopted Starfish Retention Solutions, which, among other features, sends positive feedback or kudos to students' mobile devices; and University of Michigan is building its early warning tool, called Student Explorer, which keeps advisors in the (shortened) loop.

The examined life should mean developing a sense of urgency, a driving desire to evaluate the effectiveness of our efforts in a timely fashion so that we have the information we need to catalyze advancement.

Closing

Generating feedback is only step 1. The problem is that too often, especially in an accountability-driven environment, it ends there. We can check something off. We fill out a form that states that we have met a minimum requirement. But step 2 involves "closing the loop" such that positive adjustments are possible. A simple illustration is the ubiquitous campus climate survey. These surveys are administered, results are tabulated, and a report is distributed. It is almost like saying, "There, we asked your opinion," with little or no effort to use the results in any meaningful way to challenge assumptions or change current practices.

A more specific example comes from the earlier-mentioned report, "Knowing What Students Know and Can Do," which documented the increased use of assessments such as the Community College Survey of Student Engagement (CCSSE) and the University of California's Undergraduate Experience Survey. But the lead author, George Kuh, also comments that "by far the most disappointing finding" was the degree to which institutions actually put the data to use. They didn't. They measured, they congratulated themselves for being so reflective, and then they walked away. The loop never gets closed and changes are never made.

In summary, colleges and universities that become better practitioners at embracing feedback (and all of its component gerunds) benefit in another critically important way—*buffering*. The amplifying effect of virtuous cycles creates an abundance of goodwill and makes the institution much more resilient. We know that bad things will happen. A high-velocity environment almost ensures there will be bumps and bruises along the way. But like shock absorbers on a car or truck, virtuous cycles build on the organizational capability to deal with those negative events and quickly bounce back.

EMBRACING SUMMARY

The advertisement for a free webinar offered by *Inside Higher Ed* is titled "The Evolving Curriculum: Measuring Effectiveness of Change." The initial paragraph states:

> Colleges and universities are constantly rethinking what they teach—at just about every level. Individual professors consider what worked (or didn't) in their courses. Departments ask whether their requirements for majors need revisions. Entire colleges and universities debate approaches to general education, majors and graduation requirements. In American higher education today, there is no one single curricular trend—one college may focus on reading lists or general education, while another explores the use of badges or competency education to move away from relying on traditional courses and degrees.[18]

So far, so good.

The next paragraph, however, begins with the following sentence, "But the common thread in these shifts is that colleges are responding to increased demands for accountability by asking for more evidence that particular approaches work, and looking for ways to measure the outcomes of their reforms." This statement reinforces everything that is wrong with accountability as a driving force for change. By allowing ourselves to be held accountable, we are, as the statement says, "responding" and the necessary result is denial, obfuscation, and other characteristics of a threat-rigidity response. Apparently, we measure, we rethink, and we evolve because we are told to do so. And we will be held accountable if we don't.

The contrasting paradigm—one that is purpose driven, intrinsic, and seeks to demonstrate responsibility—can be found in a quote by Robert Fritz:

> There is one major telltale sign that an organization is advancing: Its achievements are a platform for further achievements. For an organization that is advancing, everything counts; even those things that don't work are transformed into significant learning that eventual leads to success.[19]

If an institution develops the capacity for reflection, for examination, it embraces the process of asking difficult questions. When those questions suggest positive outcomes, it doesn't get comfortable but instead looks to push its collective ambition. It seeks to create new tensions around even greater aspirations. And "when things don't work," the discrepancy is embraced as an opportunity to seek understanding and then to take positive, corrective actions.

This is flourishing; the other is merely trying to survive.

NOTES

1. Chris Argyris, *On Organizational Learning* (Malden, MA: Blackwell, 1999).

2. "Voice of the Graduate," McKinsey & Co., May 2013, http://mckinseyonsociety.com/downloads/reports/Education/UXC001%20Voice%20of%20the%20Graduate%20v7.pdf.

3. Michael Cochran, "Creating Upward Spirals of Change of Positive Well-Being: A Psychological Approach," PhD dissertation, April 2010, available at Proquest, http://gradworks.umi.com/34/00/3400971.html.

4. Rosabeth Moss Kanter, *Confidence* (New York: Crown Business, 2004).

5. See Daniel H. Kim, *Introduction to Systems Thinking* (Waltham, MA: Pegasus Communications), 1999.

6. John Kilbourne, "Moving at the Speed of Academe," *Chronicle of Higher Education*, October 8, 2012, http://chronicle.com/article/Moving-at-the-Speed-of-Academe/134890.

7. Erland Stevens, "Measuring Success Is Not Easy," *Inside Higher Ed,* August 11, 2014.

8. Spurgeon Thompson, "The Unnecessary Agony of Student Evaluations," *Chronicle of Higher Education*, March 1, 2013, http://chronicle.com/blogs/conversation/2013/03/01/the-unnecessary-agony-of-student-evaluations.

9. Allison M. Vaillancourt, "Do You Want Feedback or Validation?," *Chronicle of Higher Education*, December 9, 2013, http://chronicle.com/blogs/onhiring/do-you-want-feedback-or-validation-2/42539.

10. See Dana H. Lindsley, Daniel J. Brass, and James B. Thomas, "Efficacy-Performance Spirals: A Multilevel Perspective," *Academy of Management Review* 20, no. 3 (1995).

11. Chris Argyris, "Teaching Smart People How to Learn," *Harvard Business Review*, May 1991.

12. Steven Kolowich, "Can Universities Use Data to Fix What Ails the Lecture?," *Chronicle of Higher Education*, August 11, 2014, http://chronicle.com/article/Can-Colleges-Use-Data-to-Fix/148307.

13. George D. Kuh, Natasha Jankowski, Stanley O Ikenberry, and Jillian Kinzie, "Knowing What Students Know and Can Do: The Current State of Student Learning Outcomes Assessment in U.S. Colleges and Universities," National Institute for Learning Outcomes Assessment, January 2014, www.learningoutcomesassessment.org/knowingwhatstudentsknowandcando.html.

14. Jack Stripling, "How a College Took Assessment to Heart: An Accreditor's Warning Forced Lebanon Valley to Take a Hard Look at the Cost of Its Quest for Survival," *Chronicle of Higher Education*, September 30, 2013, http://chronicle.com/article/How-a-College-Took-Assessment/141963.

15. Maria Shine Stewart, "Evaluations Should Nudge Growth, Not Beat Up or Coddle," *Inside Higher Ed*, June 13, 2013, www.insidehighered.com/advice/2014/06/13/evaluations-should-nudge-growth-not-beat-or-coddle-essay.

16. Sanford C. Shugart, "Moving the Needle on College Completion, Thoughtfully," *Inside Higher Ed*, February 7, 2013, www.insidehighered.com/views/2013/02/07/moving-needle-college-completion-thoughtfully-essay.

17. Peter Schmidt, "Great Places to Work for 2012," *Chronicle of Higher Education*, August 5, 2012, http://chronicle.com/article/AdministratorsProfessors/133307.

18. The June 11, 2014, webinar, "The Evolving Curriculum: Measuring Effectiveness of Change," can be seen at www.insidehighered.com/audio/2014/06/11/evolving-curriculum-measuring-effectiveness-change.

19. Robert Fritz, *The Path of Least Resistance for Managers* (San Francisco: Berrett-Koehler, 1999).

Chapter 10

Gumption Junction

Demonstrating the Courage to Create

In Robert Pirsig's classic work, *Zen and the Art of Motorcycle Maintenance* (1974), he explores the underlying metaphysics of Western culture on a motorcycle trip from Minneapolis to San Francisco with his young son. At some point in his long journey he states, "I like the word 'gumption' because it's so homely and so forlorn and so out of style it looks as if it needs a friend and isn't likely to reject anyone who comes along." I like it also because it describes exactly what happens to someone who connects with quality. He gets filled with gumption:

> A person filled with gumption doesn't sit around dissipating and stewing about things. He's at the front of the train of his own awareness, watching to see what's up the track and meeting it when it comes. That's gumption.
>
> If you're going to repair a motorcycle, an adequate supply of gumption is the first and most important tool. If you haven't got that you might as well gather up all the other tools and put them away, because they won't do you any good.[1]

This is a very personal, inwardly focused observation. At the very soul of any worthwhile endeavor is a commitment to the work itself. Having the appropriate set of resources is a "necessary but insufficient condition" for completing any meaningful effort. First and foremost is having the guts and the grit to actually make things happen. All the wrenches and ratchets in the world won't help if you don't have the gumption necessary for committing to and completing the task at hand—motorcycle maintenance or otherwise.

Momentum caused by virtuous cycles cannot be announced by the board of trustees. Individuals can't do it. The most charismatic, grit-filled CEO is incapable of creating momentum on her own. Events can't do it, either. A large, impressive grant won't be enough. A redesigned website and an aggressive marketing campaign don't generate sustainable growth. A spike in enrollment is just an event.

But imagine what might happen if we were able to bring together groups of individuals who were willing and able to demonstrate the courage to create?

In a 2010 TED Talk by Derek Sivers titled "How to Start a Movement," he narrates a video that begins with dozens of people calmly sitting on a hillside listening to music.[2] Then, off to the side, a solitary, shirtless, young man is inspired to dance. He flails around. His arms pump upward and his legs shoot out in impossibly different directions. What he profoundly lacks in technique, he more than makes up for in sheer joy. A short time later a second person joins the young man. Sivers analyzes this interaction. First, he emphasizes that the leader embraces the "first follower" as an equal by dancing *with* him. Almost immediately it is apparent that it isn't about the leader anymore; it is about *them* (plural). Sivers then describes the crucial role of the first follower by observing, "He's going to show everyone else how to follow." Moreover, by joining the solitary reveler the first follower plays another important role: "The first follower is what transforms a lone nut into a leader."

Before long, another person joins the festivities—"Now it's not a lone nut, it's not two nuts, three is a crowd and a crowd is news." As a few more people join in, Sivers goes on to say, "So a movement must be public. It's important to show not just the leader but the followers because the new followers emulate the followers not the leader." He then adds in describing the rapidly changing scene, "Now here come two more people and immediately after three more people. Now we've got momentum. This is the tipping point. Now we've got a movement." And by the end of the three-minute video the mildly tranquil scene is transformed into a vibrant dance party.

What happens if we are able to bring together groups of individuals who are able to demonstrate the courage to create? Gumption junction.

This final chapter begins by contrasting two different futures—one extending the current loosely coupled, threat-rigidity model into the future and the other taking responsibility for creating a new future based on the dynamics of virtuous cycles. Courage, it is explained, is central to a compelling, shared future. Next, it will be shown that the lessons described in the previous chapters are not easily implemented without a healthy dose of that same gumption.

The forces of gravity—and mediocrity—will not give up without a fight.

CONTRASTING FUTURES

Inertia is largely what we are currently experiencing in our colleges and universities and it is having profound, headline-grabbing consequences. A high-velocity environment is a given. We can't argue or explain that away. As was described in the first chapter, environmental factors are interacting in powerful ways. The strong emergence we are experiencing, in turn, places an enormous strain on our loosely coupled systems that have worked well for us in the more stable environments of the past. The lack of interdependency, coordination, and information flow didn't really matter. Indeed, you may recall (in chapter 1) the fictitious head of Huxley College, President Wagestaff, who invoked the credo: "If it's working, keep doing it. If it's not working, stop doing it. If you don't know what to do, don't do anything."

Unfortunately, the result of this mismatch of environment and system is a structure that often oscillates because the organizational learning is only adaptive in nature. It is largely about reacting to problems. And as the number and scale of problems mount, the primary posture adopted is an increasingly defensive one. Problems are interpreted as threats to the status quo and to the professionals' autonomy. The resulting rigidity is then interpreted by our external stakeholders as arrogance, with predictable calls to hold higher education more accountable. In the end, the tendency is to do nothing and the system remains unchanged—inertia.

A "new order of things" begins with colleges and universities embracing a desire to create their own futures. A conscious choice is made to be responsible for that future by taking action no matter what the circumstances. The primary tool is a virtuous cycle that is generative in terms of its organizational learning and has an advancing structure that amplifies growth in this structure. Problems are interpreted as opportunities for improvement. The system moves in the direction of more interdependence, more coordination, and more information flow. It becomes increasingly resilient, and in spite of the high-velocity environment, the organization is able to gain traction and experience real momentum.

These contrasting futures are summarized in Table 10.1.

One of these futures requires a tremendous amount of courage; the other does not.

Threat-Rigidity and Accountability

With this future it is important to reemphasize a singular truth: while inertia is a powerful force in any organization, it possesses Herculean qualities in

Table 10.1 Contrasting Futures

	Inertia	*Momentum*
Environment	High velocity	High velocity
System	Loosely coupled	Moderately coupled
Structure	Oscillating	Advancing
Learning	Adaptive	Generative
Tools	Threat-rigidity	Virtuous cycles
Paradigm	Accountability	Responsibility

higher education. You may remember what Henry Mintzberg stated were the major challenges associated with Professional Bureaucracies: (1) they do not work well in complex unstable environments and (2) they do not have much capacity to develop and pursue a single, integrated strategy. While we have written in detail about the former reality—and the resulting event-management dynamic of finding and fixing problems—it is also critical to elaborate a bit more on the second challenge.

There are many cohesive ways to move an organization forward with each option having its own set of pros and cons. After the appropriate amount of analyses, most organizations are capable of choosing a path forward.

The defining challenge for higher education, however, has been simply stated by Clark Kerr, the former president of the University of California: "The status quo is the only solution that cannot be vetoed."

Trying to align faculty, staff, and administrators around a compelling shared vision is tough enough, but then choosing a distinct set of strategies for advancing the institution is often vetoed by any one of the many individuals or internal stakeholder groups. The result is inaction because individual elements act in their own self-interest. That inertia, then, results in the use of threat-rigidity tools to deal with the inevitable problems that arise in a dynamic, high-velocity environment.

The essence of this threat-rigidity is on full display in a 2013 *Chronicle of Higher Education* opinion piece by one professor of sociology titled, "A Machiavellian Guide to Destroying Public Universities in 12 Easy Steps":

1. Denigrate public education, and public institutions in general, a drains on private wealth and "job makers" to the point that no one would dare ask for increased support.
2. Take advantage of economic downturns to instigate "taxpayer outrage" in order to remove support from public universities so that they must either raise tuition or cut back on their programs.
3. As state support recedes, encourage student loan system that will create a "market for higher education."
4. Install new public-management tactics borrowed from public-interest theory to wrestle control from faculty governance systems.
5. Out into place various "oversight instruments," such as quality-assessment exercises, "outcomes matrices," or auditing mechanisms, to assure "transparency" and "accountability to stakeholders."
6. Increase the reliance on part-time faculty members and one-year contracts to teach most courses.
7. Scream about the high cost of higher education and increases in tuition.
8. Promote narrow vocationalism and STEM areas to show that you are in tune with the demands of the "knowledge economy" and will no longer tolerate puffy and useless subjects like history or literature.

9. Limit the contractual rights of faculty members.
10. Bring in outside consultants such as Bain & Company or McKinsey & Company to convince boards and administrators of the urgent need for "disruptive innovation" or other ideas championed by Harvard Business School gurus.
11. Introduce a "competency-based" education model that allows students to bypass many of the traditional requirements of the university.
12. Finally, use public relations and advertising campaigns to divert attention from the nasty consequence of all of those reforms.[3]

While this quotation-mark-laden diatribe inspired 174 comments, many of which sought to add to the number of "easy steps," the totality of the responses can be distilled down to: "Leave me alone and let me get back to what I have been doing." Even if you agree, as many would, with some of the destructive forces being presented, it does not acknowledge our need to accept responsibility for creating a new and different future.

As loosely coupled institutions, being *less* interdependent, *less* coordinated, and with *less* information flow is easy. Heaps really are easy. Adopting the status quo by default is not an act of courage, nor are impassioned displays of victimhood. As Pirsig suggests, while "sitting around dissipating and stewing about things" may be cathartic, it doesn't actually change anything.

Rather, these approaches amount to nothing more than a future that is, essentially, *an abdication of responsibility*.

Responsibility and Virtuous Cycles

This future begins at a very different point. Whereas the accountability paradigm is the *effect* that a loosely coupled, threat-rigidity model *causes*, a responsibility paradigm is the *cause* of virtuous cycles of change that lead to the *effect*—momentum in our colleges and universities. And at the very core of this alternative future is a conscious choice rather than a future by default. The authors of *Lift* (2009), referenced in chapter 2, describe that choice:

> The question "What result do I want to create?" energizes people because it leads them to pursue results that are self-determined and that challenge them in positive ways. Creating implies doing something positive, difficult, and new rather than relying on existing expectations about what can and cannot be done.[4]

A future that begins with accepting responsibility is one empowered by a sense of self-determination. The research on Positive Organizational Scholarship discussed earlier is clear that self-determination facilitates positive deviance. When people experience self-determination, they see themselves in control of their own destiny—their reasons for taking action are internally motivated rather than coerced by external forces. Rather than playing the role of the victim, self-determination moves individuals and organizations into a realm of positivity even to the point that it is shown to lead to increasing levels of transcendent behavior (i.e., behavior that goes beyond ordinary standards or expectations).[5] At best, calls for holding higher education more accountable will result in compliance. It is only through a conscious choice to create a different future that real commitment will happen in our institutions.

The Aspen Institute has awarded the Aspen Prize for Community Excellence every two years since 2011. Selection is based on exceptional student outcomes in four areas: student learning, certificate and degree completion, employment and earnings, and high levels of access and success for minority and low-income students. In the foreword to the book *What Excellent Community Colleges Do* (2014), which describes the program, Anthony Carnevale states:

> The community colleges featured in this book are almost a decade into a significant reform movement aimed toward sorting out missions and measureable outcome standards. They are exceptional not only for the outcomes they have achieved for students—which is, let's be clear, the most important measure of success—but also because these institutions have achieved these reforms and practices absent the kinds of widespread incentives and shifts that drive change in industry.[6]

Carnevale continues that while community colleges face enormous pressure from shifting demands to unpredictable and insufficient funding, some institutions have not waited to be reformed through various market mechanisms. Some have reformed—and perhaps never stopped reforming—themselves. They are practicing self-determination.

For example, Santa Barbara City College is the cowinner of the 2013 prize. The school's Express to Success program is described as offering learning communities in developmental math and English for underprepared students. Students in each cohort have the same instructors for their courses, sign commitment agreements, work collaboratively both inside and outside of the classroom, and take at least twelve units a semester. The program has a noteworthy 90 percent retention rate. But what is remarkable is the development and implementation of Express to Success occurred during the recession years as state funds for California community colleges were being cut by $1.5 billion and course offerings reduced by 25 percent.

A similar sentiment concerning the importance of choice and self-determination has been voiced by Shah Ardalan, the president of Lone Star College's University Park campus. The Completion Agenda, as we have discussed, has generated a certain amount of push back from colleges and universities.

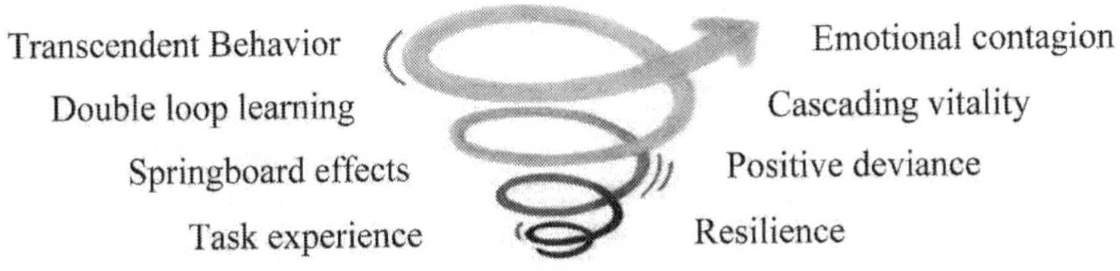

Transcendent Behavior   Emotional contagion

Double loop learning   Cascading vitality

Springboard effects   Positive deviance

Task experience   Resilience

Figure 10.1   Spiral Dynamics

Some argue that those external agencies that have driven the debate are solely interested in results—at any cost—and the quantity versus quality argument is usually then invoked. At the community college level, the additional concerns are that the historical focus on access will be diluted and, of course, the standard complaint that students are just not college ready. President Ardalan dismisses these arguments by refocusing on what is possible: "As for 'completion,' the students took the hardest step and came. The rest is my and my team's responsibility to help them reach their highest potential."[7]

No excuses. Take people where you find them and help them go as far as they can.

Taking responsibility is the necessary starting point. With that in hand, a college or university has a license to aspire and can turn its attention to approaches and strategies that will allow it to gain traction and move forward. Reinforcing loops that are virtuous, as we have seen, can be powerful tools to be used for exercising such responsibility. Indeed, all of the spiral dynamics that have been described in earlier chapters are there waiting to be unleashed (Figure 10.1), if and only if there is that commitment to a new and different future.

In the end, being held accountable is all about compliance. Our own inaction has led to stark choices: comply or don't comply with the wishes of others. This passivity is simply the default option resulting in energy-draining skirmishes and ever-increasing defensive wounds. We need to commit to our own preferred future, one that will take more than a little gumption to create.

A BIAS FOR COURAGEOUS PRINCIPLED ACTION

Talking is not doing. In both of our contrasting futures, the paradigms have modifiers. As we have discussed, adhering to the status quo results in a paradigm whose modifier is often "holding" or "being held." While this is certainly an action, it is usually within the context of being punitive. Also, the locus of control is predominantly external. Someone else is holding us accountable in order to generate conformance or compliance to their standards. Most people chafe under such circumstances and academics are certainly no exception (in fact they are probably the rule).

This final section speaks to the importance of the modifier that has been associated with the responsibility paradigm. The term *demonstrating* responsibility has been used throughout this book on purpose. *Demonstrating* within the context of this future involves purposeful action. This is focused behavior. It is conscious and intentional, guided by an institution's desire to achieve a specific goal. It also involves energy. Purposeful action implies that the institution is willing to exert effort to achieve that goal.

Monica Worline and Ryan Quinn devote an entire chapter in *Positive Organization Scholarship* (2003) to this topic. It is titled "Courageous Principled Action" and can be summarized as follows:

> Courageous principled action unlocks the possibility for change because it presents news ways to develop relationships, adaptations to existing rules and roles, alterations for goals, and new ways to approach problems and choice opportunities. Courageous principled action is risky, and can end up with the courageous actor becoming ostracized, leaving the organization, or engendering angry reactions. However, courageous principled action can also be adopted, encouraged, and replicated—especially if the action succeeds in its desired effect, or if it reflects values that others also feel are important. Courageous principled action can also engender positive emotion that inspires others to act as well.[8]

The last point is worth expanding on. As Albert Bandura states in *Social Learning Theory* (1977), "Most human behavior is learned observationally through modeling: from observing others one forms an idea of how new behaviors are performed, and on later occasions this coded information serves as a guide for action."[9] Much of the energy associated with virtuous cycles comes from people watching other people engaged in purposeful actions. Witnessing acts of benevolence and courage inspires others to engage in similar behaviors themselves. The trajectory of the organization is built on deeds that serve to underpin and then amplify future positive acts.

Each of our lessons requires courageous principled actions that, in many ways, are the key to unlocking the powerful dynamics of virtuous cycles or upward spirals of change.

Man's Search for Meaning

Chapter 3 was structured around a model that created discrepancy between a desired state and an actual state. That discrepancy, in turn, led to structural tension. It was argued this structural tension—or man's search for meaning—was ultimately resolved through purpose-filled actions. This is the essence of advancement.

But it is extraordinarily difficult to realize this level of divine discontent. First, we usually don't want to hear, "We can do better." Much of the research described earlier noted the profound lack of uniqueness in most vision statements. The words *is* or *will continue to be* were more often used than *will be* or *aspires to be*. The statements themselves were dominated by generalizations about excellence and quality that made it impossible to discriminate one institution from another. A vision like "VWX College will continue to be an active partner in building and maintaining the academic excellence and economic vitality of the diverse communities it serves" is hardly an act of courage. It may provide solace to some that the institution has proclaimed to have already achieved "academic excellence," but it does not inspire anyone to strive for a better future.

The other part of the equation involves speaking truth about the actual state. Jim Collins puts it simply in *Good to Great* (2001) when he writes, "Yes. Leadership is about vision. But leadership is equally about creating a climate where the truth is heard and the brutal facts confronted."[10] The example used earlier involved Martin Luther King's understanding that, while his vision of the mountaintop was critical, it was equally important to showcase the day-to-day, brutal realities of segregation. It was the discrepancy between his dream and the truth that provided the energy and focus for the equal rights movement (emphasis on *movement*).

For our purposes, one of the best illustrations of the importance of truth is what happens in its absence. After facing a series of controversies, Pima Community College was placed on probation by its accreditor in 2012, all the while generally defending its actions. Among other things, the college had been accused of ignoring issues of sexual harassment and moving too quickly to change its admission policies. But the college's 2013 report in response to its accreditation woes took a very different, and gutsy, approach by both admitting the problems and apologizing for them. The college's statement as reported by the *Arizona Daily Star* includes:

- "We accept full responsibility and say we are profoundly sorry for the serious breaches of integrity."
- "The era of inattention and heedlessness is over."
- "We failed to respond quickly and give proper credence to allegations of sexual misconduct."
- "Our constituents, stakeholders and colleagues spoke, but we did not listen. For this, we are truly sorry."[11]

Vicious cycles exist in part because of a lack of veracity; virtuous cycles exist largely because of a presence of it. Pima may well have used the simple, courageous act of being truthful to change the trajectory of its future.

Again, it needs to be emphasized that the nature of higher education is to lean toward comfort rather than purpose. It is who we are (or who we have been). Any organized change effort is initially perceived as a threat to individuals' independence, often wrapped in the cloak of academic freedom and shared governance. Then we go to great lengths to demonize and marginalize efforts to alter the status quo (e.g., "The Machiavellian Guide . . .") and promote policies and people who will deliver on the assurance of safety and security.

A useful example is described by Jim Walker, the former president of Moorpark College and a search consultant with Community College Search Services for over a decade. He says that most search committees ask fairly predictable questions and most candidates have the experience to do well in answering those questions. So, what makes the difference? Walker states, "When the candidates are evaluated after the interviews—what matters? It's all about personality, warmth, enthusiasm, perceived accessibility and 'will he/she leave me alone and let me do my job.' In other words it's an intangible 'comfort level' with the candidate that matters most."[12]

The act of creating structural tension in a college or university takes gumption.

The War Canoe

The metaphor of the war canoe in chapter 4 spoke to the need of having a pointy end to our vessel (mission, vision, and values) and then filling it with capable, like-minded oarsman (faculty, staff, and administrators) who can dig deep and lean in. Using Senge's arrow models, intentional movement only occurs when personal visions of individuals (the little arrows) begin to align with a compelling shared vision for the institution (the big arrow). Aligning people and processes was described as being essential to creating coherence and momentum in our colleges and universities.

But the obvious challenge is that Mintzberg's "Professional Bureaucracy," Wieck's "loosely coupled system," and Birnbaum's "cybernetics" are all based on a structure that empowers individuals to act autonomously. Indeed, as we know from previous research, individuals self-select into the academy for precisely that reason—an environment in which they are free to act independent of others.

Steven Salaita's appointment to the faculty at the University of Illinois–Urbana Champaign should have been routine after a search committee in the American Indian Studies program recommended his hiring. But after bloggers and others drew attention to Salaita's "uncivil" comments on Twitter, the university's chancellor, Phyllis Wise, made the decision to not forward the recommendation to the board of trustees for approval. She subsequently stated in a message to the campus, "What we cannot and will not tolerate at the University of Illinois are personal and disrespectful words or actions that demean and abuse either viewpoints themselves or those who express them." Tenure, she went on to say, brought with it "a heavy responsibility to continue the traditions of scholarship and civility upon which our university is built."

What followed were threats to cancel conferences at the institution, an avalanche of letters in various publications denouncing the impact on academic freedom, demonstrations at subsequent board meetings, votes of no-confidence, and the additional threat of legal action. And then it got ugly. Other campus leaders (Ohio University, Pennsylvania State University, and UC Berkeley) were similarly accused of seeking to silence speech rather than simply lowering its tone. "Civility," as Peter Schmidt begins a *Chronicle of Higher Education* article, "just might be academe's newest fighting word."[13]

Regardless of your views of this admittedly unique case, it serves to reinforce several important points. If you wish to view a college or university as a heap—independent parts that have no obligation to the whole—then difficult decisions can be rendered (or avoided altogether) fairly easy. But if, indeed, institutions of higher education are systems (any group of interacting, interrelated, or interdependent parts that form a unified whole with a specific purpose), then this requires people who are responsible for the care and feeding of the whole—and that takes significant courage.

The exact nature of that courage is the difficult struggle to find balance. The reason the system described in the responsibility paradigm has been termed "moderately coupled" is that a loosely coupled system based on a principle of "If it's working, keep doing it. If it's not working, stop doing it. If you don't know what to do, don't do anything" does not require any courageous principled actions. It merely requires a keen sense of survivability. At the other extreme, trying to implement a "tightly coupled" system in higher education (at least in the nonprofit realm) is often characterized by limited dialogue and a one-size-fits-all approach. Inevitability, this leads to the appearance of autocratic, noninclusive means that invite inevitable votes of no-confidence. Such actions also tend to put the brakes on any momentum.

The challenge is to encourage lively, and even extended, debates that are inclusive while discouraging any individual or groups from exercising a perceived right to veto power. Trying to strike the right balance that both celebrates academic freedom while also developing a collective ambition requires a healthy dose of gumption.

Black or white is a piece of cake. Gray is the color that requires guts.

The Accumulators

Deciding what assets you want to grow would seemingly be a fairly straightforward exercise. It is not. The broad issue revolves around the "deciding."

College and universities are largely populated with people who perceive themselves as being egalitarian—*asserting, resulting from, or characterized by belief in the equality of all people, especially in political, economic or social life.* These open, democratic principles are fine when it comes to much of academic life but present a challenge when it comes to such hard-edged operational issues as the allocation of scarce resources. To an economist, land, labor, and capital are the scarce resources. The growing of assets, then, is the investment of time, energy, and money in specific ways. The issue is that these are in limited supply—hence the term *scarce*. And the dilemma should be obvious: our wants are to grow all possible assets but our ability is limited to only growing some of them.

The impact is easiest to see with planning and budgeting. If step 1 (the vision) is "What do we want to create?," then step 2 (the plan) is "How do we get there?" Over the course of the last several decades, colleges and universities have gotten better at developing strategic plans with enumerated priorities and action items that are linked to mission, vision, and values. But what about step 3, which links the plan to the budget? This is where things often break down. As long as revenues are increasing, the exercise is easy because "new money" is allocated to those assets we wish to grow and those strategies that are most likely to advance the institution. But what happens when—as often has been in our recent past and probably will be for the foreseeable future—we are scrambling to just maintain what we have?

What we do is roll over the budgets. What you had is what you get. Why? Because rolling over budgets is the least contentious option. It is the accepted default. Unfortunately, there are two bad outcomes to this approach. First, any enthusiasm for planning (if there ever was any) is undermined once people figure out that it doesn't matter how well they do—they won't be rewarded for it. Indeed, the axiom is: if you don't link planning and budgeting, your budget really is your plan. Second, the rollover exercise ensures that there probably won't be any additional institutional resources dedicated to momentum-inducing assets. And the institution just bump, bump, bumps along.

Of course, the courageous allocation of scarce resources also involves human capital. An illustration is offered by Gene Hickok and Tom Shaver in a 2013 article titled "Higher Education Can't Wait" in which they speak to the issue of student costs. Conventional wisdom focuses on high tuition costs, but they note a related problem that is often overlooked—the costs associated with students graduating in five or six years instead of four. In addition to the extra 25 to 50 percent tuition costs, there are all the living expenses as well as the opportunity costs of not working. Recent data show that "bottleneck courses," that is, courses where student demand outstrips available seats, play a significant role in delaying degree completion. It explains why "access to courses" consistently ranks as the biggest student complaint about higher education, according to the Noel-Levitz annual student satisfaction survey.

According to Hickok and Shaver:

> The fix is relatively straightforward: offer those bottleneck courses more often. Just 5 to 10 percent of course are responsible for the vast majority of bottlenecks, so colleges and universities can address the shortages quickly. For instance, they can ensure that their most valuable resources—professors—are teaching the right mix of courses to prevent bottlenecks, rather than spending limited resources on courses offerings that are not needed (15–20 percent of a typical school's schedule.[14]

But, just like budgets, class schedules are notoriously rolled over with little investment being made in the design of schedules (including room-allocation software and models) that best meet students' rather than faculty members' needs. Deciding to do so is an act of courage.

Icebergs

We discussed at length in chapter 6 the problems associated with event management or the dynamic of reacting to what one sees at the surface level. The key result is oscillation in which the organization engages in daily fire drills, seemingly just trying to survive. In order to thrive, however, we needed to peek beneath the surface and examine underlying patterns and then the structures that cause those patterns to occur. All of this takes grit to accomplish because it is always easier to just glide along the surface, pretend things are okay, and, if not, blame others for the problems you are facing.

But the real need for gumption occurs even deeper. It occurs with our own mental models or those "deeply ingrained assumptions, generalizations, or even pictures or images that influence how we understand the world and how we take action." James O'Toole, a senior fellow in business ethics at Santa Clara University and the author of many leadership books, states:

> All organizations—nations, colleges, businesses and families—hold on to such fundamental and unexamined myths. While such shared values and assumptions are necessary to hold a group together, if the glue that binds them is in fact, toxic, it can result in organizational morbidity. That's why managers in companies with healthy cultures continually challenge old assumptions, rethink basic premises, question, revise, and unlearn outmoded truths.[15]

Looking through the pages of this book, it can be seen that virtually every aspect of various bold imaginings has been a function of *unlearning an outmoded truth*. The most comprehensive outmoded truth is that each institution, each organizational unit, and each program of study is some-how special. In spite of the fact that more and better studies are being done now than ever before (e.g. the Completion Agenda) this canard is used to dismiss the results as not being relevant to "us" due to the special and deli-cate nuances of any particular institution. This is the functional opposite of NIMBY (Not in My Back Yard) or OIMBY (Only in My Back Yard). If my institution didn't develop it, vote on it, and implement it successfully, it doesn't warrant my attention. This is a toxic mental model.

The list of outmoded truths in higher education is stubbornly long. For example, for years many community colleges clung to the belief that shorten-ing an eighteen-week semester would negatively impact student success. This idea was especially prevalent among professors in specific disciplines who believed that (1) there was so much critical content in their courses and (2) the students were not well prepared and didn't have the ability to move at a faster pace. This "truth" remained unexamined until the evidence made clear that with eighteen-week semesters "life gets in the way," causing most students to drop out not because of the tortuous pace but because of car problems, work conflicts, and so on.

Others on the list? There is the long-held belief that more choice is good and that students really just need access and opportunity—exploration is the key. But the evidence is clear that more structure and fewer choices in many programs increase student success. Having late registration was good because, again, it is all about access. But the data are clear that you are not doing students any favors at all. Those same students drop out and fail at significantly higher rates than those who are ready to learn on the very first day. We assumed that remediation (non-credit) worked and was needed to get students "college ready." But it doesn't work. What works is a clear path to graduation with redesigned first-year classes and built-in, just-in-time tutor-ing and support.

We have a lot of unlearning to do, and unlearning takes a lot more gump-tion than learning.

Bootstrapping

Managing the angle of approach is not for the faint of heart. In a high-velocity environment there is pressure to do something dramatic—to go big. President Sullivan of the University of Virginia, you may recall, was roundly criticized by members of her board for being an "incrementalist." The implication was that she lacked vision and was unable to bring the kind of "strategic dynamism" needed to advance the institution. Similarly, California public universities were pushed toward developing and offering MOOCs in an effort to cut costs amid pressure from Governor Jerry Brown. The governor had complained that the state's public universities were "stumbling into the future" as Silicon Valley disrupted traditional education.[16]

Of course, those in responsible positions within the academy need to balance the perceived desire to engage in disruption from outside influences with a culture that is not particularly interested in being disrupted. The ability to manage expectations in an overly stimulated environment is the key. Not doing enough will cause the board or other stakeholders to demand your resignation; doing too much, too soon, will cause the kind of embarrassment suffered by San Jose State as its MOOC experiment with Udacity crashed and burned.

But perhaps the greater challenge (and the greater need for a healthy dose of gumption) comes from our inherent tendency to play small ball. There is no doubt that many individual units within individual institutions can and do develop high-performing approaches. These are the kind of initiatives that should provide the platform for further advances. Confidence grows and winning streaks are born. But it doesn't. Instead, each best practice remains isolated and starved of the oxygen it needs to start a wildfire of amplification and growth.

A useful illustration of this challenge can be seen in the studies and reports done by the Center for Community College Student Engagement (CCCSE). The first report, "A Matter of Degrees: Promising Practices for Community College Student Success," was released in 2012. It drew attention to thirteen strategies for increasing retention and graduation rates, including fast-tracking remedial education, providing students with experiential learning, and requiring students to attend orientation. Still, it was noted that the study found "pockets of success rather than widespread improvement."

The second report came in 2013—"A Matter of Degrees: Engaging Practices, Engaging Students"—and described a dozen highly effective practices. But, again, as Kay McClenney, the director of the student engagement center comments, "Because colleges aren't requiring them. You have these innovative practices arrayed around the margins, but the rest of the college goes along untransformed."[17]

The gumption challenge is at the junction. It isn't the approaches that are the problem; it is the lack of deployment. In order to get to scale and provide the platform for further successes, leaders need to be that solitary, shirtless, young man in the TED video and "start a movement."

Peripheral Vision

Everyone is familiar with the saying of "being unable to see the forest for the trees." Systems thinking is a discipline for seeing the whole—the forest. Unfortunately, when most of us step back and peruse the landscape, we just see lots of trees. The big picture requires a different level of abstraction. You almost have to reprogram your brain to put the details on hold for a moment until the landscape comes in to focus. As simple as that sounds, it can be extremely difficult for people to step backward and work to understand the structure of the whole that emerges from the clutter of the minutiae.

This phenomenon is exacerbated in our loosely coupled institutions. While disciplinary specialization certainly has its benefits, the problem is that we are supposedly more than a collection of specialists. If our whole is greater than the sum of our parts, we need mechanisms in place to nurture that interconnectedness. We also need increased information flow that allows us to develop and share a broader understanding of the enterprise. It should be about coherency; instead, it is usually about comfort. The fact is that there is a great deal of comfort associated with limiting one's field of vision: I can deny any responsibility for any institutional issues that aren't directly related to me; I can criticize others because, again, I wasn't part of the original conversation; and I can also avoid the hard work of collaboration.

Donald Schon makes this point abundantly clear in his classic *Educating the Reflective Practitioner* (1987) when speaking about the powerful norm of individualism in universities:

> Faculty members tend to think of themselves as free-standing agents of intellectual entrepreneurship. Collaboration in groups of larger than two is rare. Prestige tends to be associated with movement out beyond the boundaries of a department to other scholarly or practice settings around the world. Hence, it is extremely difficult in a university setting to achieve focused, long-term continuity of attention and commitment to work on the institutional and intellectual problems of a school.[18]

We desperately need people—not just faculty members—within the academy to have courageous conversations about their responsibility for understanding and improving their own ecosystem, their own forest.

The Examined Life

Learning—individual and organizational—is dependent on feedback. But the examined life, one that is reflective and open to change, sometimes presents us with a conundrum: *we might not like what we see*. At its broadest level, new knowledge creation comes through experimentation, which is a trial-and-error process often resulting in failure. Research suggests that individuals who are "focused on learning" are more likely to attempt novel and difficult tasks where they are likely to fail, persevere in the face of setbacks, and take advantage of opportunities where they can gain new skills.

In contrast, individuals who are "focused on demonstrating competence" are less likely to engage in such tasks. In effect, learning and creating new knowledge is related to the individual's willingness to incur failures. The same is true for organizations. When failure is an option in organizations, individuals are less motivated to cover up their own mistakes, and more likely to use past failures from others as a source of learning and improvement.[19]

Failure due to incompetence, though, is another matter entirely. As such, there has been a lot of discussion of the what, when, and why aspects of failure in recent years across many disciplines. One of the more interesting viewpoints has been offered by Atul Gawande, a surgeon and author, in a 2012 *New Yorker* article titled "Failure and Rescue." First, he correctly notes that no one really wants a surgeon to be a "risk taker." But the research in a health care setting shows that the best hospitals aren't the ones that control or minimize risks. Their complication rates after surgery were almost the same as others. Instead, what they proved to be really good at was rescuing people when they had a complication—that is, they didn't fail less; they rescued more.

The business world is equally enthralled with failure. An April 2011 issue of *Harvard Business Review* is devoted to it—"The Failure Issue: How to Understand It, Learn from It, and Recover from It." The author of the lead article, Amy Edmondson, explores aspects of the blame game, building a learning culture, analyzing failure, and comes to the conclusion that not all failures are created equal; there are preventable failures in predictable operations, unavoidable failures in complex systems, and intelligent failures at the frontier.[20]

How do colleges and universities think about failure? We don't, really.

The primary reason goes back to our earlier discussions of Argyris' "Teaching Smart People to Learn," and the learning disabilities associated with overvaluing one's own experience. Single loop learners simply don't engage themselves and others in questioning basic assumptions. They take things for granted because those assumptions have worked for them in the past. Our resulting conversation patterns are more concerned with advocating as opposed to inquiring. We eschew vulnerability or doubt. Instead, we constantly seek to demonstrate our competence. Help-seeking behavior is another factor. Research suggests individuals who see themselves as being independent (in a loosely coupled system) are less likely to seek help. Unfortunately, help-seeking behavior has been shown to be associated with new knowledge creation. +-9

This challenge is currently being played out with our MOOC experimentation. Certainly the expectations around MOOCs were overblown in the media and, perhaps, in certain parts of higher education. The democratization of learning, a huge reduction in costs, and the Silicon Valley twist created a powerful front-page narrative. The results, predictably, are beginning to show that this is no magic bullet. But Harvard University and MIT, who together have registered more than 1 million people in seventeen MOOC courses, have "de-identified" student records and released the data to researchers. Moreover, they have also developed a suite of tools, named Insights, which will "help to guide instruction while courses are running and deepen our understanding of the impact of courses after they are complete."[21]

The promise of the technology and its ability to impact the world remains. But the question is whether higher education can embrace failure. In an NPR interview with Udacity's CEO Sebastian Thrun, his reaction was, "We try things out, we look at the data, and we learn from it." Meanwhile, back in the halls of academe, too many "no-gos" are simply eager to celebrate the bump in the road, use it as an excuse to say, "I told you so," and return to their comfort on the quad.

Why the emphasis on courage across all these elements of virtuous cycles? Why is it important to man's search for meaning, the examined life, and everything in between? Perhaps Winston Churchill said it best: "Courage is rightly esteemed the first of human qualities . . . because it is the quality which guarantees all others."

IMAGINING A DIFFERENT FUTURE

It should be clear that all of this will take some gumption. The status quo is our status quo. While we may not be thrilled with all the buffeting and badgering we are receiving, we can take solace in what we know. And we know that colleges and universities in this country have been beacons of democracy and hope, and the envy of the world for decades and decades. Change, any change, is perceived as perilous because we cannot be sure of what that change will bring.

It is, simply, incredibly difficult to imagine a different future.

Patrick Awuah was born in Ghana. He came to the United States and graduated from Swarthmore College with degrees in engineering and economics and then received an MBA from UC Berkeley's Haas School of Business. He worked as a program manager for Microsoft, where, among other things, he spearheaded the development of dial-up internet working technologies and gained a reputation for bringing difficult projects to completion. After living and working in the United States for two decades, Awuah returned to his native Ghana in 2001 and founded Ashesi University in Accra, the capital, with thirty students.

The private, not-for-profit institution was designed to blend the liberal arts method of education with majors in computer science, management information systems, and business administration. Ashesi quickly gained a reputation for innovation and quality education in Ghana and, more than a decade later, is partnering with the Melton Foundation to add a global citizenship program and with the Clinton Global Initiative to begin offering an engineering degree. It now has 630 students, half of whom are women, and has clearly set its sights even higher—"By raising the bar for higher education in Ghana we aim to make a significant contribution towards a renaissance in Africa."[22]

In 2013, Ashesi's president traveled to Babson College in Massachusetts to receive an honorary doctorate and deliver the commencement address. In part, Awuah said:

> To really make change, we must have courage: the courage to imagine something new, the courage to act, and the courage to persist through setbacks. We all recognize leaders whose dramatic acts of courage changed the world.
>
> We are well familiar with the actions of political leaders such as Abraham Lincoln, Marin Luther King, Mohandas Gandhi, and Nelson Mandela; of innovators such as Steve Jobs, Thomas Edison, and Alexander Bell; and of pioneering scientists such as Isaac Newton, Albert Einstein, and Charles Darwin.
>
> But courage is not always about big, dramatic events. It is often about quiet, determined action every day, at work and at home. The courage to say "Sorry" when you've wronged someone. The courage to be introspective and honest with yourself. The courage to join a cause you believe in and to do all you can to help it succeed. The courage to even imagine a different future.[23]

Indeed, it takes courage to even imagine a different future. But we can do this. We have all the tools at our disposal. We certainly have the incentive to do so. We just need to be bold about what that future looks like, be honest with ourselves about how we are doing, apply what we know will work to amplify change, and support and encourage one another along the way. Our smaller victories will feed on each other. Before too long, our expectations will change. What was good enough before will no longer be good enough.

A narrative will begin to take hold: "You know, this place is really on a roll." Good results will confirm those expectations and poor results will be seen in a different light—as bumps in the road that we need to analyze, reflect on, and then make adjustments. With all this scaffolding in place, we can learn and we can grow.

The upward trajectory that emerges will be evidence that momentum is on our side.

NOTES

1. Robert Pirsig, *Zen and the Art of Motorcycle Maintenance* (New York: William Morrow Publishers, 1974).

2. Derek Sivers, "How to Start a Movement," TED Blog, February, 2010, http://blog.ted.com/2010/04/01/how_to_start_a.

3. Steven Ward, "A Machiavellian Guide to Destroying Public Universities in 12 Easy Steps," *Chronicle of Higher Education*, October 2, 2013, http://chronicle.com/blogs/conversation/2013/10/02/a-machiavellian-guide-to-destroying-public-universities-in-12-easy-steps.

4. Ryan W. Quinn and Robert E. Quinn, *Lift: Becoming a Positive Force in Any Situation* (San Francisco: Berrett-Koehler, 2009), 59.

5. See Gretchen M. Spreitzer and Scott Sonenshein, "Positive Deviance and Extraordinary Organizing," in Kim S. Cameron, Jane E. Dutton, and Robert E. Quinn (eds.), *Positive Organizational Scholarship* (San Francisco: Berrett-Koehler, 2003).

6. Cited in Joshua S. Wyner, *What Excellent Community Colleges Do: Preparing All Students for Success* (Cambridge: Harvard Education Press, 2014), and also see the Aspen Institute for details of the program, www.aspeninstitute.org/policy-work/college-excellence/overview.

7. Personal conversation, September 2, 2014.

8. Monica C. Worline and Ryan W. Quinn, "Courageous Principled Action," in Kim S. Cameron, Jane E. Dutton, and Robert E. Quinn (eds.), *Positive Organizational Scholarship* (San Francisco: Berrett-Koehler, 2003), 155.

9. Albert Bandura, *Social Learning Theory* (Englewood Cliffs, NJ: Prentice Hall, 1977).

10. Jim Collins, *Good to Great* (New York: Harper Business, 2001).

11. Cited in and adapted from Scott Jaschik, "An Apology from Pima Community College," *Inside Higher Ed*, July 18, 2013, www.insidehighered.com/quicktakes/2013/07/08/apology-pima-community-college.

12. Personal conversation, September 5, 2014.

13. Peter Schmidt, "Please for Civility Meet Cynicism," *Chronicle of Higher Education,* September 10, 2014, http://chronicle.com/article/Pleas-for-Civility-Meet/148715.

14. Gene Hickok and Tom Shaver, "Higher Education Can't Wait," *Inside Higher Ed*, April 26, 2013, www.insidehighered.com/views/2013/04/26/colleges-cant-wait-systemic-reform-must-make-changes-now-essay.

15. James O'Toole, "Speaking Truth to Power: A White Paper," Santa Clara University, Markkula Center for Applied Ethics, www.scu.edu/ethics/practicing/focusareas/business/truth-to-power.html.

16. See Tyler Kingkade, "San Jose State University Begins MOOC Partnership as California School Pushed to Online Education," *Huffington Post*, January 16, 2013, www.huffingtonpost.com/2013/01/16/san-jose-state-state-univ_n_2488734.html#.

17. Two of the three intended reports have been published so far by CCCSE. The first is "A Matter of Degrees: Promising Practices for Community College Student Success" (2012), and see Jennifer Gonzalez, "Multiyear Study of Community College Practices Asks: What Helps Students Graduate?," *Chronicle of Higher Education*, February 2, 2012, http://chronicle.com/article/Community-College-Study-Asks-/130606/. The second is "A Matter of Degrees: High Impact Practices for Community College Student Engagement" (2013), and see Katherine Mangan, "Tactics That Engage Community College Students Get Few Takers, Study Finds,"

Chronicle of Higher Education, October 17, 2013, http://chronicle.com/article/Tactics-That-Engage/142373.

18. Donald Schon, *Educating the Reflective Practitioner* (San Francisco: Jossey-Bass, 1987).

19. See Fiona Lee et al., "New Knowledge Creation in Organizations," in Kim S. Cameron, Jane E. Dutton, and Robert E. Quinn (eds.), *Positive Organizational Psychology* (San Francisco: Berrett-Koehler, 2003).

20. See Amy. C. Edmondson, "Strategies for Learning from Failure," *Harvard Business Review*, April 2011.

21. "Harvard and MIT Release Visualization Tools for Trove of MOOC Data," *Chronicle of Higher Education*, February 20, 2014, http://chronicle.com/blogs/wiredcampus/harvard-and-mit-release-visualization-tools-for-trove-of-mooc-data/50631.

22. See Ashesi University College, http://ashesi.edu.gh.

23. Cited in "On Courage and Difference: Excerpts from Graduation Speeches," *Chronicle of Higher Education*, May 28, 2013, http://chronicle.com/article/On-CourageDifference-/139461.

Index

About the Author

Daniel Seymour is the author of 15 books in higher education and business including the best-selling classic *Once Upon a Campus* (1995) as well as the recent books *Noble Ambitions* (2013) and *Future College* (2015). He teaches in the graduate business program at California State University, Channel Islands and is a consultant with the Collaborative Brain Trust. Dr. Seymour has worked in the financial services industry and served in senior administrative positions in higher education. His B.A. degree is from Gettysburg College and his M.B.A. and Ph.D. from the University of Oregon. He lives in Santa Barbara, California.

Made in the USA
Charleston, SC
15 June 2016